Effective Communication for School Administrators

A Necessity in an Information Age

Theodore J. Kowalski
George J. Petersen
Lance D. Fusarelli

Rowman & Littlefield Education
Lanham, Maryland • Toronto • Plymouth, UK
2007

Published in the United States of America
by Rowman & Littlefield Education
A Division of Rowman & Littlefield Publishers, Inc.
A wholly owned subsidary of The Rowman & Littlefield Publishing Group, Inc.
4501 Forbes Boulevard, Suite 200, Lanham, Maryland 20706
www.rowmaneducation.com

Estover Road
Plymouth PL6 7PY
United Kingdom

British Library Cataloguing in Publication Information Available

Library of Congress Cataloging-in-Publication Data

Kowalski, Theodore J.
  Effective communication for school administrators : a necessity in an information age / Theodore J. Kowalski, George J. Petersen, Lance D. Fusarelli.
      p. cm.
  Includes bibliographical references and index.
  ISBN-13: 978-1-57886-587-1 (hardcover : alk. paper)
  ISBN-13: 978-1-57886-588-8 (pbk. : alk. paper)
  ISBN-10: 1-57886-587-5 (hardcover : alk. paper)
  ISBN-10: 1-57886-588-3 (pbk. : alk. paper)
  1. School management and organization—United States. 2. Communication in education—United States. I. Petersen, George J. II. Fusarelli, Lance D. (Lance Darin), 1966– III. Title.

  LB2801.A2K68 2007
  371.2'011—dc22   2006037985

∞™ The paper used in this publication meets the minimum requirements of American National Standard for Information Sciences—Permanence of Paper for Printed Library Materials, ANSI/NISO Z39.48-1992.
Manufactured in the United States of America.

Contents

Preface

Historically, effective communication was commonly cited as an essential skill for school administrators; but neither licensing criteria nor curricula in preparation programs required the study of this discipline. This indifference had relatively few consequences in the past, and most observers believed that educators would learn to communicate effectively once they entered practice. This erroneous assumption became increasingly problematic for at least three reasons:

1. America is now an information-based society in which many citizens can access information quickly. Computers, the Internet, and the World Wide Web have helped to shape new expectations about the manner in which administrators disseminate, receive, and exchange information.
2. Circa 1990s, school restructuring emerged as the preferred strategy for improving elementary and secondary schools. This approach magnified the importance of school climate and, most notably, school culture. Today, scholars agree that systems will not improve unless the influence of prevalent change-resistant cultures is attenuated.
3. A nexus between communication and culture change is well established in the literature. In order to diagnose and then change existing cultures, superintendents and principals must be able to develop positive relationships with employees so that pertinent information can be exchanged.

Unfortunately, negative assumptions remain prevalent in many schools. For example, teachers and administrators often believe that they are more productive by virtue of working individually and in seclusion and that schools are more productive when they insulate themselves from community interventions. Highly effective schools, however, have been able to replace such change-resistant cultures. The new belief systems treat communication and information as being central to organizational effectiveness.

Communication and culture change are interlaced. Cultures are created and sustained by communication, and once established, cultures determine communicative behavior. Therefore, administrators failing to communicate appropriately are unlikely to build learning organizations. This is because they do not establish open relationships with others and because they model behavior that actually ensures the survival of an unproductive culture.

The primary premise of this book is that administrators must be effective communicators if they are to be effective reformers. Specific purposes include defining communicative competence in school administration, establishing relational communication as the normative standard for communicative behavior, and demonstrating the application of relational communication across critical school improvement activities. In this vein, this is truly a unique text within the education profession. The content has been designed to serve the needs of both aspiring and practicing administrators.

CONCEPTUAL FRAMEWORK

The book contains 11 chapters divided into two parts. The first part, consisting of five chapters, is intended to provide a foundation for understanding communication in relation to public relations and school reform. Communication is described as the nucleus of public relations, a component of school administration that involves not only building goodwill and persuasion, but also developing open and constant information exchanges. The practice of school public relations is then interfaced with organizational improvement generally and school culture change specifically. Lastly, communicative competence is defined in the context of an information-based and reform-minded society.

The second part of the book, consisting of six chapters, focuses on applications of relational communication. This concept is examined relative to (1) making a school a learning organization, (2) practicing democratic leadership, (3) performing critical tasks such as visioning and planning, (4) managing conflict, (5) building positive relationships, and (6) working with school councils.

INTENDED AUDIENCE

The book is designed as a text to be used in courses taken by both aspiring and practicing school administrators. It can be a primary text in a course on administrative communication or communication in schools. The book also is intended to be used as a reference by experienced practitioners seeking to improve their communicative behavior.

Acknowledgments

Many individuals contributed directly or indirectly to the completion of this book. We are especially thankful to Sally A. Morrison, an education consultant in San Luis Obispo, California, for her contributions to chapters 9 and 10. Appreciation is also expressed to the following individuals who assisted with research or preparation of the manuscript: Elizabeth Pearn, administrative assistant, University of Dayton; Cheryl Marcus, doctoral student at the University of Dayton and assistant to the president of Central State University; and Lucianne Lilienthal, doctoral student at the University of Dayton.

I

PUBLIC RELATIONS, COMMUNICATION, AND SCHOOL REFORM

1

Seeking Reform in an Information-Based Society

Edgar Smith spent his entire career in the Ruston School District. During the first 13 years, he served as the agriculture teacher, assistant principal, and principal at Ruston High School; in the last 25 years, he was the district superintendent. Over time, Mr. Smith became one of the most influential persons in this rural farming community, and his autocratic management style was rarely challenged. He spoke with authority and unilaterally decided whether and how he would share information. School board members not only approved of this behavior, they applauded it. They appreciated having a superintendent who was in control totally. He knew how many miles there were on every school bus, he knew where every penny was spent, and he made sure that resources were never wasted.

During the 1980s, however, conditions in the community and school district started changing. District employees and taxpayers gained access to new technologies such as the web and e-mail; the state legislature passed a school reform act requiring every public school to include teachers and parents on school councils. Superintendent Smith treated these changes as temporary nuisances. For example, he initially resisted spending money on computers, both for instruction and for administration; he changed his position only after parents and teachers started writing letters to school board members indicating the district's students were being denied a vital resource. In addition, he told the district's principals that school councils were relatively unimportant. He reminded principals that they had a legal obligation to form the councils, but they had no obligation to relegate authority to them. He also predicted that the law requiring councils would be rescinded once legislators realized that the law created more problems than it solved.

In 1990, a group of disgruntled parents organized and demanded progressive changes in the district. At first, the group was small, fewer than 20 parents, because most citizens did not want to anger the superintendent. But over the next 2 years, the group's membership increased to over 100. Even more noteworthy, two candidates endorsed by the group defeated incumbent school board members. Even so, Superintendent Smith continued to be the stern, steely-eyed boss he had always been. Two years later, two other incumbent board members were defeated. The new coalition of four board members outlined changes they wanted in the school district. After Superintendent Smith reacted with disapproval, they demanded his resignation. Realizing that dismissal was his only other option, he reluctantly complied. After 38 years of service to the school district, he retired a bitter and dismayed person.

INTRODUCTION

The preceding vignette demonstrates two critical points about the relevance of context in relation to organizational behavior norms. First, community and organizational context play an influential role in shaping perceptions of effective administrative behavior (Kowalski, 2005). For nearly two decades, the residents in Ruston, a small, farming community, considered their superintendent to be a highly competent manager—a judgment that would have been far less probable if this superintendent was serving in a larger city or suburban school district. Second, major societal transitions play an influential role in shaping perceptions of effective communication (Kowalski, 2005). For most of his career in Ruston, the superintendent was thought to be an effective communicator, but as residents acquired technology and as they became aware of the need to improve schools, they became increasingly dissatisfied with his one-way, top-down approach to communicating.

This initial chapter explores America's transition to become an information-based society and incremental demands for school reform, arguably the two most important developments that have affected normative standards for communication in districts and schools. The primary intent is to demonstrate why both events have set new quantitative and qualitative standards for information management and, hence, for the communicative behavior of administrators.

HISTORY OF SCHOOL REFORM

Efforts to reform education in the United States have been documented from the earliest days of public schools (Urban & Wagoner, 2000). These periods of dissatisfaction waxed and waned, often without having had a lasting effect on schools. The current quest to transform public elementary and secondary education, however, stands apart from previous reform movements in that it has endured for more than 25 years. Circa 1980, several factors converged to spawn dissatisfaction and, subsequently, proposals for eliminating perceived deficiencies in local schools. One of those issues occurred at the national level. As control of the administrative and legislative branches of the federal government changed, so too did the emphasis on guiding values for public education. For example, President Jimmy Carter established the Department of Education, and his administration focused largely on adequacy and equity issues. President Ronald Reagan initially opposed the Department of Education, and his administration focused on issues of excellence and liberty (Kowalski, 2003). At approximately the same time, America was being affected by the rapid development and deployment of technology; the availability of microcomputers, for instance, changed role expectations for teachers (Donlevy & Donlevy, 1997) and administrators (Mehlinger, 1996). Perhaps most notable, the evolution of a world economy caused top business executives to focus on public education, and they quickly became some of this institution's harshest critics. Their access to elected officials, their financial resources, and their economic perspectives made them a powerful political voice (Cuban, 1992).

Reform Before 1990

Some authors (e.g., Finn, 1991) believe that the modern era of school reform started as early as the late 1970s. Nevertheless, public awareness clearly commenced after an influential group of business and political

leaders comprising the National Commission on Excellence in Education
(NCEE) (1983) summarized their negative opinions in the highly publi-
cized report, *A Nation at Risk*. The sentiments expressed are captured in
the following passage:

> If an unfriendly power had attempted to impose on America the mediocre
> educational performance that exists today, we might well have viewed it as
> an act of war. As it stands, we have allowed this to happen to ourselves. We
> have even squandered the gains in achievement made in the wake of the
> Sputnik challenge. Moreover, we have dismantled essential support systems
> which helped make those gains possible. We have, in effect, been commit-
> ting an act of unthinking, unilateral educational disarmament. (p. 5)

In the aftermath of this report, governors and state legislators raced to
enact mandates intended to mollify the critics. The political intent of their
actions was evidenced by the fact there was little or no nexus between the
reforms proposed and state funding policies. Many policymakers ration-
alized this disjunction by claiming that schools could be improved without funding increases, although they provided little or no evidence to support their claim (Hertert, 1996). Most reform initiatives, although state
centered, were developed or supported by national networks consisting
largely of political and business elites. Until the very late 1980s, traditional education interest groups had relatively little influence on reform
policy (Feir, 1995).

Despite intense efforts to change school performance during the 1980s,
improvements were either minor or nonexistent. Cuban (1988, 1990) postulates that state reforms usually failed because the reformers framed the
problems incorrectly. More precisely, they viewed education problems as
being simple and solvable when they "were instead persistent dilemmas
involving hard choices between conflicting values. Such choices seldom
get resolved but rather get managed; that is, compromises are struck until
the dilemmas reappear" (p. 329). According to Pogrow (1996), the reformers often relied on myths rather than empirical evidence; for example, he argued that their perspectives of the preparation of education professionals and of the profession's existing knowledge base were at best
narrow and at worst incorrect.

Reformers relied primarily on two strategies to change schools: the use
of power and coercion and the introduction of new ideas through staff de-

velopment. The former approach has never really worked well in public education, because reliance on laws, regulations, and mandates flies in the face of conventional wisdom (Finn, 1991). Teachers and administrators obviously had the power to derail such efforts, and their resentment toward being treated as nonprofessionals often prompted them to do just that. Staff development strategies, on the other hand, only proved to be effective when the change initiatives being proposed were congruous with the basic values and beliefs of educators (Fullan, 2000; Louis, Toole, & Hargreaves, 1999). In addition, many of the reforms proposed during the 1980s were contradictory in nature (Orlich, 1989), disjointed, and unrelated to philosophical discourse about the purposes of schooling (Soltis, 1988)—conditions Fullan (2000) describes as *fragmentation*. Resistance also stemmed from a realization that the risks associated with changing schools far outweighed possible benefits. As an example, teachers realized that changing practices in their classrooms involved considerable risk, but at the same time they would not be rewarded financially if the changes proved to be successful (Glickman, 1991; Shanker, 1990).

Two other oversights contributed significantly to reform failure during the 1980s. In large measure, the reformers were ignorant of or indifferent toward evidence indicating that student performance was tempered by social and personal conditions. A hungry or abused child, for instance, is unlikely to achieve at a level commensurate with his or her potential unless social services are coordinated so that the total needs of the student are met (Smrekar & Mawhinney, 1999). Moreover, the reformers appeared to not understand the critical nexus between organizational change and organizational culture. Studying failed reforms, noted psychologist Seymour Sarason (1996) concludes that behavior in schools was controlled by a long-standing culture that was passed from one generation of educators to the next. He observes that reformers basically disregarded culture and that educators, including administrators, either were unwilling to change their institutional culture or were incapable of doing so.

Reform After 1990

After studying attempted reforms during the 1980s, several scholars (e.g., Henkin, 1993; Murphy, 1994) concluded that change needed to be pursued locally, that efforts had to focus on real student needs in relation to

the organizational structure of schools, and that superintendents and principals had to function as primary change agents. Gradually, insights and
conclusions guiding reforms changed as educators were given an opportunity to participate in policy development. In the previous decade, most
reformers assumed that they could improve schools sufficiently by tinkering with selected components of the education process—a supposition
commonly referred to as the "fix the broken parts" mentality. In addition,
they assumed that educators would act rationally and comply with mandates (Louis et al., 1999). As previously noted, neither of these convictions was accurate.

Reforms introduced after 1990 were anchored in the assumption that
higher levels of effectiveness required school restructuring. More specifically, the structure of schools (e.g., curriculum, daily schedules) needed to
be reorganized; authority needed to be redistributed so that teachers could
have a professional role in improving education; decisions needed to be
made democratically so that parents and other stakeholders could be included; institutional cultures resistant to change needed to be revamped
(Bauman, 1996). And in pursuing these objectives, educators were encouraged to abandon assumptions that schools were simple, predictable,
and static organizations (Louis et al., 1999). The concept of restructuring,
however, has been interpreted in different ways ranging from top-down,
ruthless retrenchment to power sharing and professionalism (Hargreaves,
1994). For most educators, restructuring has become synonymous with
specific reform initiatives such as educator empowerment, decentralization, and professionalism (Tyack, 1990).

Since 1990, several reform principles have been widely embraced.
They include the following beliefs:

- *Both centralization and decentralization are essential.* This principle
  suggests that school improvement requires a situation-specific blend of
  top-down and bottom-up authority. Whereas total centralization limits
  liberty (i.e., the right of citizens to exert control of public education)
  and provides too much control, complete decentralization limits equity
  (i.e., reasonably equal educational opportunities) and provides too little control (Fullan, 1999; Timar & Kirp, 1989). The degree to which restructured schools balance centralization and decentralization depends
  on contextual variables, most notably the unique elements of communities, school districts, and individual schools.

- *Meaningful reform is much more likely if it is pursued locally.* The relevancy of national and state initiatives varied considerably among districts and even among schools in a given district. In light of this fact, most reformers now realize that effective change needs to be tailored to real student needs (Louis et al., 1999).
- *Local reform requires community participation.* Reformers now recognize that essential functions, such as visioning and planning, require collaboration that crosses organizational boundaries. By involving the community, school officials are more likely to identify real education needs and more likely to garner political and economic support to implement change (Fullan, 1999).
- *Schools cannot be sufficiently improved unless organizational cultures are reshaped.* What actually occurs in classrooms on a daily basis is heavily influenced by school culture. Improving schools requires underlying values and beliefs to be identified and discussed; those detrimental to school improvement should be altered (Sarason, 1996).
- *Reform requires educators to develop an internal capacity to change.* Newer strategies for reform rely on professionalism and democratic decision making. These concepts are attenuated, however, if educators are incapable of or unwilling to assume the responsibilities inherent in them (Louis et al., 1999).
- *Reform requires philosophical compromise.* Policy for public education has always been guided by basic values that are widely supported in society—even when the values conflict with each other (Swanson & King, 1997). Rather than seeing reform as a win-lose political contest, administrators are expected to sculpt acceptable compromises that allow schools to become excellent without becoming inequitable and that allow citizen involvement without creating substantial disparities among school resources.

EVOLUTION OF THE INFORMATION AGE

Noted futurist Alvin Toffler (1970) was among the first authors to chronicle the transition of American society from an agriculture base to a manufacturing base to an information base. Nearly 25 years ago, typewriters were replaced by microcomputers, and more recently, the Internet provided a distributed, failproof network that could connect computers. With the subsequent invention of the World Wide Web, the Internet became a global network. Examples of other information technology that has been developed since 1970 include facsimile (fax) machines, electronic data-bases, voice mail, digital copiers, and cellular telephones. The phenome-nal growth of the Internet, however, has been the major factor in the information revolution. In just 1 year, the number of U.S. citizens with access to the Internet increased from 158.9 million in 2001 to 168.6 million in 2002—an astonishing 9.8% increase (Nielsen/Net Ratings, 2005).

The broadcast media has been another source of information. Just 40 years ago, citizens relied on three national television networks and limited radio news broadcasts to gain information. Today, they have access to hundreds of cable channels, many of them providing continuous news and commentary, even at the local level. In addition, they can listen to a myriad of political talk shows, again national and local, that offer information and viewpoints across the political spectrum.

By the late 1970s, scholars had become confident that technology would improve access to information and increase the value of information in organizational management (Lipinski, 1978). West (1981), one of the first authors to analyze these trends as they applied to school administration, concluded that they would change normative standards of practice. Noting how previous efforts to generate high levels of interaction between school and community had routinely failed, he predicted that technology would allow practitioners to narrow the divide between theory and practice in this important area. The paradigm shift he envisioned centered on a combination of communication and techno-relations—the former being a process utilizing electronic options devoid of physical contact. However, West cautioned that while technology could increase the quantity of communication, it did not ensure that school and community relations would improve. Instead, he concluded that positive relationships through technology depended on administrators using such tools in a way that did not sacrifice human interaction for efficiency (West, 1985).

Today, state departments of education and virtually all districts and schools have Web pages offering the public access to information and an entry point for exchanging information with educators. As citizens learned how to use the Internet, their appetite for information and communication expectations increased.

The information age also has had a profound influence on administrator behavior. Prior to e-mail, superintendents and principals could exercise considerable control over personal communication. As an example, a teacher who wanted to discuss a problem with her principal usually had to gain access through a secretary. With computer networks, she could simply send an e-mail message and verify that it was delivered. Not unexpectedly, many principals disliked e-mail initially because the medium required them to be more interactive. By the mid-1990s, technology had become so prevalent in education that many administrators were evaluated formally with respect to deploying it (Lare & Cimino, 1998). Even so, studies of principals often found that experienced practitioners were slow to develop computer literacy skills. For example, Testerman, Algozzine, and Flowers (2002) found that assistant principals and graduate students aspiring to be principals had computer skills that exceeded those of practicing principals.

CONNECTING REFORM, INFORMATION, AND COMMUNICATION

The current reform movement has evolved through several stages in which perceived problems, change strategies, and proposed solutions have been altered (Kowalski, 2003; 2006). Table 1.1 contains information regarding these changes. Although the transitions are quite clear, they

Table 1.1.   Evolution of School Reform: 1983–2006

Factor	1983–1989	2000–2006
Primary reform targets	Students and educators	Schools
Primary change strategy	Fix noneffective elements	Organizational restructuring
Primary change tactic	Intensification mandates	Changing institutional culture
Primary governance strategy	Centralized control	Mix of centralization and decentralization
Power and authority	Autocratic	Democratic
Locus of policy development	National and state levels	District and school levels
Coupling of reform ideas	Fragmented	Coordinated
View of schools as organizations	Rational and ordered	Political, emotional, and complex

need to be analyzed in relation to the social environment in which they are being pursued. In this vein, America's status as an information-based society functioning in a global economy is highly relevant to determining normative standards for contemporary school administrators.

Moving the reform policy arena to local communities has magnified the importance of community and institutional cultures. Emphasizing this fact, analysts (e.g., Bauman, 1996; Sarason, 1996) have concluded that school systems do not improve appreciably unless change-resistant cultures are transformed. Institutional culture is erected on shared fundamental values and beliefs, and in the case of schools, they instruct employees, via norms, how to address their work (Schein, 1996; Trimble, 1996). Equally important, various facets of school culture influence administrator and teacher attitudes toward promoting and accepting change (Duke, 2004; Leithwood, Jantzi, & Fernandez, 1994). The possible effects of negative culture are evidenced by two beliefs that unfortunately are still held by many educators. The first is that teachers are more productive when they work individually and in seclusion (Gideon, 2002); the second is that community involvement undermines a school's efficiency and productivity (Blase & Anderson, 1995). Noted organizational theorist Edgar Schein (1992) argues that to be highly effective, organizations must change resistant cultures into *learning cultures*. A learning culture is a belief system built "on the assumption that communication and information are central to organizational well-being and must therefore create a multichannel communication system that allows everyone to connect to everyone else" (p. 370).

Connections between organizational culture and communication have been detailed in the literature. Hall (1997), for instance, points out that communication and culture are inextricably linked, a nexus equally relevant to community and organizational cultures. Conrad (1994) writes, "Cultures are communicative creations. They emerge and are sustained by the communicative acts of all employees, not just the conscious persuasive strategies of upper management. Cultures do not exist separately from people communicating with one another" (p. 27). Despite the fact that most organizational research has categorized culture as a causal variable and communication as an intervening variable (Wert-Gray, Center, Brashers, & Meyers, 1991), their relationship also has been deemed reciprocal. Axley (1996), for instance, contends that "communication gives rise to culture, which gives rise to communication, which perpetuates culture" (p. 153).

Initiating and facilitating change, however, are especially risk-laden assignments for administrators. Many lack a deep understanding of organizational culture and its effects on change (Sarason, 1996), and most have not had experience functioning as change agents (Murphy, 1994). Organizational change strategies discussed in the literature (e.g., Brown, 1965; Kilmann, 1984; Schein, 1996) describe the process as requiring a visualization of a destination and the development of a plan for reaching it. In the case of public education, visioning and planning should be inclusive activities; and to meet this expectation, administrators must engage stakeholders in discussion of seemingly intractable governance, power, and organizational design problems (Carlson, 1996; Heckman, 1993). Clearly, then, reform discussions in local districts will not be productive as long as participants believe that substantial change is neither necessary nor politically advantageous (Sarason, 1996; Streitmatter, 1994). This fact, more than any other, links organizational culture to school reform; and because effective communication is essential to culture change, effective communication is essential to school reform.

CONCLUDING COMMENTS

Organizational change in general and culture change specifically become more probable when top executives provide direction (King & Blumer, 2000), symbolic leadership (Fullan, 2001; Murphy, 1994), and facilitation through effective communication (Corbett, 1986; D'Aprix, 1996; Goodman, Willis, & Holihan, 1998; Quirke, 1996; Walker, 1997). Although communication has received considerably more attention in school administration during the past 15 years, many preparation programs and practitioners continue to treat this topic casually. In part, this neglect may be attributable to the erroneous belief that everyone can communicate effectively and, accordingly, school administrators learn and adapt once they are immersed in practice. Linkages between communication competence and organizational effectiveness have been studied more intensely in business administration than they have in school administration. Relatively recent studies in that profession have found that most embattled business executives shared a common characteristic—they were ineffective communicators (Perina, 2002). Therefore, it is reasonable to conclude that principals and superintendents are no more capable of developing communication competence naturally than are top business executives.

The primary objective of this book is to analyze the role of communication in the context of school administration. In the remaining chapters, organizational communication is examined in relation to public relations and communication competence is defined in relation to contemporary practice. The argument is made that communication has become a pervasive administrative role, and as such, the discipline needs to be studied, both in pre-service and in-service learning experiences.

REFERENCES

Axley, S. R. (1996). *Communication at work: Management and the communication-intensive organization.* Westport, CT: Quorum Books.

Bauman, P. C. (1996). *Governing education: Public sector reform or privatization.* Boston: Allyn & Bacon.

Blase, J., & Anderson, G. (1995). *The micropolitics of educational leadership: From control to empowerment.* New York: Teachers College Press.

Brown, A. F. (1965). Two strategies for changing climate. *CAS Bulletin, 4*, 64–80.

Carlson, R. V. (1996). *Reframing and reform: Perspectives on organization, leadership, and school change.* New York: Longman.

Conrad, C. (1994). *Strategic organizational communication: Toward the twenty-first century* (3rd ed.). Fort Worth, TX: Harcourt Brace.

Corbett, W. J. (1986). Corporate culture: An opportunity for professional communicators. *Bulletin of the Association for Business Communication, 49*(2), 14–19.

Cuban, L. (1988). How schools change reforms: Redefining reform success and failure. *Teachers College Record, 99*(3), 453–477.

Cuban, L. (1990). Reforming again, again, and again. *Educational Researcher, 19*(1), 3–13.

Cuban, L. (1992). The corporate myth of reforming public schools. *Phi Delta Kappan, 74*(2), 157–159.

D'Aprix, R. (1996). *Communicating for change: Connecting the workplace with the marketplace.* San Francisco: Jossey-Bass.

Donlevy, J. G., & Donlevy, T. R. (1997). Teachers, technology, and training. Perspectives on education and school reform: Implications for the emerging role of the teacher. *International Journal of Instructional Media, 24*(2), 91–98.

Duke, D. (2004). *The challenge of educational change*. Boston: Allyn & Bacon.

Feir, R. E. (1995). *Political and social roots of education reform: A look at the states in the mid-1980s*. (ERIC Document Reproduction Service No. ED 385925).

Finn, C. E. (1991). *We must take charge*. New York: Free Press.

Fullan, M. (1999). *Change forces: The sequel*. Philadelphia: Falmer.

Fullan, M. (2000). The three stories of education reform. *Phi Delta Kappan, 81*(8), 581–584.

Fullan, M. (2001). *Leading in a culture of change*. San Francisco: Jossey-Bass.

Gideon, B. H. (2002). Structuring schools for teacher collaboration. *Education Digest, 68*(2), 30–34.

Glickman, C. (1991). Pretending not to know what we know. *Educational Leadership, 48*(8), 4–10.

Goodman, M. B., Willis, K. E., & Holihan, V. C. (1998). Communication and change: Effective change communication is personal, global, and continuous. In M. B. Goodman (Ed.), *Corporate communication for executives* (pp. 37–61). Albany: State University of New York Press.

Hall, E. T. (1997). *The silent language*. New York: Doubleday.

Hargreaves, A. (1994). Restructuring: Postmodernity and the prospects for educational change. *Journal of Education Policy, 9*(1), 47–65.

Heckman, P. E. (1993). School restructuring in practice: Reckoning with the culture of school. *International Journal of Educational Reform, 2*(3), 263–272.

Henkin, A. B. (1993). Social skills of superintendents: A leadership requisite in restructured schools. *Educational Research Quarterly, 16*(4), 15–30.

Hertert, L. (1996). Systemic school reform in the 1990s: A local perspective. *Educational Policy, 10*(3), 379–398.

Kilmann, R. H. (1984). *Beyond the quick fix*. San Francisco: Jossey-Bass.

King, M., & Blumer, I. (2000). A good start. *Phi Delta Kappan, 81*(5), 356–360.

Kowalski, T. J. (2003). *Contemporary school administration: An introduction* (2nd ed.). Boston: Allyn & Bacon.

Kowalski, T. J. (2005). Evolution of the school superintendent as communicator. *Communication Education, 54*(2), 101–117.

Kowalski, T. J. (2006). *The school superintendent: Theory, practice, and cases* (2nd ed.). Thousand Oaks, CA: Sage.

Lare, D., & Cimino, E. (1998). Not by print alone. *American School Board Journal, 185*(12), 40–41.

Leithwood, K., Jantzi, D., & Fernandez, A. (1994). Transformational leadership and teachers' commitment to change. In J. Murphy & K. S. Louis (Eds.), *Reshaping the principalship* (pp. 77–98). Thousand Oaks, CA: Corwin.

Lipinski, A. J. (1978). Communicating the future. *Futures, 10*(2), 126–127.

Louis, K. S., Toole, J., & Hargreaves, A. (1999). Rethinking school improvement. In J. Murphy & K. S. Louis (Eds.). *Handbook of research on educational administration* (2nd ed., pp. 251–276). San Francisco: Jossey-Bass.

Mehlinger, H. D. (1996). Achieving school reform through technology. *TECHNOS, 5*(1), 26–29.

Murphy, J. (1994). The changing role of the superintendency in restructuring districts in Kentucky. *School Effectiveness and School Improvement, 5*(4), 349–75.

National Commission on Excellence in Education. (1983). *A nation at risk: The imperative for educational reform*. Washington, DC: U.S. Department of Education.

Nielsen/Net Ratings (2005). *Global Internet population grows four percent year-over-year*. Retrieved October 5, 2005, from www.nielsen-netratings.com/pr/pr_030220_hk.pdf#search='Internet%20and%20access%20and%20percent%20and%20population'.

Orlich, D. C. (1989). Education reforms: Mistakes, misconceptions, miscues. *Phi Delta Kappan, 70*(7), 512–517.

Perina, K. (2002). When CEOs self-destruct. *Psychology Today, 35*(5), 16.

Pogrow, S. (1996). Reforming the wannabe reformers: Why education reforms almost always end up making things worse. *Phi Delta Kappan, 77*(10), 656–663.

Quirke, B. (1996). *Communicating corporate change*. New York: McGraw-Hill.

Sarason, S. B. (1996). *Revisiting the culture of the school and the problem of change*. New York: Teachers College Press.

Schein, E. H. (1992). *Organizational culture and leadership* (2nd ed.). San Francisco: Jossey-Bass.

Schein, E. H. (1996). Culture: The missing concept in organization studies. *Administrative Science Quarterly, 41*(2), 229–240.

Shanker, A. (1990). A proposal for using incentives to restructure our public schools. *Phi Delta Kappan, 71*(5), 344–357.

Smrekar, C. E., & Mawhinney, H. B. (1999). Integrated services: Challenges to linking schools, families, and communities. In J. Murphy & K. S. Louis (Eds.). *Handbook of research on educational administration* (2nd ed., pp. 443–462). San Francisco: Jossey-Bass.

Soltis, J. F. (1988). Reform or reformation? *Educational Administration Quarterly, 24*(3), 241–245.

Streitmatter, J. (1994). *Toward gender equity in the classroom: Everyday teachers' beliefs and practices*. Albany: State University of New York Press.

Swanson, A. D., & King, R. A. (1997). *School finance: Its economics and politics* (2nd ed.). New York: Longman.

Testerman, J. C., Algozzine, R., & Flowers, C. P. (2002). Basic technology competencies of educational administrators. *Contemporary Education, 72*(2), 58–63.

Timar, T. B., & Kirp, D. L. (1989). Education reform in the 1980s: Lessons from the states. *Phi Delta Kappan, 70*(7), 504–511.

Toffler, A. (1970). *Future shock.* New York: Random House.

Trimble, K. (1996). Building a learning community. *Equity and Excellence in Education, 29*(1), 37–40.

Tyack, D. (1990). Restructuring in historical perspective: Tinkering toward utopia. *Teachers College Record, 92*(2), 170–191.

Urban, W., & Wagoner, J. (2000). *American education: A history.* New York: McGraw-Hill.

Walker, G. (1997). Communication in leadership. *Communication Management, 1*(4), 22–27.

Wert-Gray, S., Center, C., Brashers, D. E., & Meyers, R. A. (1991). Research topics and methodological orientations in organizational communication: A decade of review. *Communication Studies, 42*(2), 141–154.

West, P. T. (1981). Imagery and change in the twenty-first century. *Theory into Practice, 20*(4), 229–236.

West, P. T. (1985). *Educational public relations.* Beverly Hills, CA: Sage.

2

Public Relations in Districts and Schools

Recently, a school board in a rural district rejected unanimously a recommendation made by their new superintendent to allocate $75,000 in next year's budget for district public relations (PR). Summarizing the sentiments of the other members, the board president commented, "We should not be using tax dollars to prepare and distribute propaganda. There are far more important issues that require funding." Just 3 months earlier, however, the board members, meeting with the district's new superintendent, unanimously agreed that changes were needed to make the schools more effective. Moreover, they told their new executive that she would have to allow both district employees and community members to play integral roles in the change process and then garner their support for the proposed changes.

Unfortunately, failing to see a nexus between the realities of school improvement and the deployment of public relations is not uncommon. While the school board members are arguably correct that broad participation and support are essential to reform, their narrow perspective of PR severely limits the resources the superintendent will require to meet their expectations. In large measure, the board's ambivalence toward PR stems from an erroneous belief that the superintendent's motive in recommending this budget item is self-promotion, for the school district generally and for herself specifically. Their myopic perspective, however, leads them to essentially dissociate organizational change from communication, information management, and conflict resolution. In other words, their disapproval of a PR budget is de facto a serious detriment to their own avowed goal of producing school improvement.

Two realities help us understand how narrow perspectives of PR thwart school improvement. The first is that inclusive approaches to school reform are more effective than other approaches. Unless visions and strategic plans, especially for public schools, are developed collaboratively, and unless they are then embraced politically by employees and taxpayers, meaningful educational improvements are improbable (Bauman, 1996; Fullan, 2004). The second is that effective communication is essential to the success of inclusive change strategies. Collaborative visioning, planning, and coalition building are communication-intensive activities requiring administrators to exchange information openly and continuously with employees and patrons (Kowalski, 2004; 2005). Consequently, narrow PR definitions almost always set inappropriate benchmarks for administrator communication. As examples, they often reinforce a conviction that administrators are supposed to selectively disseminate carefully crated information and lead many board members, employees, and district residents to believe that manipulation of public opinion, especially if intended to enhance district or school interests, is acceptable administrator behavior (Kowalski, 2005).

The knowledge base on school improvement helps us comprehend the complexity of education institutions and the critical nature of communication in organizational change and development. However, this information is not always understood or accepted. For instance, an administrator's effectiveness as a change agent is seriously attenuated if he or she fails to treat districts and schools as social systems. Yet, efforts to improve education during the 1980s often reflected a fix the "broken parts" mentality; that is, superintendents and principals presumed performance would be improved by replacing or mending one element (e.g., adopting a new mathematics program) while ignoring other dimensions of the organization (e.g., the quality of instruction, assessment and evaluation procedures) (Hall & Hord, 2001). Even if administrators understand that schools are intricate social systems, they may fail to see a nexus between systemwide improvement and effective communication, inclusion, and information management—all core functions of a comprehensive PR program (Kowalski, 2004).

The content of this chapter is rooted in the conviction that systems thinking, inclusive change strategies, and PR programming are equally essential factors in relation to school improvement. The content is divided into three subtopics. The first is an accurate definition of school PR; the second is the nexus between a systems approach to change and open communication; the third is the political, social, and economic contexts of contemporary practice.

THE TRUTH ABOUT PUBLIC RELATIONS

In the eyes of the public, a profession's or academic discipline's social importance is determined by the quantity and quality of governmental controls placed on its practitioners. Consequently, occupations that are difficult to enter (i.e., they have the most stringent requirements for academic study and licensing) are the most revered. In the case of PR, preparation, licensing, and practice have not been subjected to governmental regulations (Seitel, 2004). When we consider this fact in relation to common misperceptions of the purposes of PR, we are apt to understand why the public may lack respect for those who apply this process. Therefore, it is essential for school administrators to first dispel misperceptions and then share their wisdom with the public.

At varying times during the past century, PR was described as a concept, a profession, a process, and even a goal—and its intended meaning was often modified by the context(s) in which it was being discussed or applied (e.g., in business vs. education) (Gordon, 1997). The most damaging images describe PR as nothing more than press agentry, propaganda, or advertising (Kowalski, 2004). Press agentry involves disseminating carefully crafted messages intended to benefit clients (either individuals or corporations) by keeping them before the public's eye. Propaganda involves creating and spreading ideas, facts, or allegations intended to influence public opinion—and it can include spreading misinformation, typically to enhance the organization's image or to destroy the image of competing organizations. Advertising also entails the preparation of carefully controlled messages and their transmission to the public. Here, however, the messages almost always are sent through purchased mechanisms such as paid television or newspaper ads. The origin of narrow or erroneous PR perspectives can be traced to the formative years when some practitioners "played fast and loose with the truth" (Dilenschneider, 1996, p. xxi). As the discipline matured, however, a disjunction between perception and reality became increasingly wider.

Definitions are either *descriptive* or *normative*. Those in the former category seek to explain what actually occurs across organizations. The accuracy of descriptive definitions can be diminished by researcher bias; as an example, a person opposed to school PR may describe practices in a district that are more reflective of a political agenda than reality. Moreover, descriptive definitions are often context specific; that is, they describe what is occurring in the environment of a specific organization. Therefore, a descriptive definition of PR derived from studying a cosmetic company may have little or no applicability to public schools. Despite their limitations, however, descriptive definitions can be important for school administrators, especially if they are relatively objective and derived from observations of organizations that share common characteristics with schools. Descriptive definitions are inherently rhetorical and, therefore, usually influence perceptions of reality (Gordon, 1997).

Normative definitions, by comparison, seek to influence practice by prescribing standards for shaping public opinion (e.g., how administrators attempt to influence public perceptions or opinions) or for practitioner behavioral standards (e.g., the degree to which administrators should be candid or accessible) (Grunig & Hunt, 1984). Organizational goals are often included in normative statements. For example, a normative definition may stipulate the organization's intent with respect to engaging in PR, or it may detail the organization's intended relationships with its many publics. Notwithstanding the maturity of PR over the last half of the 20th century, one of the earliest normative definitions, developed over 60 years ago by Edward Bernays, still is widely cited in the literature. His standard sets three objectives: to *inform* the public, to *persuade* (i.e., modifying attitudes and opinions), and to *integrate* the actions and attitudes of the organization and its publics (Cohen, 1987). Persuasion has been and remains the most controversial of these objectives because the word implies domination, an action deemed by most PR specialists to be unethical (Gordon, 1997). Consequently, contemporary scholars (e.g., Dilenschneider, 1996) advocate substituting the word *influence*.

Recognizing that conflicting definitions can be confusing, Wilcox, Ault, and Agee (1992) suggest that an accurate understanding of PR could be more readily accomplished by applying six key terms:

- *Deliberate process*
- *Planned process*
- *Performance-based process*
- *Public interest*
- *Two-way communication*
- *Management function*

For school PR purposes, the last term, *management function*, should be changed to *administrative function* since school administration texts (e.g., Hoy & Miskel, 2005; Kowalski, 2003) typically identify administration as a broad concept entailing both leadership and management.

Historically, many education writers and practitioners have referred to school PR as *community relations* because they equate PR with Madison Avenue persuasion tactics (West, 1985), deception, obfuscation, and even lying (Martinson, 1995). In fact, community relations are more accurately either a PR component (functions that pertain to interactions between organizations and their external environments) or a PR goal (an outcome to be achieved via PR). Equally important, viewing school PR as community relations overlooks an important fact—PR is not restricted to relationships between an organization and its external environment; it also includes internal relationships (those occurring among organizational members) (Kowalski, 2004).

The National School Public Relations Association (NSPRA) (1986) defines educational PR as "a planned and systematic two-way process of communications between an educational organization and its internal and external publics designed to build morale, goodwill, understanding, and support for that organization" (p. 28). West (1985) offers this description: "Educational public relations is a systematically and continuously planned, executed, and evaluated program of interactive communication and human relations that employs paper, electronic, and people mediums to attain internal as well as external support for an educational institution" (p. 23). The focus on human relations in these two definitions is highly relevant because school PR addresses how people feel about issues, services, and individual or organizational personalities. Alluding to this fact, Norris (1984) suggests that PR might be better understood if it were called "public relationship" because the process involves building connections with a great many different publics.

James Grunig developed the most widely used typology for understanding the communication options in public relations. Employing two factors, *communication direction* and *symmetry*, he describes four types of communication. Direction refers to the flow of information; symmetry refers to intended beneficiaries of the information exchange. Grunig's four paradigms, as explained by Dozier (1995), are summarized as follows:

- *One-way asymmetrical.* In this model, the intention is to disseminate positive publicity and to restrict unfavorable information. Therefore, it is arguably a form of propaganda closely aligned with press agentry and is intended to benefit only the organization. As an example, a principal communicates with parents only when it serves to enhance his or the school's reputation. All other information, and especially negative information, is suppressed. The principal is interested neither in helping parents understand more about the schools nor in receiving feedback from parents.
- *One-way symmetrical.* In this model, the intention is to disseminate accurate public information without volunteering negative information. Therefore, it is more neutral than press agentry and is intended to benefit both the organization and society. As an example, a principal sends a letter to parents detailing the school's homework policy. He expects the letter to benefit both the school (e.g., increasing overall student performance) and parents (e.g., improving individual student performance). However, his letter does not encourage questions or comments.
- *Two-way asymmetrical.* In this model, the intention is to engage in two-way communication, but the motive is one-sided. As an example, a principal holds several discussion sessions with parents who are carefully selected because they are known to support him politically. The principal's sole intention is to enhance his reputation directly and the school's reputation indirectly by demonstrating that he engages parents in dialogue. Although information is exchanged in these sessions, the discussions are not intended to benefit the participating parents or the larger community they represent.

- *Two-way symmetrical.* In this model, the intentions are to establish mutual understanding and to resolve conflict between the organization and its publics. It requires extensive knowledge and understanding of publics and is intended to benefit both the organization and society. As an example, a principal creates a variety of activities (e.g., open forums, parent coffees) designed to have parents interact with him and other school employees. The intentions are to allow parents to have an active role in the school, to allow them to state and test their opinions, and to build collaborative visions for ongoing school improvement.

Clearly, the two-way symmetrical model is the preferred alternative in an information-based, reform-minded society.

In summary, school PR can be viewed in three dimensions: what it is, what it relies on, and what it should accomplish (see Figure 2.1). Here it is defined as "an evolving social science and leadership process utilizing multimedia approaches designed to build goodwill, enhance the public's attitude toward the value of education, augment interaction and two-way symmetrical communication between schools and their external communities, provide vital and useful information to the public and employees, improve decision-making and problem solving, and facilitate school reform efforts" (Kowalski, 2004, pp. 10–11). The essential nature of this administrative process in governmental agencies,

What It Is
- An evolving social science
- A leadership process

What It Relies On
- Multimedia approaches

What It Should Accomplish
- Building goodwill
- Enhancing the public's attitude toward the value of education
- Augmenting interaction and two-way symmetrical communication between schools and their broader communities
- Providing vital and useful information to the public and employees
- Improving decision making and problem solving
- Facilitating school reform

Figure 2.1. Elements of School Public Relations

including public schools, is based on the following three philosophical convictions:

1. A democratic government is best served by a free two-way flow of ideas and accurate information so citizens and their government can make informed choices.
2. A democratic government must report and be accountable to the citizens it serves.
3. Citizens, as taxpayers, have a right to government information—but with some exceptions (exceptions to disclosing information may be predicated on laws and administrative judgments about balancing public interests with citizens' rights). (Baker, 1997, p. 456)

THE PURPOSES OF SCHOOL PUBLIC RELATIONS

Even if school PR is defined accurately, some school board members and administrators may still reject the process because they see it as unessential. In an environment of restricted resources and persistent criticism, the temptation is to yield to political pressures and reject funding for what appear to be non-instruction-related programs. In the case of PR, however, such a decision is impetuous and detrimental. First, ongoing and genuine community involvement often has a positive effect on student success and helps ensure that schools are addressing real needs (Arriaza, 2004). Second, schools are social-political systems affected continuously by internal forces (e.g., employee unions) and external forces (e.g., special interest groups) (Fowler, 2000; Wirt & Kirst, 2001). Superintendents and principals typically fail when they attempt to eradicate or minimize political influence and the tensions it creates by simply insulating themselves from employees and the public (Cooper, Fusarelli, & Randall, 2004). Furthermore, an out-of-hand rejection of PR is unwarranted in light of three important facts regarding the communicative behavior of administrators:

- Their behavior influences how others communicate, both within and outside the organization.
- Their behavior influences quantity and quality of relationships that are developed between school personnel and relevant publics.

• Their behavior influences how members of the organization identify and address the needs of clientele (Kowalski, 2004; 2005).

A justification for school PR is embedded in seven goals and directly or indirectly, each of them is relevant to school improvement. The following is a summary of the relationships between the goals and school reform.

1. *Improving the quality of education.* Armistead (2000) points out that a sound PR program can provide policy and process that facilitates communication essential to identifying and addressing real education needs. For example, an effective program plays a pivotal role in environmental scanning (i.e., identifying changing conditions in the ecosystems surrounding the school)—a process deemed essential to strategic planning (Beach, 2004).

2. *Ensuring open political dialogue.* In both public and private schools, primary stakeholders (e.g., employees, parents, patrons) expect administrators to express ideas, but they also desire to be a part of an open and fair debate about these ideas (Baker, 1997). Such discourse allows rival views to be expressed and evaluated (Martinson, 1999). Those denied an opportunity to be involved often resort to covert political activities to express their views, a divisive action that makes school reform even more improbable (Kowalski, 2004).

3. *Enhancing the district or school image.* For more than two decades, the public's confidence in education has been diminished by negative news (Peck & Carr, 1997). Typically based on problems experienced in the largest and most troubled school systems, downbeat media coverage gives rise to the generalization that all schools are basically the same. Imaging is a strategy that can be used to combat this erroneous deduction. To engage in imaging, administrators first establish an accurate institutional identity (including strengths, weaknesses, and needs) that separates a district or school from other districts and schools; they then communicate this identity accurately and repeatedly to stakeholders (Pfeiffer & Dunlap, 1988).

4. *Managing information.* Information management is more than controlling data. In modern organizations, this function has a broadening scope that includes seeking and obtaining information—from employees, students, parents, governmental agencies, other educational

institutions, and the community at large. It also extends to storing, analyzing, and distributing information, especially with respect to visioning, planning, and decision making (Place, McNamara, & McNamara, 2004).

5. *Marketing programs.* Prior to 1990, most public school officials paid little attention to marketing because their organizations faced only token competition for students. However, various reform initiatives, namely charter schools and vouchers, move public schools from a noncompetitive to a competitive market. Marketing is a process used by organizations to identify and analyze consumer needs and wants. Applied to schools, it has three purposes: (a) to produce a voluntary exchange of values between school officials and stakeholders, (b) to identify targeted audiences, and (c) to sensitize school personnel to stakeholder needs and wants (Kotler, 1975). Hanson (2003) wrote that educational marketing involves "developing or refining *specific* school programs in response to the needs and desires of specific target-markets (e.g., 'at risk' families, parents of pre-school children, voters)" (p. 235).

6. *Establishing goodwill and sense of ownership.* Unfortunately, many taxpayers now see their relationship with public schools as being unbalanced—that is, one in which they provide financial support but receive little or no benefit in return. This perspective is understandably most prevalent among residents without children enrolled in the district. In truth, public schools belong to the community, and they represent investments in human capital. Communities tend to develop more positively when they support education (McGaughy, 2000), and in this vein, every resident arguably benefits. This sense of ownership and the potential for societal improvements must be communicated and reaffirmed continuously to ensure the public's political and economic support.

7. *Building support for change.* Organizational development, including school improvement, requires change (Hanson, 2003). Public schools, however, evolved as institutions of stability (Spring, 1990), and in this context, administrators were socialized to avoid failure rather than to take risks (Kowalski & Björk, 2005). Analysts (e.g., Bauman, 1996; Duke, 2004; Fullan, 2004) note that school reform requires departures from traditional management perspectives. Most

notably, administrators are unlikely to succeed by unilaterally selecting change targets and then ordering others to implement the
changes. Instead, they are more apt to be successful if they explain
the need for change, engage the public in discourse that produces a
vision for change, and build support for acquiring the resources necessary for change.

Like any other administrative function, PR should be guided by goals
and objectives identified in an organizational PR plan—a document
that helps ensure that goals remain focused and effective. Goals represent desired ends or purposes, and they are usually broad, long-term
(i.e., extending beyond 2 or 3 years), philosophical statements providing a normative perspective. In addition to the PR plan, goals also may
be found in policy manuals, planning documents, and annual reports.
There can be, and often is, a substantial difference between stated and
real goals. For example, the policy manual in one school district states
that the purposes of the PR program are to foster open communication
and improve community relations, but in reality the program has focused exclusively on efforts to influence the taxpayers to support se-
lective district initiatives.

WHY DISTRICTS AND SCHOOLS AVOID PUBLIC RELATIONS

At this point, you may be asking, "If PR is so essential, why do many administrators spend little or no time engaging in this function?" The diversity of educational institutions and administrators obviously makes it difficult to provide a universally correct response. In general, however,
programming of any type can be blocked by three types of problems (see
Figure 2.2). The first type relates to comprehension (Connor & Lake,
1988). As discussed earlier, PR has been and continues to be defined in
different ways. When school officials and the public define PR narrowly—that is, as a form of press agentry and persuasion—they overlook
or undervalue the potential of this process relative to improving (a) relationships among school personnel, (b) relationships between school personnel and the community, and (c) efforts to achieve meaningful organizational improvement.

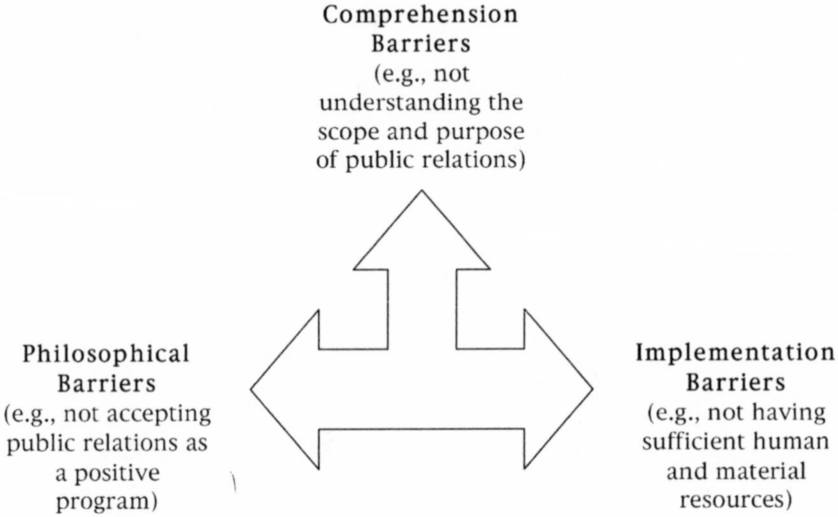

Chapter 2

Comprehension
Barriers
(e.g., not
understanding the
scope and purpose
of public relations)

Philosophical
Barriers
(e.g., not accepting
public relations as
a positive
program)

Implementation
Barriers
(e.g., not having
sufficient human
and material
resources)

Figure 2.2. Obstacles to Implementing Public Relations

Correctly understanding PR, however, does not ensure that the process will be deployed. Philosophical resistance can come from four sources:

1. *Individual dispositions.* An administrator or board member may oppose PR because the process, even when defined properly, is incongruous with personal values and beliefs (Kowalski, 2004). As an example, a principal may believe that exchanging information with others creates more problems than benefits.

2. *Professional culture.* Professions maintain belief systems that communicate behavioral norms to practitioners. These standards are transmitted via professional preparation and exposure (both formal and informal) to experienced practitioners (Daresh, 2004; Heck, 1991). Historically, the culture of educational administration has been influenced predominately by principles of management theory (Hanson, 2003), but more recently, principles of democratic leadership have become increasingly influential (Petersen & Kowalski, 2005). Since neither professional preparation nor exposure to experienced practitioners is uniform in school administration, the values transmitted through socialization are not consistent. As a result, some principals and superintendents embrace PR as a professional responsibility while others do not.

3. *Organizational culture.* Institutions also have cultures; thus, district and school employees socialize new employees to accept prevailing values and beliefs (Hanson, 2003). At times, new administrators experience internal conflict because their professional beliefs are not consistent with their workplace norms (Kowalski, 2003). As an example, a principal may accept open communication as a professional norm but be pressured to adopt closed communication in order to be accepted by peer principals and the superintendent.

4. *Community culture.* Community cultures consist of shared values and beliefs held by relevant publics. They are almost always a potent political force determining the limits of acceptable behavior. As an example, taxpayers may view PR as unessential because they believe effective communication can occur without such a program.

The last group of problems obstructing PR pertains to implementation. School officials may not be able to implement PR programs because they lack necessary fiscal and human resources. School officials uniformly face the reality that they must allocate scarce resources (Wirt & Kirst, 2001), and in this vein, PR budget decisions are no different than the decisions for other elective programs. Frequently, the choices made are not rational (i.e., based on data and made objectively) but rather political or emotional (Hoy & Miskel, 2005). Barriers to implementing are the most difficult to diagnose correctly because school officials often use insufficient resources as an excuse not to implement PR (Kowalski, 2004).

The three categories of barriers provide an effective diagnostic tool for administrators interested in deploying a comprehensive PR program. Spending considerable time trying to persuade the public to accept PR, for example, may be futile if the concept is not properly understood. Moreover, a willingness to appropriate adequate resources becomes much more probable when school board members understand and accept the potential of PR to improve education.

PUBLIC RELATIONSHIPS

In all likelihood, PR would be more readily understood and embraced if it were called *public relationships*. In truth, PR is really all about relationships—among educators, between schools and other institutions, and between educators and the publics they serve. From a communication perspective, relationships are a measure of participant perceptions or a function of those perceptions (Broom, Casey, & Ritchey, 2000). Thus, a principal, for example, may view her relationship with teachers as being positive because of the manner in which she and the teachers treat each other. Often, however, our perceptions of relationships are not accurate and therefore, we fail to know when they are deteriorating or already negative.

Millar and Rogers (1976) observe that "people become aware of themselves only within the context of their social relationships" (p. 87). These relationships may be positive or negative, interpersonal or role-specific, but always "bestowed, sustained, and transformed through communicative behavior" (p. 87). Relationships formed between administrators and others are either objective or subjective realities. In either instance, the relationships provide behavioral contexts that determine how principals and superintendents act toward other people. Moreover, these perceptions shape an administrator's understanding of others and determines how he or she will predict and interpret the behavior of others (Surra & Ridley, 1991).

The importance of positive relationships has been elevated by the current school reform context, a topic discussed in detail in chapter 4. At this point, however, it is important to understand how relationships between schools and their relevant publics affect perceptions about the need for change and shape dispositions toward pursuing change. Equally important, you should understand how PR serves to build and sustain productive relationships.

Modern PR theory offers new perspectives on organizational success that are congruous with democratic administration and social justice. Grunig and Huang (2000), for example, summarize four approaches that theorists have used to determine organizational effectiveness. These approaches, discussed primarily in relation to business and industry, are clarified here in relation to districts and schools.

1. *Goal attainment.* Success is predicated on the extent to which institutional goals are met. This approach has limited utility in education because stakeholder goals are totally ignored. Consequently, school officials may declare success because the organization's goals have been met; however, those goals are not embraced by the public.

2. *Systems perspective.* Success is predicated on survival in the context of community environment. That is, this approach determines success by the degree to which an organization's resources are sufficient to continue an acceptable level of operations. This perspective has limited utility to public schools because they are quasi-monopolies; that is, public schools face limited competition almost ensuring their continued existence. Although this approach recognizes forces outside the organization, it does not detail environmental elements essential to effectiveness (e.g., specifying which needs and wants must be satisfied).

3. *Strategic constituencies.* Success is predicated on identifying power structures in the district (or school) and in the community and then satisfying the interests of these constituencies. This approach provides a political perspective to organizational success. In education, it involves administrators (a) identifying political elites (both inside the organization and in the community), (b) determining the needs and wants of the elites, and (c) satisfying those needs and wants. This approach to success obviously is unacceptable in a democratic society where the interests of all citizens are relevant and need to be protected.

4. *Competing values.* Success is predicated on determining values and goals for all publics and then incorporating those values into the district's or school's goals. With this approach, success is determined at three levels. First, the needs and interests of all citizens are balanced (e.g., in a collective vision); second, these needs and interests are translated accurately into goals; third, those goals are met.

Success based on analysis from the first two approaches is not dependent on a comprehensive PR program. The third approach requires a limited PR program targeted exclusively to political elites. Only the fourth approach requires a comprehensive PR program, and it is in this vein that true success and PR are connected.

Unfortunately, administrators do not always understand how relationships influence school improvement efforts and how PR influences positive relationships. The quality of relationships is determined by four variables described by Huang (1997):

1. *Control mutuality*—mutual agreements about power sharing
2. *Trust*—the extent to which persons in a relationship trust each other

3. *Satisfaction*—feelings that the relationship is successful and mutually beneficial
4. *Commitment*—feelings that the relationship is sufficiently important to warrant effort and resources

Administrators may attempt to manipulate or otherwise control relationships unilaterally; such behavior often has been observed in relationships between superintendents and school board members (Kowalski, 2006). This form of relationship management, however, usually produces misunderstandings and dissatisfaction (Grunig & Huang, 2000). One of the attributes of comprehensive PR is that the process provides a framework for mutuality concerning control, trust, satisfaction, and commitment.

CONCLUDING COMMENTS

Experts (e.g., Newsom, Turk, & Krukeburg, 2004; Seitel, 2004) believe that organizations benefit from a well-conceived PR program even in the best of times because two core functions, information management and open communication, are incessant activities linked to effective operations (Razik & Swanson, 2001). In the past, however, public schools faced limited competition; therefore, continuously accessing information to identify and solve problems was not necessarily a high priority. Today, administrators face noticeably different circumstances. In this information-based and reform-minded society, there can be dire consequences for superintendents and principals unable or unwilling to engage in organizational imaging, effective communication, marketing, and information management (Kowalski, 2003).

Image problems have played a major role in heightening interest in PR. During much of the 1960s and 1970s, for example, opinions of public education were damaged by incessant conflict between teacher unions and school boards (Campbell, Corbally, & Nystrand, 1983). Even today, some detractors argue that schools are controlled politically by national and state teacher unions. More recently, public education's image has been injured by a protracted and unusually intense demand for school reform. During this period, the primary critics have been individuals outside the education profession who by virtue of their stature are able to influence public opinion; the most notable examples include captains of business and industry, politicians (governors, mayors), and media representatives. Public schools always have been vulnerable politically and, for much of their existence, have been blamed for jeopardizing the nation's welfare (e.g., militarily after *Sputnik* and economically after an elevation of global competition) (Kowalski, 2004).

REFERENCES

Armistead, L. (2000). Public relations: Harness your school's power. *High School Magazine, 7*(6), 24–27.

Arriaza, G. (2004). Making changes that stay made: School reform and community involvement. *High School Journal, 87*(4), 10–24.

Baker, B. (1997). Public relations in government. In C. L. Caywood (Ed.), *The handbook of strategic public relations and integrated communication* (pp. 453–480). New York: McGraw-Hill.

Bauman, P. C. (1996). *Governing education: Public sector reform or privatization*. Boston: Allyn & Bacon.

Beach, R. H. (2004). Planning in public relations: Setting goals and developing strategies. In T. J. Kowalski (Ed.), *Public relations in schools* (3rd ed., pp. 227–250). Upper Saddle River, NJ: Merrill/Prentice Hall.

Broom, G. M., Casey, S., & Ritchey, J. (2000). Concept and theory of organization: Public relationships. In J. Ledingham & S. Bruning (Eds.), *Public relations as relationship management* (pp. 3–22). Mahwah, NJ: Erlbaum.

Campbell, R. F., Corbally, J. E., & Nystrand, R. O. (1983). *Introduction to educational administration* (6th ed.). Boston: Allyn & Bacon.

Cohen, P. M. (1987). *A public relations primer: Thinking and writing in context.* Upper Saddle River, NJ: Prentice Hall.

Connor, P., & Lake, L. (1988). *Managing organizational change.* New York: Praeger.

Cooper, B. S., Fusarelli, L. D., & Randall, E. V. (2004). *Better policies, better schools: Theories and applications*. Boston: Allyn & Bacon.

Daresh, J. (2004). Mentoring school leaders: Professional promise or predictable problems? *Educational Administration Quarterly, 40*(4), 495–517.

Dilenschneider, R. L. (1996). Public relations: An overview. In R. L. Dilenschneider (Ed.), *Public relations handbook* (pp. xix–xxix). Chicago: Dartnell.

Dozier, D. M. (with Grunig, L. A., & Grunig, J. E.). (1995). *Manager's guide to excellence in public relations and communication management.* Mahwah, NJ: Erlbaum.

Duke, D. (2004). *The challenge of educational change*. Boston: Allyn & Bacon

Fowler, F. C. (2000). *Policy studies for educational leaders: An introduction*. Upper Saddle River, NJ: Merrill/Prentice Hall.

Fullan, M. (2004). *Leadership and sustainability*. Thousand Oaks, CA: Corwin.

Gordon, J. C. (1997). Interpreting definitions of public relations: Self assessment and a symbolic interactionism-based alternative. *Public Relations Review, 23*(1), 57–66.

Grunig, J. E., & Huang, Y. H. (2000). Antecedents of relationships and outcomes. In J. Ledingham & S. Bruning (Eds.), *Public relations as relationship management* (pp. 23–54). Mahwah, NJ: Erlbaum.

Grunig, J. E., & Hunt, T. (1984). *Managing public relations*. New York: Holt, Rinehart &Winston.

Hall, G. E., & Hord, S. M. (2001). *Implementing change: Patterns, principals, and potholes*. Boston: Allyn & Bacon.

Hanson, E. M. (2003). *Educational administration and organizational behavior* (5th ed.). Boston: Allyn & Bacon.

Heck, R. H. (1991). Organizational and professional socialization: Its impact on the performance of new administrators. *Urban Review, 27*(3), 31–49.

Hoy, W., & Miskel, C. (2005). *Educational administration: Theory, research and practice* (7th ed.). New York: McGraw-Hill.

Huang, Y. H. (1997). *Public relations strategies, relational outcomes, and conflict management strategies*. Unpublished doctoral dissertation, University of Maryland, College Park.

Kotler, P. (1975). *Marketing for nonprofit organizations*. Upper Saddle River, NJ: Prentice Hall.

Kowalski, T. J. (2003). *Contemporary school administration* (2nd ed.). Boston: Allyn & Bacon.

Kowalski, T. J. (2004) School public relations: A new agenda. In T. J. Kowalski (Ed.), *Public relations in schools* (3rd ed., pp. 3–29). Upper Saddle River, NJ: Merrill, Prentice Hall.

Kowalski, T. J. (2005). Evolution of the school superintendent as communicator. *Communication Education, 54*(2), 101–117.

Kowalski, T. J. (2006). *The school superintendent: Theory, practice, and cases* (2nd ed.). Thousand Oaks, CA: Sage.

Kowalski, T. J., & Björk, L. G. (2005). Role expectations of the district superintendent: Implications for deregulating preparation and licensing. *Journal of Thought, 40*(2), 73–96.

Martinson, D. L. (1995). School public relations: Do it right or don't do it at all. *Contemporary Education, 66*(2), 82–85.

Martinson, D. L. (1999). School public relations: The public isn't always right. *NASSP Bulletin, 83*(609), 103–109.

McGaughy, C. (2000). Community development and education: A tripod approach to improving America. *Urban Review, 32*(4), 385–409.

Millar, F. E., & Rogers, L. E. (1976). A relational approach to interpersonal communication. In G. Miller (Ed.), *Explorations in interpersonal communication* (pp. 87–103). Newbury Park, CA: Sage.

National School Public Relations Association. (1986). *School public relations: The complete book.* Arlington, VA: Author.

Newsom, D., Turk, J. V., & Krukeburg, D. (2004). *This is PR : The realities of public relations* (8th ed.). Belmont, CA: Wadsworth/Thompson Learning.

Norris, J. S. (1984). *Public relations.* Upper Saddle River, NJ: Prentice Hall.

Peck, K. L., & Carr, A. A. (1997). Restoring public confidence in schools through systems thinking. *International Journal of Educational Reform, 6*(3), 316–323.

Petersen, G. J., & Kowalski, T. J. (2005). *School reform strategies and normative expectations for democratic leadership in the superintendency.* Paper presented at the Annual Conference of the University Council for Educational Administration, Nashville, TN.

Pfeiffer, I. L., & Dunlap, J. B. (1988). Advertising practices to improve school–community relations. *NASSP Bulletin, 72*(506), 14–17.

Place, A. W., McNamara, M., & McNamara, J. F. (2004). Collecting and analyzing decision-oriented data. In T. J. Kowalski (Ed.), *Public relations in schools* (3rd ed., pp. 299–318). Upper Saddle River, NJ: Merrill/Prentice Hall.

Razik, T. A., & Swanson, A. D. (2001). *Fundamental concepts of educational leadership* (2nd ed.). Upper Saddle River, NJ: Merrill/Prentice Hall.

Seitel, F. P. (2004). *The practice of public relations* (9th ed.). Upper Saddle River, NJ: Pearson Prentice Hall.

Spring, J. (1990). *The American school: 1642–1990* (2nd ed.). New York: Longman.

Surra, C. A., & Ridley, C. A. (1991). Multiple perspectives on interaction: Participants, peers, and observers. In B. Montgomery & S. Duck (Eds.), *Studying interpersonal interaction* (pp. 35–55). New York: Guilford.

West, P. T. (1985). *Educational public relations.* Beverly Hills, CA: Sage.

Wilcox, D., Ault, P., & Agee, W. (1992). *Public relations: Strategies and tactics* (3rd ed.). New York: HarperCollins.

Wirt, F., & Kirst, M. (2001). *The political dynamics of American education.* Berkeley, CA: McCutchan.

3

Effective Communication: The Nucleus of School Public Relations

Superintendent Alexander Jones constantly emphasized public relations with the school board, district employees, and the public. When he was employed 3 years ago, one of his first actions was to complete a detailed study of the district's communication office. After just four months in office, he reassigned the director, a former principal in one of the middle schools, and employed a public relations (PR) specialist who had been working for a department store. He then convinced the school board to double the communication office's annual budget. The two actions, he explained, were necessary to launch a campaign to improve the district's image. Over the next two years, the new director produced dozens of brochures, videotapes, and information packets designed to recapture taxpayer confidence in a school system that had lost one-third of its enrollment in less than 20 years. At the same time, student test scores plummeted, and half of the district's schools had been placed on academic probation by the state department of education.

Superintendent Jones expected the district's employees to be goodwill ambassadors. He told them to encourage community involvement and to make themselves available to the district's residents. His availability to the public and even employees, however, remained restricted. Excepting emergencies, principals had to make appointments several days in advance to see him privately. After a disgruntled principal raised a question about his accessibility to the public at a monthly administrative meeting, Superintendent Jones responded, "My job is to coordinate. I make sure that I have the right people in the right jobs and encourage them to do the right things. My position is different from yours. I'm the chief executive officer of this organization. CEOs of a major company don't spend their time meeting with customers."

INTRODUCTION

This vignette conveys a powerful message about the role of communication in school PR. All too often, administrators admit that they should interact with the public, but privately they view such contacts as being inconvenient, unimportant, and often unpleasant. Therefore, they relegate this responsibility to subordinates. Experiences with effective PR programs, however, inform us that every employee, and especially top-level administrators, must be competent communicators. Moreover, they must have dispositions that cast open information exchanges as being essential to maintaining organizational equilibrium. That is, the organization is in harmony with the external environment by virtue of making adaptations to ensure that the changing needs and wants of consumers or clients are satisfied (Schmuck & Runkel, 1994). Superintendents and principals should realize that their behavior is symbolically important; therefore, asking others to do what they are unwilling or incapable of doing almost always produces resentment (Bolman & Deal, 2002).

This chapter examines the significance of communication. First, the unfortunate disjunction between the importance placed on communication and the realities of administrator preparation and licensing is reviewed. Then the process of communication is examined from both personal and organizational perspectives. The purposes are to demonstrate the complexity of communication and to broaden your understanding of why communication competence has become essential to effective practice for district and school administrators.

DISJUNCTION BETWEEN THEORY AND PRACTICE

The relevance of communication should be viewed in two dimensions. From a personal perspective, there is compelling evidence that communication is a key variable in determining how others perceive a principal or superintendent. For example, people readily detect when an administrator has poor writing skills, poor verbal skills, or poor listening skills. Several studies (e.g., Davis, 1998) have identified weak communication skills as a primary reason why administrators get dismissed and, conversely, other studies (e.g., Mahoney, 1996; O'Hair & Reitzug, 1997) find that communication proficiency is a critical variable in successful practice.

Communication also is relevant to organizational success. For example, administrative communication styles and skills often influence how people treat each other, how they treat conflict, how they exchange information, and how they react to the need for change. The direct and symbolic effects are especially noteworthy. During planned organizational change initiatives, administrators must provide accurate information in order to prevent less informed individuals from making and interpreting education news. By using communication effectively, administrators are better able to counteract rumors and misinformation that is being distributed among staff and other stakeholders (Spaulding & O'Hair, 2004). Equally important, by engaging in open and continuous two-way communication, they are modeling expected behavior.

The centrality of communication in school administration is certainly evident in both the profession's literature and its symbolic gestures. Since 1980, many authors (e.g., Bredeson, 1988; Carter & Cunningham, 1997; Gousha & Mannan, 1991; Hunt, Simonds, & Cooper, 2002) stress that effective communication has become a normative standard for practice. Others (e.g., Friedkin & Slater, 1994; Morgan & Petersen, 2002; Petersen & Short, 2002) note that communication influences both school culture and institutional productivity. These assertions are not atypical in the literature on organizational leadership; authors studying organizations other than schools (e.g., Toth, 2000; Vihera & Nurmela, 2001) also conclude that there is a nexus between effective executive communication and organizational success. In recognition of the critical role communication plays in school administration, several authors (e.g., Geddes, 1993; Kowalski, 2005; Lester, 1993; Osterman, 1994) recommend changes in licensing laws that would require the study of communication.

Communication also has enjoyed the spotlight in the realm of practice. In awarding what is arguably its most prestigious honor, the National Superintendent-of-the-Year Award, the American Association of School Administrators (AASA) relies on just four criteria; communication and community relations (or PR) are two of them. However, objective analysis discloses that neither intellectual discourse nor practitioner awards have had the effect of producing uniform and defensible requirements for the study of communication within school administration (Kowalski, 2001, 2005). Research conducted among principals (e.g., Kowalski, 1998) indicates that most have not had any graduate-level instruction in this discipline, and, even more disconcerting, a relatively high percentage have never even completed an undergraduate communication course. Similarly, meta-analysis of superintendent preparation (e.g., Kowalski, 2005; Kowalski & Keedy, 2003; 2006) indicates that a majority of these administrators did not study communication theory or have clinical experiences that integrated communication systematically and formally into the superintendency (Kowalski, 2005).

UNDERSTANDING COMMUNICATION

Long ago, Lasswell (1948) stated that communication is shaped by "Who says What, to Whom, in Which channel, with What effect?" (p. 37). This simple definition, however, captures only one side of the communication equation. The other side might be stated as "Who heard What, from Whom, When, through Which channel, with What effect?" (Kowalski, 2003, p. 233). Communication also can be conceived in relation to its integral parts: a sender, a receiver, a sent message, a time when it was sent, a medium, and an outcome.

Lysaught (1984) writes that "problems of language, and meaning, and their transmission are among their [administrators] most important, persistent, and ubiquitous organizational difficulties" (p. 102). He argues that failures in communication result in a myriad of organizational problems including difficulties with visioning, goal-setting, productivity, and evaluation. One can reasonably conclude that there is a nexus between an organization being dysfunctional and executives being incompetent communicators. Consequently, communication competence is viewed appropriately as both an individual and organizational goal. A first step to competence is an accurate understanding of communication. Five characteristics shown in Figure 3.1 provide a foundation to acquiring this knowledge.

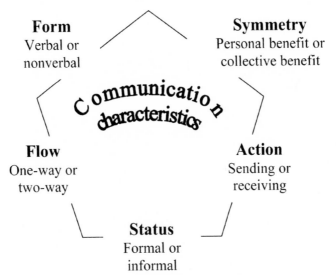

Form
Verbal or
nonverbal

Symmetry
Personal benefit or
collective benefit

Flow
One-way or
two-way

Action
Sending or
receiving

Status
Formal or
informal

Figure 3.1. Communication's Five Defining Characteristics

Form

Communication is commonly described by form, either *verbal* or *nonverbal*. Verbal communication entails the transmission or exchange of words; nonverbal communication involves behaviors that convey meaning without the use of language (Spaulding & O'Hair, 2004). Examples of nonverbal communication include gestures, expressions, and other forms of body language. According to Argyle (1988), nonverbal communication may serve four functions:

1. Expressing emotions
2. Expressing interpersonal attitudes
3. Presenting one's personality
4. Augmenting verbal communication (by reinforcing, regulating, complementing, or contradicting what is said)

The augmentation function is especially noteworthy because skilled communicators often interpret verbal messages in the context of the speaker's behavior (e.g., eye contact, voice inflections).

The importance of nonverbal communication has increased as districts and schools become more diverse culturally, racially, socially, and politically.

For example, cultural differences in areas such as visual contact and gestures have been well documented (Spaulding & O'Hair, 2004). Often school officials unfamiliar with cultural communication differences can make two serious errors: misinterpreting nonverbal behaviors and expressing nonverbal behaviors that are offensive to persons with a different cultural background.

Flow

The flow of communication is almost always described as being either one-way or two-way. The line between these categories, however, is not necessarily clean and crisp. Schmuck and Runkel (2004), for example, describe two forms of one-way communication, *unilateral* and *directive.* The former is one-way communication occurring in some manner other than face-to-face; an example is a principal's memorandum reminding employees that they have an obligation to arrive at work at least 20 minutes prior to the start of the homeroom period. Unilateral messages neither encourage the receiver to respond nor give the receiver an opportunity to respond. The sender typically is unable to verify if the message was received or interpreted correctly. *Directive communication* is described as being one-way but occurring face-to-face. Here, the receiver is simply asked to acknowledge that he or she understands the message rather than being given an opportunity to ask questions, seek explanations, or present a dissenting opinion. For example, a student who has been sent to the principal's office for misconduct is warned that the next time such an infraction occurs, he will be suspended from school. Rather than giving the student an opportunity to explain his behavior, the principal terminates the conversation by asking, "Do you understand what I just said?"

Two-way communication is interactive; that is, information travels between or among the individuals involved (individuals involved in communication are referred to as *interactants*). It too can occur face-to-face or in some other way. Examples of two-way communication where the interactants are not physically together include e-mail (provided the interactants exchange information), Internet chat rooms, and telephone conferences. The greatest opportunity for mutual understanding and mutual benefits occurs in two-way, face-to-face exchanges because interactants are able to transmit messages and seek clarifications both through their words and through their expressions.

Status

Communication is classified as being either *formal* or *informal*. Formality relates to organizational purpose. For example, when a principal communicates with others in her official capacity as an administrator, the communication is formal regardless of whether it occurs verbally or nonverbally or regardless of whether it occurs face-to-face or in some other way. Communication status may be affected by both intent and interpretation. As an example, a principal may make a casual comment to a neighbor over the fence about the poor performance of the school's football coach. Although the principal considers the conversation being informal, the neighbor interprets it differently; for example, he may infer that the principal intends to recommend the coach's dismissal. Because administrators live in a public "fishbowl," they must always be cautious about informal conversations and how they will be interpreted.

Action

Communication involves either sending information or receiving it. The former requires *encoding* skills; that is, the competency to prepare a message that conveys its intended meaning accurately. The latter entails *decoding* skills, or the ability to listen effectively and interpret accurately.

Action typically involves clarity. Consider two examples of communication problems created by principals. In the first, a middle school principal wrote the following sentence in the school's monthly newsletter: "Parents should be cautious about encouraging their children to participate in extracurricular activities." This ambiguous statement could be interpreted in several different ways. For example, some parents might conclude that the principal is generally opposed to extracurricular activities; others might interpret his words to mean that some activities are better than others. What the principal really meant to say is that parents should consider academic performance in relation to the amount of extracurricular activities their children pursue. In another situation, a high school principal prepared a progress report for the superintendent and parents on block scheduling in her school. She used terms like *block eight* and *teaming* without defining them. Thus, many parents were unable to grasp the full meaning when they read the report.

Organizational conflict often begins with encoding and decoding problems. This is why administrators should always recognize the differences
between encoding and decoding and why they should seek to improve
their performance in each area. Testing whether people interpret your
messages as they are intended and testing whether others interpret messages as you do are two effective ways to increase competency.

Symmetry

Communication can be *symmetrical* or *asymmetrical*. The former includes
exchanges designed to benefit all interactants; the latter includes exchanges designed to benefit only one interactant. The issue of symmetry
was introduced in the previous chapter in relation to PR. In organizations,
communication is more effective when it is directed toward the general
goal of improving individual and group behavior; that is, it is supposed to
affect behavior positively and in turn, the improved behavior facilitates
organizational goal attainment (Hanson, 2003). Consider a principal who
is required by policy to inform a first-year teacher that his performance,
observed by the principal during a classroom observation, was unsatisfac-
tory. If the principal's intent is solely to perform his duty, he can give the
teacher a memorandum detailing the deficiencies; this action provides
him with evidence that he followed policy. It does not provide the teacher
an opportunity to dispute the assessment or to ask questions. If the principal's intent is to ensure that the teacher and the teacher's students also
benefit from the evaluation, the communication would have to be structured differently. A face-to-face conference, for example, would make it
more likely that the goal of symmetrical communication would be met.

COMMUNICATION CHANNELS

How information gets transferred within districts and schools is another
essential issue for superintendents and principals. In communication literature, distribution processes are called *channels*, networks composed of
interconnected individuals (Hanson, 2003). These information conduits
may be formal or informal. *Formal channels* are created by or sanctioned
by the organization for the purposes of facilitating its mission and meet-

ing its goals (Kowalski, 2006). Two readily recognized examples of formal channels in districts and schools are the traditional chain of command and a network for informing employees, the media, and the public when schools must close unexpectedly (e.g., due to inclement weather). A chain of command is usually found in the district's line and staff chart (see Figure 3.2), and it becomes a communication channel when policy or rules require employees to adhere to the authority relationships when communicating. For example, an assistant elementary school principal could not converse with the superintendent unless he did so through the school's principal or by receiving the principal's permission to meet with the superintendent. The purpose of following the chain of command is to avoid conflict and to enhance efficiency. In actuality, this regimented arrangement can stifle creativity, open communication, and positive relationships.

Informal channels are essentially grapevines; they are neither created by nor sanctioned by the district or school (Kowalski, 2006). A depiction of an informal communication network in a small elementary school is shown in Figure 3.3. In this school, the second-grade teacher who is the sister of a school board member is a primary conduit for information from and to the school board. The network is designed to bypass both the principal and superintendent. Describing informal channels, Shockley-Zalabak (1988) writes, "These networks emerge as a result of formal networks and are

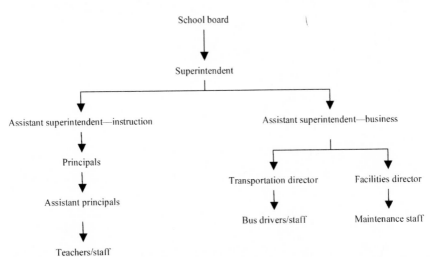

Figure 3.2. Formal Network Based on the Chain of Command in a 2,000-Student School District

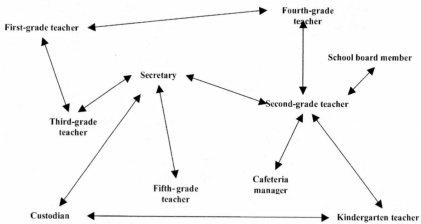

Figure 3.3. Informal Network in a Small Elementary School Designed to Bypass Administrators

formed by individuals who have interpersonal relationships, who exchange information across reporting chains, and who disregard formal status and timing" (pp. 47–48). People develop and use informal networks when they do not trust the formal networks or when they are dissatisfied with the information they receive from them. Although informal networks can be productive (e.g., a conduit for teachers to share ideas about their experiences with new teaching methods), they more frequently are counterproductive (e.g., they are rumor mills or sources of misinformation).

Administrators can decrease dependency on informal channels by strengthening formal networks. This is especially important during stressful periods, such as those involving organizational change. Katz and Kahn (1978) urge executives to focus on five issues in relation to formal networks:

1. *Inclusiveness.* This refers to the extent to which the communication loop includes all organizational subsystems (e.g., schools in a district, departments or grade levels in a school).
2. *Transmission.* This refers to the extent to which messages remain unaltered as they pass through different organizational levels.
3. *Feedback capacity.* This refers to the network's provisions for two-way communication.
4. *Efficiency.* This refers to the speed and accuracy of transmissions.

5. *Organizational fit.* This refers to the appropriateness of the network in relation to the organization's characteristics, mission, and vision.

In constructing formal channels, administrators should consider organizational design and availability of information technology (Hoy & Miskel, 2005). *Design* refers to the degree to which the district or school centralizes authority. Overall, however, formal communication networks are most effective in education institutions when they have the following qualities:

- *Interactive.* They facilitate two-way, continuous communication.
- *Symmetrical.* They distribute information equally.
- *Recurrent.* They provide information frequently.
- *Accessible.* Everyone has access to them.
- *Recognized.* They are known to all who are a part of them (Kowalski, 1999).

The topic of formal and informal networks is discussed in greater detail in chapter 8.

COMMUNICATION PROBLEMS

Administrators do not become effective communicators naturally. Competence depends largely on personal knowledge and skills; that is, one must know about communication and be able to apply that knowledge within the context of practice. Consider a principal who has been directed by the superintendent to transfer a teacher involuntarily to another school. The principal has to make several critical decisions in carrying out the order. Three questions are especially cogent:

1. *How should the message be sent?* The principal can convey the message to the teacher in several different ways—for example, through a formal letter, a routine memorandum, an e-mail message, a telephone conversation, a third party contact (e.g., having an assistant principal or department chair tell the teacher), or a face-to-face conference. A wide array of personal, professional, political, and legal

factors should be weighed before deciding which medium is most appropriate. In some cases, more than one medium may be needed—for example, having a face-to-face conference and giving the teacher a formal letter during the conference.

2. *When should the communication occur?* A number of factors could be weighed in deciding when to present the message to the teacher. Some are legal (e.g., complying with state law, district policy, and the master contract with the teachers' union), some are professional (e.g., determining when to send the message given the teacher's responsibilities to students), and some are political (e.g., determining when to send the message based on an attempt to avoid or reduce conflict).

3. *What quantity of information is necessary?* The principal needs to decide how much to say in the message. For example, this could range from simply saying, "I hereby notify you that you are being transferred to another assignment effective . . ." to providing both a legal explanation and a personal note (e.g., an expression of sorrow that the transfer must take place). More than a few principals have discovered that the content of the message can produce legal or political problems.

Organizations also manifest communication problems. These difficulties are associated with elements of institutional climate that range from a lack of material resources to social behavior, to organizational design, to shared values and beliefs (Hanson, 2003). Perhaps the most common organizational problem is strict adherence to the chain of command. This practice limits information for key officials who set policy and guide the organization. Additionally, it almost always spawns political problems as influential individuals bypass the chain. Other common communication problems are summarized here:

- *Poor listening skills.* Far too many of us devalue the importance of listening skills in communication and underestimate the degree to which others recognize if we are poor listeners. Trying to capture the deeper meanings in messages (e.g., by observing nonverbal behavior or by reading between the lines), improving comprehension and memory skills, and asking clarifying questions in a conversation are ways that we can improve as listeners (Spaulding & O'Hair, 2004).

- *Poor language skills.* Difficulties with grammar, vocabulary, or linguistics result in encoding and decoding problems, and these errors are particularly detrimental when an organization is pursuing planned change (Quirke, 1996). For example, a principal who uses inappropriate words may convey an unintended message to parents and staff.
- *Lack of credibility and trust.* No matter how well structured and delivered, a message can fail to produce its intended effect if an administrator lacks credibility or trust. Credibility pertains to believability. In schools, principals may lack credibility with teachers in the area of instructional supervision. That is, teachers believe that the administrator knows little about pedagogy; therefore, the principal's suggestions for improved teaching performance are ignored. Trust involves confidence. It is often destroyed by telling untruths or by not honoring confidentiality. For example, a principal lies to employees by telling them that the superintendent and school board are not considering staff reductions. Her motive is noble; she does not want to lower morale. Her gain is temporary, however, and is eventually outweighed by negative consequences after the truth surfaces. The punishment for lying can be a loss of public respect and trust (Howard & Mathews, 1994), and the employees may mistrust any future messages. Ensuring that communication is accurate is the best way to avoid credibility and trust problems.
- *Communication oversights.* Administrators may fail to be inclusive in their communication. Therefore, some individuals requiring or desiring information do not receive it. This problem has been especially evident in school-to-home communication (Kowalski, 2003). Consider the principal who did not inform parents that a proposal to adopt block scheduling was being considered. When parents learned about the proposal via the grapevine, they formed their own conclusions about the merits of block scheduling and about the principal's motives for not discussing the issue with them. In today's world, the Internet and intense media coverage make it nearly impossible for administrators to conceal pertinent information from stakeholders. Groups and individuals affected by administrative decisions understandably want to have input, and increasingly, they are willing to bypass formal networks if their participation is obstructed.

- *Inaccessibility.* Stakeholders expect administrators to be accessible, and if their attempts to communicate are ignored, they often complain to higher level officials or school board members (Kowalski, 2006). E-mail and fax machines allow people to initiate communication freely and they provide a record that an attempt to communicate occurred. Although it is unfair to expect that administrators in larger districts and schools will respond personally and immediately to every contact, most employees and patrons anticipate that their questions and comments will not be totally ignored. This is an area where a well-developed public relations program can be very beneficial.
- *Elitism.* Some administrators make themselves accessible only to select individuals. Like the more general problem of accessibility, this difficulty may be encouraged by organizational conditions (e.g., a highly structured environment in which top-level executives are discouraged from fraternizing with subordinates). More directly, however, it stems from two personal convictions: spending your time with power elites (persons of considerable influence) is in your best interest and the school's best interest; you enhance your professional stature by remaining aloof (Kowalski, 1999). Both views ignore the condition that separates school administration from most other service professions. Administrators face the seemingly contradictory challenge of providing intellectual leadership (based on their professional knowledge) while being sensitive to the political will of the people (Wirt & Kirst, 2001).
- *Inadequate attention to effect.* Administrators may fail to determine whether a communication has produced its intended effect. The potential for this problem is highest when principals and superintendents engage primarily in one-way communication. Frequently, administrative messages are not decoded in the intended manner; for example, using emotion-producing terms, such as *redistricting* or *reductions in force*, produces contextual noise (the effect of situational conditions that influence decoding), resulting in a discrepancy between the sent message and the received message (Lysaught, 1984). The most expedient and effective way to reduce such problems is to rely on two-way communication. Misinterpretations often become known when receivers are allowed to ask questions or comment. This is why very serious matters (e.g., issuing a reprimand to an employee) should provide some face-to-face communication.

- *Information overload.* Administrators usually receive a considerable amount of information from multiple sources, including many messages from outside the organization (e.g., directives from state officials, letters from angry parents). If improperly managed, this situation produces an overload resulting in problems. The more common difficulties include *omitting* (e.g., failing to process information), *queuing* (e.g., not processing information until time is found to do so), *filtering* (e.g., incorrectly determining that some information may be nonessential), *generalizing* (e.g., reducing the specificity of information by skimming through it), *relegating* (e.g., having a secretary read communication to determine its relevance even though she may not be properly qualified to do so), and *escaping* (not dealing with information, such as tossing letters in the wastebasket without reading them) (Miller, 2003). Unfortunately, no simple recipe solves overload problems because each administrator's situation is somewhat unique. However, two actions are helpful. The first is ensuring that you have sufficient time to deal with information; this is a time management issue. The second is utilizing technology to process information. Personal computers, fax machines, and other equipment have made it possible for us to handle increasing amounts of information.

- *Excessive use of informal channels.* Often administrators do not recognize that their behavior actually encourages others to develop their own information sources. Historically, formal organizational channels in districts and schools were designed so that information came from the top without provisions for receiver interaction. The origins of this normative standard are nested in three efficiency-related tenets of classical theory (bureaucracy): (a) administrators should protect information as a means of exercising control; (b) when necessary, administrators should disseminate information to subordinates on a "need-to-know" basis (subordinates should never receive more information than is essential, nor should they receive information that will distract them from being efficient); (c) there is no reason for communication to move upward since supervisors have more technical knowledge than subordinates (Hanson, 2003). Although administrators cannot eliminate informal communication channels, they should try to influence their value and frequency of use because many messages transmitted through them are distorted or even inaccurate. The most effective strategy for reducing the effects of informal communication channels is to devise formal channels that are inclusive, accessible, timely, and interactive (allowing for two-way communication) (Kowalski, 2003).

CONCLUDING COMMENTS

As the United States moved from being a manufacturing society to an information-based society, all professions paid more attention to practitioner communication skills. In particular, the belief that every leader learns to be an effective communicator by virtue of experience was challenged. Increasingly, school administration scholars have advocated the infusion of communication into professional preparation and licensing standards. Regrettably, this rhetoric has not yet been paralleled by action.

The objective of this book is to show that the process of school public relations is essential to completing the difficult journey to reform. In this chapter, communication is presented as a complex but essential process for school public relations. Unless administrators become effective communicators, they are unlikely to produce the leadership required for district and school-based reforms. More specifically, they will not be prepared to assume the most challenging but vital tasks, such as facilitating democratic discussions of purpose, building shared visions, and acquiring broad-based support for positive change.

REFERENCES

Argyle, M. (1988). *Bodily communication* (2nd ed.). London: Methuen.

Bolman, L. G., & Deal, T. E. (2002). Leading with soul and spirit. *School Administrator, 59*(2), 21–26.

Bredeson, P. V. (1988). Communications as a measure of leadership in schools: A portraiture of school principals. *High School Journal, 71*, 178–186.

Carter, G. R., & Cunningham, W. G. (1997). *The American school superintendent*. San Francisco: Jossey-Bass.

Davis, S. H. (1998). Why do principals get fired? *Principal, 28*(2), 34–39.

Friedkin, N. E., & Slater, M. R. (1994). School leadership and performance: A social network approach. *Sociology of Education, 67*, 139–157.

Geddes, D. S. (1993). Empowerment through communication: Key people-to-people and organizational success. *People and Education, 1*, 76–104.

Gousha, R. P., & Mannan, G. (1991). *Analysis of selected competencies: components, acquisition and measurement perceptions of three groups of stakeholders in education.* (ERIC Document Reproduction Service No. ED336 850)

Hanson, E. M. (2003). *Educational administration and organizational behavior* (5th ed.). Boston: Allyn & Bacon.

Howard, C. M., & Mathews, W. K. (1994). *On deadline: Managing media relations.* Prospect Heights, IL: Waveland.

Hoy, W. K., & Miskel, C. G. (2005). *Educational administration: Theory, research, and practice* (8th ed.). New York: McGraw-Hill.

Hunt, S. K., Simonds, C. J., & Cooper, P. J. (2002). Communication and teacher education: Exploring a communication course for all teachers. *Communication Education, 51*(1), 81–94.

Katz, D., & Kahn, R. (1978). *The social psychology of organizations* (2nd ed.). New York: Wiley.

Kowalski, T. J. (1998). Communication in the principalship: Preparation, work experience, and expectation. *Journal of Educational Relations, 19*(2), 4–12.

Kowalski, T. J. (1999). *The school superintendent: Theory, practice, and cases.* Upper Saddle River, NJ: Merrill, Prentice Hall.

Kowalski, T. J. (2001). The future of local school governance: Implications for board members and superintendents. In C. Brunner & L. Björk (Eds.), *The new superintendency* (pp. 183–201). Oxford, UK: JAI, Elsevier Science.

Kowalski, T. J. (2003). *Contemporary school administration: An introduction* (2nd ed.). Boston: Allyn & Bacon.

Kowalski, T. J. (2005). Evolution of the school superintendent as communicator. *Communication Education, 54*(2), 101–117.

Kowalski, T. J. (2006). *The school superintendent: Theory, practice, and cases* (2nd ed.). Thousand Oaks, CA: Sage.

Kowalski, T. J., & Keedy, J. (2003, November). *Superintendent as communicator: Implications for professional preparation and licensing.* Paper presented at the Annual Conference of the University Council for Educational Administration, Portland, OR.

Kowalski, T. J., & Keedy, J. (2006). Preparing superintendents to be effective communicators. In L. Björk & T. Kowalski (Eds.), *The contemporary superintendent: Preparation, practice and development* (pp. 207–226). Thousand Oaks, CA: Corwin.

Lasswell, H. D. (1948). The structure and function of communication in society. In L. Bryson (Ed.), *The communication of ideas* (pp. 39–51). New York: Harper.

Lester, P. E. (1993). *Preparing administrators for the 21st century.* Paper presented at the Annual Meeting of the New England Educational Research Organization, Portsmouth, NH.

Lysaught, J. P. (1984). Toward a comprehensive theory of communications: A review of selected contributions. *Educational Administration Quarterly, 20*(3), 101–127.

Mahoney, J. (1996). The secrets of their success. *Executive Educator, 18*(7) 33–34.

Miller, K. (2003). *Organizational communication: Approaches and processes* (3rd ed.). New York: Wadsworth.

Morgan, C. L., & Petersen, G. J. (2002). The role of the district superintendent in leading academically successful school districts. In B. S. Cooper & L. D. Fusarelli (Eds.), *The promises and perils facing today's school superintendent* (pp. 175–196). Lanham, MD: Scarecrow Education.

O'Hair, M. J., & Reitzug, U. C. (1997). Restructuring schools for democracy: Principals' perspectives. *Journal of School Leadership, 7*(4), 266–286.

Osterman, K. F. (1994). Communication skills: A key to collaboration and change. *Journal of School Leadership, 4*(4), 382–398.

Petersen, G. J., & Short, P. M. (2002). An examination of school board presidents' perceptions of their superintendent's interpersonal communication competence and board decision making. *Journal of School Leadership, 12*(4), 411–436.

Quirke, B. (1996). *Communicating corporate change.* New York: McGraw-Hill.

Schmuck, R. A., & Runkel, P. J. (1994). *The handbook of organization development in schools and colleges* (4th ed.). Prospect Heights, IL: Waveland.

Shockley-Zalabak, P. (1988). *Fundamentals of organizational communication.* New York: Longman.

Spaulding, A. M., & O'Hair, M. J., (2004). Public relations in a communication context: Listening, nonverbal, and conflict-resolution skills. In T. J. Kowalski (Ed.), *Public relations in schools* (3rd ed., pp. 96–122). Upper Saddle River, NJ: Merrill, Prentice Hall.

Toth, E. L. (2000). From personal influence to interpersonal influence: A model for relationship management. In J. A. Ledingham & S. D. Bruning (Eds.), *Public relations as relationship management* (pp. 205–220). Mahwah, NJ: Erlbaum.

Vihera, M. L., & Nurmela, J. (2001). Communication capability as an intrinsic determinant for an information age. *Futures, 33*(3/4), 245–265.

Wirt, F. M., & Kirst, M. W. (2001). *The political dynamics of American education* (2nd ed.). Berkeley, CA: McCutchan.

4

School Reform and Effective
Administrator Communication

Dr. Catherine Walsh was described by the East Highland School District board president as a dynamic change agent who would restore the district's schools to their former glory. Now enrolling approximately 7,000 students, the district has lost nearly 30% of its enrollment in 15 years as residents with school-age children relocate to newer and more affluent suburbs or elect to send their children to new charter schools. The incremental decline in enrollment has negatively affected state aid and local tax revenues but according to the school board president, the most serious repercussion of the enrollment decline has been a downturn in the district's performance. During the last 15 years, for example, the high school graduation rate has declined from 92% to 80% and the percentage of high school graduates enrolling in 4-year colleges and universities has declined by 13%.

After successfully instituting reforms in a smaller school district, Dr. Walsh decided she was ready for new challenges. She accepted the East Highland position confident that she would replicate her previous successes. Her school improvement formula was rather basic: engage the community and district employees in visioning, establish a plan for change that included specific performance goals, and provide staff development for the employees to ensure goal attainment. Even though many district employees, including administrators, were visibly skeptical about the need for school reform, she was able to complete the first two phases in approximately 16 months. When her plan reached level 3, however, employee skepticism progressed to overt and covert resistance.

Employee defiance was perhaps most evident in relation to an improvement goal calling for cooperative learning to be deployed in elementary schools. Once teachers and principals were required to attend workshops, their reactions to school reform in general and to cooperative learning specifically were mixed. Some said they resented the fact that they had to attend workshops; some said that the values and beliefs underlying cooperative learning were flawed; some expressed enthusiasm about experimenting with the instructional strategy. Few of them, however, agreed with Dr. Walsh's assertion that curricular or instructional changes would make an appreciable difference in the district's performance. In their minds, they were not responsible for negative trends. This sentiment was summarized publicly in the following passage from a letter written by the teachers' union president and published on the local newspaper's editorial page: "Blaming teachers for lower productivity is unwarranted and unfair. We are the same teachers who produced positive outputs consistently in the past. We don't control demographic trends in this community, and therefore, we are not responsible for a loss of revenue and a changing student population."

Both the content of the letter and its tone surprised Dr. Walsh, because to that point, she had been unaware of the union's negative attitude toward her reform program. She had relied almost entirely on progress reports from principals and none of them had indicated serious opposition or even concerns. She had no direct communication with the teachers' union president and her limited contact with other teachers did not provide signals that the improvement efforts were not widely accepted.

INTRODUCTION

The brief description of change resistance in the East Highland School District demonstrates that successful reform requires more than a proven leader and good intentions. Moreover, it reveals the critical role organizational culture plays in shaping educator dispositions toward change. As discussed in chapter 1, Sarason (1996) found that between 1970 and the early 1990s, most public elementary and secondary education had not been changed and concluded that an intractable institutional culture was to blame. His analysis of institutional culture and school change has influenced the writing of many education scholars, especially in relation to the following two conclusions:

1. Meaningful improvement is unlikely to occur in schools that have change-resistant cultures (Duke, 2004; Fullan, 2001; Hall & Hord, 2001).
2. Culture change must be pursued locally with superintendents and principals providing necessary leadership (Henkin, 1993; Murphy, 1994).

The typical administrator, however, has been skeptical about the wisdom of functioning as a true change agent. Doubt has been fueled both by a conviction that society really does not want change and by a conviction that internal reform (i.e., change from within the organization) is unattainable in the case of public schools. Misgivings about trying to restructure schools or school personnel roles also are exacerbated by the fact that most administrators have neither been prepared academically nor socialized professionally to be change agents (Kowalski, 2006; Murphy, 1994). Consequently, reform pressures, and especially those coming from outside the education profession, often conflict with a prevailing conviction that public schools are intended to be social agencies of stability (Streitmatter, 1994).

The content of this chapter examines the critical nature of administrator communication in school reform. The current goal of restructuring is examined first in order to identify the basic tasks involved with this process. Second, districts and schools are analyzed as organizations; important concepts such as organizational equilibrium, organizational development, institutional climate, and school culture are given focused attention. Then, traditional strategies for organizational change and their shortcomings are identified. Lastly, culture change is presented as an essential strategy for school restructuring, and the nexus between this approach and administrator communication is detailed.

Reconstructing Schools

Imagine a manufacturing company facing the dilemma of having one out of every three products it produces being defective. You need not be an Ivy League business school graduate to realize that this company is in trouble. Yet public education's failure rate, defined here as the percentage of students who either do not graduate from high school or who graduate as functional illiterates, has been at this level for decades (Schlechty, 1990; 2001).

After studying failed attempts to improve schools during the 1980s, many analysts (e.g., Henkin, 1993; Murphy, 1991; 1994) found that generic reforms were unsuccessful because they did not address the considerable variability in (a) real student needs, (b) school resources, and (c) school cultures. They then concluded that effective reform required change to be pursued locally (i.e., at the district or even individual school level) and required principals and superintendents to be primary change agents.

Adopting the Concept of Directed Autonomy

In the face of growing evidence that their efforts to impose generic mandates had not been successful, policymakers shifted the locus of reform to the local level. That is, they adopted a form of *directed autonomy*—a strategy in which state officials set broad performance goals, give local officials greater leeway to determine how they would pursue those goals, and then hold these officials accountable for outcomes (Weiler, 1990).

Requiring school boards and superintendents to set reform policy has both professional and political repercussions. From a professional standpoint, directed autonomy presents an opportunity for educators to play a significant role in shaping school improvement strategies; from a political perspective, it makes it more probable that educators, and not policymakers, will be blamed if reforms fail (Kowalski, 2006). After completing two national studies of failed reforms spanning several decades, Sarason (1996) warns that specific initiatives would have little effect on improving schools unless counterproductive beliefs regarding organizational change were diagnosed, challenged, and altered. Consider two beliefs pivotal to reinforcing convictions that restructuring schools is unnecessary: educators often believe that teachers are more productive when they work individually and in seclusion (Gideon, 2002); educators often believe that schools are more productive when they evade community interventions (Blase & Anderson, 1995).

Essential Administrative Tasks

The literature identifies six administrative tasks essential to school restructuring (see Figure 4.1). Each is affected by the prevailing atmosphere in a school and each has the potential to change that atmosphere. The first task is *building an open school climate*. School climate is often described with respect to the organization's disposition toward external interventions—that is, intercessions from groups and individuals outside the organization (Hanson, 2003). In a closed climate, school officials attempt to isolate their organization so that policy and decision making can be controlled internally; in an open climate, administrators encourage stakeholder participation in an effort to ensure that the organization adapts to changing social needs (Kowalski, 2006).

The differences between closed and open climates are illustrated in Figure 4.2 and exemplified by practices in two rural districts located just 50 miles apart. The school board in the first district, the one having a closed climate, meets once a month at 8:00 A.M. on a Saturday. The meeting is held in the superintendent's conference room, an environment that provides little space and no seating for visitors. The school board in the other

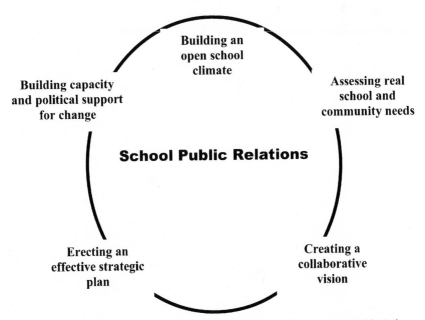

Figure 4.1.   Possible Contributions of School Public Relations to Systemwide Reform

Closed

Political pressure groups

Local government officials

Administrators exert energy discouraging and repelling interventions from community groups and agencies in an effort to avoid conflict and maintain efficiency.

Athletic booster clubs

Taxpayers association

Open

Political pressure groups

Local government officials

Administrators encourage interactions with community groups and agencies and view conflict as a catalyst for necessary changes.

Athletic booster clubs

Taxpayers association

Figure 4.2.   Closed-School and Open-School Climates

district meets twice a month on Tuesday evenings at 7:00 P.M. The meetings rotate among the six schools and are held in the school libraries. The intent is to have as much community participation as possible.

Public schools do not operate in a vacuum; they are repeatedly influenced by a myriad of legal, social, political, and economic forces. Historically, however, administrators have been socialized to believe that citizen and employee participation in problem solving and decision making inevitably produces conflict which then results in organizational inefficiency (Hanson, 2003). In essence, they were influenced by more experienced administrators who treated democratic leadership as a counterproductive administrative style (Kowalski, 2003). Such behavior was less consequential in the past because citizens usually were content having school boards, superintendents, and principals make important decisions. Today, primary stakeholders (e.g., employees, parents, patrons) expect administrators to lead by expressing ideas but they insist on being included in open and fair debates about these ideas (Baker, 1997). When denied such opportunities, disgruntled patrons often resort to covert political actions that serve to divide communities into competing interest groups.

Forward-thinking administrators treat conflict as a catalyst for needed change; hence, widespread participation is not only tolerated, it is encouraged. This perspective of conflict was summarized by Uline, Tschannen-Moran, and Perez (2003):

> Conflict is a natural part of collective human experience. In our efforts to cooperate with one another, we have differences of opinion about how best to accomplish our common goals. We seek to protect our individual interests within these efforts and forestall outside influences, fearing discord in the face of these conflicting forces. Conflict is often unsettling. It can leave participants shaken and ill at ease, so it is often avoided and suppressed. Yet conflict, when well managed, breathes life and energy into relationships and can cause individuals to be much more innovative and productive. (p. 782)

Within this open climate perspective, administrators not only engage in conflict management for pragmatic reasons (i.e., to control disputes and maintain working relationships), they also attempt to capitalize on conflict as a medium for organizational change.

Assessing real school and community needs is the second administrative responsibility. A need is a gap between what is and what is required. For instance, if a high school's graduation rate is 63% and the state benchmark for accreditation is 85%, improving the rate by 22% is a real need. Needs assessment is a formal process through which administrators identify and analyze such gaps (Kirst & Kelley, 1995). Much of the information required for a needs assessment that exists outside the school district itself must be collected periodically through a process called *environmental scanning* (Beach, 2004)—one of the defining characteristics of strategic planning (Poole, 1991). School officials can conduct surveys, public opinion polls, and similar techniques to obtain data that identify changing trends that alter stakeholder needs and wants (Stellar & Kowalski, 2004).

Creating a collaborative vision is the third administrative responsibility. Unfortunately, the concept of vision remains an enigma for many practitioners; for example, many administrators confuse mission and vision statements (Rozycki, 2004). Properly written, the former describes an organization's overall purpose—its reason for existing (Kowalski, 2006). Historically, administrators have taken mission statements for granted because much of what public schools should do is determined by state laws and policy (Coleman & Brockmeier, 1997). Mission statements, however, can be augmented at the local level. They serve multiple purposes including informing the public and employees, cultivating unity of purpose, providing a frame of reference for strategic planning goals, and guiding difficult decisions (e.g., resource allocation decisions) (Kowalski, 2006).

A vision has its own purpose. Visions are instrumental in that they provide a guide for long-term action, a symbolic statement that gives meaning to action (Conger, 1989), and a sociological force that generates shared commitment essential to intended change (Björk, 1995). In most basic terms, a vision is an image of what a district or school should look like in meeting its mission at some point in the future (Winter, 1995). Clearly, then, a vision statement will be flawed if the mission statement on which it is based is inaccurate or considered unimportant. Visions are indispensable to planned change because they define gaps between the present and desired future.

Today, the notion that an administrator should unilaterally determine a district's or school's vision is not only politically unacceptable, it is inconsistent with prevailing thought on organizational development (discussed later; see also Kowalski, 2006). Lessons learned from organizational change research indicate that visions are more supportable and effective when they are an amalgam of individual visions and widely supported by the various publics affected. In the case of public schools, all stakeholders should be given an opportunity to state their personal visions and to react to those proposed by others (Tomal, 1997). However, reaching consensus, even in a small school system, requires open and candid communication and skilled conflict management allowing administrators to "effectively monitor, interact, and react to key groups within the organizational environment" (Lamb & McKee, 2005, p. 1).

Erecting an effective strategic plan is the fourth responsibility. Planning is a process through which data are analyzed and then integrated with mission and evolving social conditions so that informed resource allocation decisions can be made in relation to achieving the approved vision (Cunningham & Gresso, 1993). Establishing goals and selecting strategies for achieving them are essential planning tasks (Sergiovanni, 2001). Strategy development encompasses both process and technique (organizational change strategies are discussed later in this chapter). Process details the sequence of steps to be taken whereas technique identifies approaches that will be used at each stage (that is, tactics for reaching goals) (Nutt, 1985). One of the most popular processes is a five-step continuous planning cycle that integrates needs assessment and visioning:

1. Formulating—interfacing current conditions with a vision to identify needs
2. Conceptualizing—breaking needs into small components and selecting a planning paradigm appropriate to the task
3. Detailing—identifying and refining contingency approaches (plausible alternatives) to meeting the identified needs
4. Evaluating alternatives—determining costs, benefits, potential pitfalls, and selecting the best alternative
5. Implementing—identifying implementation techniques and adopting strategies to gain acceptance of the planning process (Nutt, 1985).

Ideally, planning for school improvement is a strategic process. *Strategic plan*ning is a long-range activity (extending beyond one year) (McCune, 1986) that has three notable characteristics:

1. *Environmental scanning*—monitoring the environment consistently and continuously to identify opportunities and needs
2. *Inclusive stakeholder participation*—allowing all segments of the school's various publics to participate or have input
3. *Vision-driven*—the process is focused on achieving an approved vision (Justis, Judd, & Stephens, 1985; Verstegen & Wagoner, 1989)

Inclusion reflects a social system perspective to planning (Schmidt & Finnigan, 1992); that is, the process recognizes that all school subsystems are interrelated and educational outcomes are rarely, if ever, attributable to a single cause (Kowalski, 2006).

To reiterate, a mechanism for information exchanges between a school and its relevant publics is pivotal to environmental scanning and thus to strategic planning (Beach, 2004). Similarly, established communication channels, information management, and conflict resolution are important to an organization's capacity to include stakeholders (Kowalski, 2004).

Building capacity and political support for change is the fifth responsibility. Once plans for achieving a vision are in place, superintendents and principals must lead and facilitate their implementation. Firestone (1989) defines capacity as "the extent to which the district has knowledge, skills, personnel, and other resources necessary to carry out decisions" (p. 157). Duke (2004) identifies three facets of district or school change capacity: (1) a supportive organizational structure, (2) a culture that embraces change, and (3) adequate resources to support capacity-building efforts.

Numerous authors (e.g., Berliner & Biddle, 1995; Björk, 1993; Duke, 2004; Hopkins, 2001; Short & Greer, 1997; Short & Rinehart, 1992) have identified the following conditions underlying capacity building:

- Altering governance and decision-making structures to institutionalize distributed and transformational forms of leadership
- Aligning and delivering professional development activities with distributed leadership and instructional improvement tasks to enhance the capacity of teachers and principals to successfully implement change initiatives
- Recruiting and selecting teachers, principals, and key central office staff whose views on the future of schooling are consistent with district goals
- Providing adequate resources to support planned change initiatives
- Valuing and the use of data in improving learning and teaching
- Building community capacity

These factors promote collective action and nurture a change-receptive culture. In addition, Björk (1993) and Firestone (1989) note that district superintendents occupy a strategic position in the organization and have managerial levers at their disposal that can be employed to launch and sustain education reform.

Enabling others to be productive also includes staff development. The complexity of the education process and the challenges of educational change often make it unlikely that necessary skills will be acquired by administrators and teachers without planned interventions (Duke, 2004). During recent years, professional development has been moving away from short-term venues that emphasize "seat time" and "credit hours" to research-based, continuous, performance-assessed, and systemic learning experiences (Björk, Kowalski, & Browne-Ferrigno, 2006).

Districts and schools are dependent on local communities for political and financial support; therefore, administrators must assess and nurture this support to ensure that reforms get implemented (Duke, 2004; Hoyle, Björk, Collier, & Glass, 2005). Public schools derive substantial benefits from working with stakeholders including: (a) political capital in the form of increased financial support (Valenzuela & Dornbush, 1994), (b) social capital in the form of positive dispositions and interrelationships among citizens (Smylie & Hart, 1999), and (c) human capital in the form of increased citizen knowledge and skills (Bourdieu, 1986; Coleman, 1990). Too often, however, administrators have viewed community collaboration as a process that could be turned off and on at will. Symbiotic relationships between schools and their stakeholders require more than intermittent information exchanges, especially when those exchanges occur only when school officials seek more money (Kowalski, 2004).

DISTRICTS AND SCHOOLS AS ORGANIZATIONS

Administrative tasks associated with school restructuring are carried out in an organizational context. Organizations have been described as integrated systems of independent structures known as groups; and in all organizations, these groups are composed of individual members (Berrien, 1976). Despite being immersed in organizations, many individuals do not understand them, nor do they comprehend how these social and political systems influence behavior.

Some authors have used metaphors to explain organizations. Owens (2001), for instance, compares organizations to the human body by noting that groups and individuals in the former function much like cells and molecules in the latter. That is, components in both organizations and the human body are interdependent, and over time none becomes self-governing.

Morgan (1986) offers several other metaphors for organizations. For example, he likens bureaucratic organizations to machines—entities where some parts were purposely designed to interface with other parts, and to do so with a minimum loss of energy. He also postulates that organizations could be viewed as systems of political activity in which groups vie for power.

Organizational behavior is the term identifying individual and group attitudes and actions within an organizational context (Johns, 1988). At the individual level, behavior is the product of interactions between personal conditions (e.g., employee personality and needs) and organizational structure (e.g., prescribed roles and rules). At the group level, behavior is the product of shared personal conditions (e.g., positions taken by a teachers' union toward forced change) and organizational structure (Hanson, 2003). Much of school administration involves diagnosing organizational behavior and then attempting to change it when it has a negative influence on organizational productivity.

Organizational Uncertainty

Organizational uncertainty makes administrative work difficult (Thompson, 1967). This condition is created by ambiguity in philosophy, mission, and structure. Its presence causes confusion regarding institutional mission (i.e., knowing what the organization is supposed to accomplish). Uncertainty also results in greater risk for administrators making decisions because it causes individuals to question the value of their work and the organization's motives (March & Simon, 1958). In public schools, uncertainty is evidenced by philosophical differences regarding institutional purpose. For example, even professional staff in a school may not agree that academic excellence and social development are equally important or that being prepared for college trumps being prepared for the job market.

Uncertainty also makes it more difficult for schools to maintain *organizational equilibrium*. Equilibrium is a state in which a school is in harmony with its broader community (Hanson, 2003; Hoy & Miskel, 2005). Clearly, the degree to which equilibrium exists across districts and schools varies markedly and the actual level falls at some point on a continuum between being imbalanced or balanced (see Figure 4.3). Disequilibrium has long been recognized as a destructive force that intensifies external pressures for change.

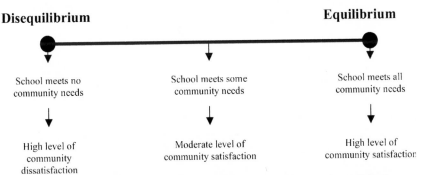

Figure 4.3.   Relationship Between School Equilibrium and Community Satisfaction

Organizational Development

Organizational development (OD) is an intervention intended to reduce disequilibrium. Schmuck and Runkel (1994) describe OD in education institutions as "a coherent, systematically planned, sustained effort at system self-study and improvement, focusing explicitly on change in formal and informal procedures, processes, norms, or structures, and using behavioral science concepts" (p. 5). They add that the purposes of OD are to improve "the quality of life of individuals as well as organizational functioning and performance with a direct or indirect focus on educational issues" (p. 5).

Although OD is not a new idea, applications have become more challenging over time because of dynamic social and political contexts. The dawn of the information age discussed in chapter 1 exemplifies the fluid nature of the ecosystem in which schools operate. Mehlinger (1996) referred to the information age as America's third revolution (following the Agriculture Revolution and Industrial Revolution as discussed in chapter 1). Connecting school reform to an information-based society, he portrayed the convergence as an "immovable object" (schools) meeting an "irresistible force" (information technology). Optimistically, he predicted that school reform would be more successful than in the past because the infusion of technology would give educators little choice but to change. The alterations that have occurred since the mid-1970s, however, have been more evolutionary than revolutionary. In addition, neither the quality nor the quantity of the transitions has been universal.

The unevenness of change in schools is evident in communicative behavior—that is the manner in which administrators and teachers relate to each other and to persons outside of their work environments (Kowalski, 2005). A study conducted in the late 1990s (Williamson & Johnston,

1998), for example, found that parents (a) complained that school personnel were unresponsive to their requests and inquiries, (b) received mixed messages from school personnel, (c) were unaware of how to get information about the school, and (d) were unaware of who they should contact regarding routine problems.

Irregular effects of change also are detectable in the manner in which school administrators have reacted to criticism and to the negative images of their organizations. Broadly speaking, the responses characterize three different types of administrators:

1. Those who remained silent hoping that damaging conditions would dissipate naturally
2. Those who counterattacked either by denying the validity of the criticisms or by denouncing the critics' motives
3. Those who initiated dialogue among stakeholders so that community needs and values pertinent to education could be stated and then tested (Amundson, 1996)

The third category of administrators relied on the *communicative view for school reform* (St. John & Clements, 2004). The value of this view rose considerably after the locus of school improvement shifted to local districts. Citizen participation is essential to local reforms. Recognizing this fact, policymakers in a growing number of states (e.g., Florida, Kentucky) and Canadian provinces (e.g., Calgary, Ontario) have required school councils to be established to ensure that inclusive visioning and planning took place. Unfortunately, evidence suggests that participation in local reform efforts often has been either bogus, superficial, or ineffective (Anderson, 1998). To be influential, participation must span stakeholders across multiple publics (Thomas, 1996), and meaningful engagement requires opportunities for stakeholders to exert leadership in critical functions such as needs assessment, visioning, and planning (Cortes, 1995).

Disjunctions between ideal and real participation are partially explained by administrative behavior; even when mandated to involve others, some superintendents and principals have covertly opposed and even obstructed such directives (Thompson, 1996). Participatory reform also has been attenuated by the quantity and quality of communication occurring between school officials and the community (Carr, 1995). As noted previously, some administrators opt to communicate with the public only when they need political or economic support.

Organizational Climate

Every organization has a unique climate. With respect to education institutions, Hoy and Miskel (2005) describe climate as "a relatively enduring quality of the school environment that is experienced by participants, affects their behavior, and is based on their collective perceptions of behavior in schools" (p. 185). Climate is commonly described in relation to its four components:

1. *Ecology*—consisting of the physical attributes of the environment (e.g., buildings, technology, books, furniture)
2. *Milieu*—consisting of social relationships (e.g., how participants treat each other and outsiders)
3. *Organizational structure*—consisting of structural designs that determine how the school functions (e.g., line of authority, curriculum, annual calendar, daily schedule, departments or grade levels)
4. *Culture*—consisting of values and beliefs shared by the school's employees (e.g., regarding the ability of all students to succeed, regarding the role of parents in education, regarding peer collaboration) (Hanson, 2003)

Restructuring can involve change in any and all of climate's four components; however, the level of difficulty for imposing change in them is not uniform (Kowalski, 2003). In fact, there is an inverse relationship between ease of change and effect of change. That is, elements of culture that are easiest to change tend to have the least amount of influence on organizational productivity (Kowalski, 2003). Changes to ecology are arguably the easiest to pursue because they spark the least resistance, especially among employees. For instance, building a new school, remodeling an existing school, or adding new technology are initiatives educators typically support. Changing curriculum (e.g., interdisciplinary courses in a middle school), scheduling (e.g., block scheduling), instructional paradigms (e.g., teaming), and calendars (e.g., year-round schooling) are likely to generate more opposition, but they typically are easier than changing a school's social structure. Revamping milieu requires either personnel changes or behavioral changes among personnel. The former is hindered by legal (e.g., tenure laws), political (e.g., pressure group support), and economic (e.g., litigation costs) barriers; the latter is hindered by the time and cost associated with therapeutic interventions.

Without question, revamping institutional culture is the most formidable task in climate change. Underlying shared beliefs that influence behavior often are difficult to identify either because employees are unwilling to talk about them or because they are unable to do so. Reluctance to discuss them usually stems from an awareness that the views in question are inappropriate professionally or incorrect politically. The inability to discuss the views results when employees suppress their views.

Understanding the varying levels of difficulty in changing elements of school climate is critical to effective administrative practice. When pressured to produce change, superintendents and principals intuitively elect to pursue aspects of climate that are easiest to change (Kowalski, 2006). This partially explains why actions such as improving facilities and implementing block scheduling are relatively common school improvement initiatives. Although these changes may improve a school's image, they do not necessarily improve student outputs, especially when they are not accompanied by behavioral changes (e.g., individualizing instruction, setting student expectations, assessment and evaluation of pupil progress) (Fullan, 2001; Hall & Hord, 2001).

School Culture

A school's culture is composed of the shared fundamental values that inform employees how to address their work (Schein, 1996; Trimble, 1996) and how they should promote and accept change (Duke, 2004; Leithwood, Jantzi, & Fernandez, 1994). They are often described in relation to two qualities: *unity of beliefs* and *appropriateness of beliefs*. The former quality is described along a continuum from weak to strong. In weak cultures, there is little unity; in a strong culture, the educators largely embrace the same beliefs. The latter quality is described along a continuum from negative to positive. A negative culture is characterized by beliefs that conflict with the professional knowledge base; a positive culture is characterized by beliefs embedded in that knowledge base (Kowalski, 2003). The two continua are shown in Figure 4.4.

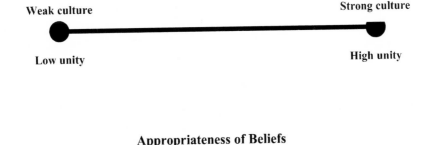

Unity of Beliefs

Weak culture   Strong culture

Low unity   High unity

Appropriateness of Beliefs

Negative culture   Positive culture

Inappropriate beliefs   Appropriate beliefs

Figure 4.4.   **Essential Characteristics of School Culture**

Schein (1992) describes culture as having three distinct layers. On the surface, one finds physical *artifacts* that usually communicate what a school's culture values. As examples, the prominent display of athletic trophies in a public school indicates that competitive sports are important and a crucifix on the wall of a classroom indicates that the school is affiliated with the Catholic Church.

The middle layer of culture contains *espoused beliefs*—that is, beliefs people communicate publicly. These beliefs may be found in philosophy statements, school handbooks, and school policy and they may or may not accurately communicate values that influence behavior. As an example, a school may claim to promote democratic decision making and student self-discipline, but in reality, the principal is an autocrat and rules governing student behavior may actually discourage self-development.

The lowest and most important layer of culture contains *underlying beliefs* influencing both the behavior of educators and their dispositions toward the necessity and value of organizational change. Unearthing these true beliefs is very difficult in most schools either because teachers and administrators will not admit to them or because they really do not recognize that they are influenced by them (Firestone & Louis, 1999). Through the process of socialization, these beliefs get transformed into routine behaviors

(Schein, 1992). Consider a situation in which teachers in an inner-city school believe that at least half of their students will not succeed regardless of instructional interventions. Consequently, they delude themselves into believing that they cannot help students predestined to fail and, therefore, devote little time to helping these students. However, when asked whether the failure of some students is predetermined, they rarely would admit to this conviction. If they do so consciously, it is because they know that this belief is either incongruent with the professional knowledge base or politically incorrect. If they do so unconsciously, it is because they have suppressed a belief that causes internal conflict (Schein, 1992).

TRADITIONAL CHANGE STRATEGIES

Organizational change has been pursued through three types of strategies described by Chin and Benne (1985). *Empirical-rational* approaches are predicated on the belief that after being given evidence demonstrating the need for change, persons will act rationally and implement proposed changes. As an example, a superintendent may develop a report showing declining student performance in the school district and then ask the district's employees to implement new instructional strategies. These approaches often fail because people do not always act rationally; that is, even in the face of compelling evidence supporting the need for change, some employees will refuse to change for political or emotional reasons.

Normative-reeducative approaches are predicated on the belief that new programs or instructional paradigms (i.e., new normative standards for teaching) will be adopted by educators after they are properly educated to implement them. As an example, a superintendent promotes block scheduling as a preferred format for secondary schools and then provides staff development programs for principals and teachers. Although this type of strategy has been widely used in education, its level of success is debatable. Educators, even when they are initially open-minded, experience a reversion after staff development if the underlying beliefs associated with the new norm are not compatible with the beliefs shared by a majority of the school's teachers (Kowalski, 2006).

Efforts to reform schools also have used power and coercion (referred to as *power-coercive approaches*). This stratagem is predicated either on a conviction that educators are unwilling to change or on a conviction that they are incapable of implementing change independently. Therefore, persons possessing power try to force educators to change, usually by deploying positional, legal, political, or economic enforcement criteria. As an example, a superintendent sends a memorandum to employees informing them that they must implement block scheduling the following school year. He then adds that all professional employees are required to attend two workshops related to the transition and notes that disciplinary actions will be taken against those who fail to comply. Though this approach to change is quick and decisive, it rarely works well in education because teachers have considerable autonomy in classrooms, allowing them to resist ideas they reject (Kowalski, 2006).

In summary, traditional change strategies have been less than effective when applied to public education largely because would be change agents have tried to alter schools without having analyzed the prevailing culture. Consequently, reform initiatives, even when well conceived, almost always were rejected if they conflicted with the underlying assumptions shared by educators expected to implement them. Accordingly, scholars who have studied failed school reforms (e.g., Fullan, 2001; Sarason, 1996) have concluded that necessary improvements are highly improbable unless change-resistant and negative school cultures are transformed.

CULTURE CHANGE AND ADMINISTRATOR COMMUNICATION

Peter Senge (1990) argues that to be highly effective organizations must replace change-resistant cultures with *learning cultures*. He describes the latter type of organization as one "where people continually expand their capacity to create the results they truly desire, where new and expansive patterns of thinking are nurtured, where collective aspiration is set free, and where people are continually learning to see the whole together" (p. 3). Learning cultures, per se, are belief systems built "on the assumption that communication and information are central to organizational well-being and must therefore create a multi-channel communication system that allows everyone to connect to everyone else" (Schein, 1992, p. 370).

Changing a school's culture is a complex and difficult task. First, administrators must properly diagnose existing culture, and as noted earlier, this task is usually quite difficult. Principals must earn the trust of school employees so that teachers will talk openly about their shared values and beliefs. Second, culture change requires a properly structured vision. Vision presents a mental image of what the school should look like in meeting its mission at some point in the future. If the vision is unrealistic or if it is not widely embraced, culture change efforts will suffer (Tomal, 1997). Third, administrators must engage members of the school community in discussions that interface prevailing values and beliefs with vision; the purpose is to determine whether current culture facilitates or impedes progress toward the vision.

A nexus between organizational culture and communication has been detailed in both school administration literature (e.g., Hanson, 2003; Kowalski, 1998; 2005) and communication literature (e.g., Hall, 1997). Describing this relationship, Conrad (1994) writes, "Cultures are communicative creations. They emerge and are sustained by the communicative acts of all employees, not just the conscious persuasive strategies of upper management. Cultures do not exist separately from people communicating with one another" (p. 27). Despite the fact that most organizational research has categorized culture as a causal variable and communication as an intervening variable (Wert-Gray, Center, Brashers, & Meyers, 1991), their relationship also has been described as reciprocal. Axley (1996), for instance, contends that "communication gives rise to culture, which gives rise to communication, which perpetuates culture" (p. 153).

Facilitating culture change is especially difficult for administrators who lack (a) a deep understanding of organizational culture (Sarason, 1996), (b) experience as a change agent (Murphy, 1994), and (c) competence as a communicator (Kowalski, 2005). Even when superintendents and principals are knowledgeable and competent, they discover that culture change is often a slow, deliberate process that may take three or more years to accomplish (Fullan 2001; Schein, 1992).

CONCLUDING COMMENTS

After attempting to improve schools by mandating higher standards for students and educators in the 1980s, policymakers moved toward directed autonomy in the 1990s (Bauman, 1996). Under this strategy, state officials set broad goals and provide leeway to local school officials to determine how those goals should be met. At the same time, however, the state officials hold local officials accountable for the outcomes. As a result of this policy shift, school restructuring has become the primary change objective; restructuring entails developing new iterations of governance and school climate. In the process of pursuing school restructuring, practitioners have learned that school culture is their most formidable barrier.

The probability of restructuring schools—that is, of changing climate in general and culture specifically—is increased significantly when the process is led by administrators who provide direction (King & Blumer, 2000), symbolic leadership (Fullan, 2001; Murphy, 1994), and facilitation through effective communication (Corbett, 1986; D'Aprix, 1996; Goodman, Willis, & Holihan, 1998; Quirke, 1996; Walker, 1997). Engaging stakeholders in discussion of seemingly intractable governance, power, and organizational design problems, however, is a risk-laden assignment for administrators even under favorable conditions (Carlson, 1996; Heckman, 1993), but it is especially perilous for administrators who are not competent communicators (Kowalski, 2005).

REFERENCES

Amundson, K. (1996). *Telling the truth about America's public schools.* Arlington, VA: American Association of School Administrators.

Anderson, G. L. (1998). Toward authentic participation: Deconstructing the discourses of participatory reforms in education. *American Educational Research Journal, 35*(4), 571–603.

Axley, S. R. (1996). *Communication at work: Management and the communication-intensive organization.* Westport, CT: Quorum Books.

Baker, B. (1997). Public relations in government. In C. L. Caywood (Ed.), *The handbook of strategic public relations and integrated communication* (pp. 453–480). New York: McGraw-Hill.

Bauman, P. C. (1996). *Governing education: Public sector reform or privatization.* Boston: Allyn & Bacon.

Beach, R. H. (2004). Planning in public relations: Setting goals and developing strategies. In T. J. Kowalski (Ed.), *Public relations in schools* (3rd ed., pp. 202–224). Upper Saddle River, NJ: Merrill, Prentice Hall.

Berliner, D., & Biddle, B. (1995). *The manufactured crisis: Myths, fraud, and the attack on America's public schools*. Reading, MA: Addison-Wesley.

Berrien, F. K. (1976). A general systems approach to organizations. In M. Dunnette (Ed.), *Handbook of industrial and organizational psychology* (pp. 41–62). Chicago: Rand McNally.

Björk, L. G. (1993). Effective schools effective superintendents: The emerging instructional leadership role. *Journal of School Leadership, 3*(3), 246–259.

Björk, L. G. (1995). Substance and symbolism in the education commission reports. In R. Ginsberg & D. Plank (Eds.), *Commissions, reports, reforms and educational policy* (pp. 133–149). New York: Praeger.

Björk, L. G., Kowalski, T. J., & Browne-Ferrigno, T. (2006). Learning theory and research: A framework for changing superintendent preparation and development. In L. G. Björk & T. J. Kowalski (Eds.), *The contemporary superintendent: Preparation, practice and development* (pp. 71–108). Thousand Oaks, CA: Corwin.

Blase, J., & Anderson, G. (1995). *The micropolitics of educational leadership: From control to empowerment*. New York: Teachers College Press.

Bourdieu, P. (1986). The forms of capital. In J. Richardson (Ed.), *Handbook of theory and research for sociology education* (pp. 141–258). New York: Greenwood.

Carlson, R. V. (1996). *Reframing and reform: Perspectives on organization, leadership, and school change*. New York: Longman.

Carr, B. (1995). Communication failure can threaten progress. *Journal of Educational Relations, 16*(4), 18–22.

Chin, R., & Benne, K. D. (1985). General strategies for effecting changes in human systems. In W. G. Bennis, K. D. Benne, & R. Chin (Eds.), *The planning of change* (4th ed., pp. 22–43). New York: Holt, Rinehart & Winston.

Coleman, D. G., & Brockmeier, J. (1997). A mission possible: Relevant mission statements. *School Administrator, 54*(5), 36–37.

Coleman, J. (1990). *Foundations of social theory*. Cambridge, MA: Harvard University Press.

Conger, J. A. (1989). *The charismatic leader: Behind the mystique of exceptional leadership*. San Francisco: Jossey-Bass.

Conrad, C. (1994). *Strategic organizational communication: Toward the twenty-first century* (3rd ed.). Fort Worth, TX: Harcourt Brace.

Corbett, W. J. (1986). Corporate culture: An opportunity for professional communicators. *Bulletin of the Association for Business Communication, 49*(2), 14–19.

Cortes, E. (1995, November 22). Making the public the leaders in education reform. *Education Week, 15*, 34.

Cunningham, W., & Gresso, D. (1993). *Cultural leadership: The culture of excellence in education*. Boston: Allyn & Bacon.

D'Aprix, R. (1996). *Communicating for change: Connecting the workplace with the marketplace.* San Francisco: Jossey-Bass.

Duke, D. (2004). *The challenge of educational change.* Boston: Allyn & Bacon.

Firestone, W. (1989). Using reform: Conceptualizing district initiative. *Educational Evaluation and Policy Analysis, 11*(2), 151–164.

Firestone, W. A., & Louis, K. S. (1999). Schools as cultures. In J. Murphy & K. S. Louis (Eds.), *Handbook of research on educational administration* (2nd ed., pp. 297–322). San Francisco: Jossey-Bass.

Fullan, M. (2001). *Leading in a culture of change.* San Francisco: Jossey-Bass.

Gideon, B. H. (2002). Structuring schools for teacher collaboration. *Education Digest, 68*(2), 30–34.

Goodman, M. B., Willis, K. E., & Holihan, V. C. (1998). Communication and change: Effective change communication is personal, global, and continuous. In M. B. Goodman (Ed.), *Corporate communication for executives* (pp. 37–61). Albany: State University of New York Press.

Hall, E. T. (1997). *The silent language.* New York: Doubleday.

Hall, G. E., & Hord, S. M. (2001). *Implementing change: Patterns, principles, and potholes.* Boston: Allyn & Bacon.

Hanson, E. M. (2003). *Educational administration and organizational behavior* (5th ed.). Boston: Allyn & Bacon.

Heckman, P. E. (1993). School restructuring in practice: Reckoning with the culture of school. *International Journal of Educational Reform, 2*(3), 263–272.

Henkin, A. B. (1993). Social skills of superintendents: A leadership requisite in restructured schools. *Educational Research Quarterly, 16*(4), 15–30.

Hopkins, D. (2001). *Improvement for real.* London: Routledge/Falmer.

Hoy, W. K., & Miskel, C. G. (2005). *Educational administration: Theory, research, and practice* (8th ed.). New York: McGraw-Hill.

Hoyle, J. R., Björk, L. G., Collier, V., & Glass, T. (2005). *The superintendent as CEO: Standards-based performance.* Thousand Oaks, CA: Corwin.

Johns, G. (1988). *Organizational behavior: Understanding life at work* (2nd ed.). Glenview, IL: Scott, Foresman.

Justis, R. T., Judd, R. J., & Stephens, D. B. (1985). *Strategic management and policy.* Englewood Cliffs, NJ: Prentice Hall.

King, M., & Blumer, I. (2000). A good start. *Phi Delta Kappan, 81*(5), 356–360.

Kirst, M. W., & Kelley, C. (1995). Collaboration to improve education and children's services: Politics and policy making. In L. Rigsby, M. Reynolds, & M. Wang (Eds.), *School-community connections: Exploring issues for research and practice* (pp. 21–44). San Francisco: Jossey-Bass.

Kowalski, T. J. (1998). The role of communication in providing leadership for school reform. *Mid-Western Educational Researcher, 11*(1), 32–40.

Kowalski, T. J. (2003). *Contemporary school administration: An introduction* (2nd ed.). Boston: Allyn & Bacon.

Kowalski, T. J. (2004). School public relations: A new agenda. In T. J. Kowalski (Ed.), *Public relations in schools* (pp. 3–29). Upper Saddle River, NJ: Merrill, Prentice Hall.

Kowalski, T. J. (2005). Evolution of the school superintendent as communicator. *Communication Education, 54*(2), 101–117.

Kowalski, T. J. (2006). *The school superintendent: Theory, practice, and cases* (2nd ed.). Thousand Oaks, CA: Sage.

Lamb, L. F., & McKee, K. B. (2005). *Applied public relations: Cases in stakeholder management*. Mahwah, NJ: Erlbaum.

Leithwood, K., Jantzi, D., & Fernandez, A. (1994). Transformational leadership and teachers' commitment to change. In J. Murphy & K. S. Louis (Eds.), *Reshaping the principalship* (pp. 77–98). Thousand Oaks, CA: Corwin.

March, J. G., & Simon, H. A. (1958). *Organizations*. New York: Wiley.

McCune, S. D. (1986). *Guide to strategic planning for educators*. Alexandria, VA: Association for Supervision and Curriculum Development.

Mehlinger, H. D. (1996). School reform in the information age. *Phi Delta Kappan, 77*, 400–407.

Morgan, G. (1986). *Images of organization*. Newbury Park, CA: Sage.

Murphy, J. (1991). *Restructuring schools*. New York: Teachers College Press.

Murphy, J. (1994). The changing role of the superintendency in restructuring districts in Kentucky. *School Effectiveness and School Improvement, 5*(4), 349–75.

Nutt, P. C. (1985). The study planning processes. In W. G. Bennis, K. D. Benne, & R. Chin (Eds.), *The planning of change* (4th ed., pp. 198–215). New York: Holt, Rinehart & Winston.

Owens, R. G. (2001). *Organizational behavior in education: Instructional leadership and school reform* (7th ed.). Boston: Allyn & Bacon.

Poole, M. L. (1991). Environmental scanning is vital to strategic planning. *Educational Leadership, 48*(4), 40–41.

Quirke, B. (1996). *Communicating corporate change*. New York: McGraw-Hill.

Rozycki, E. G. (2004). Mission and vision in education. *Educational Horizons, 82*(2), 94–98.

Sarason, S. B. (1996). *Revisiting the culture of the school and the problem of change*. New York: Teachers College Press.

Schein, E. H. (1992). *Organizational culture and leadership* (2nd ed.). San Francisco: Jossey-Bass.

Schein, E. H. (1996). Culture: The missing concept in organization studies. *Administrative Science Quarterly, 41*(2), 229–240.

Schlechty, P. C. (1990). *Schools for the twenty-first century: Leadership imperatives for educational reform.* San Francisco: Jossey-Bass.

Schlechty, P. C. (2001). *Shaking up the schoolhouse: How to support and sustain educational innovation.* San Francisco: Jossey-Bass.

Schmidt, W., & Finnigan, J. (1992). *The race without a finish line: America's quest for total quality.* San Francisco: Jossey-Bass.

Schmuck, R. A., & Runkel, P. J. (1994). *The handbook of organizational development in schools and colleges* (4th ed.). Prospect Heights, IL: Waveland.

Senge, P. (1990). *The fifth discipline: The art and practice of the learning organization.* New York: Doubleday/Currency.

Sergiovanni, T. J. (2001). *The principalship: A reflective practice perspective* (4th ed.). Boston: Allyn & Bacon.

Short, P., & Greer, J. (1997). *Leadership in empowered schools: Themes form innovative efforts.* Upper Saddle River, NJ: Merrill, Prentice Hall.

Short, P., & Rinehart, J. (1992). School participant empowerment scale: Assessment of the level of participant empowerment in the school. *Educational and Psychological Measurement, 54*(2), 951–960.

Smylie, M., & Hart, A. (1999). School leadership for teacher learning and change: Human and social capital development. In J. Murphy & K. S. Louis (Eds.), *Handbook of research on educational administration* (2nd ed., pp. 421–441). San Francisco: Jossey-Bass.

St. John, E. P., & Clements, M. M. (2004). Public opinions and political consensus. In T. J. Kowalski (Ed.), *Public relations in schools* (3rd ed., pp. 47–67). Upper Saddle River, NJ: Merrill, Prentice Hall.

Stellar, A., & Kowalski, T. J. (2004). Effective programming at the district level. In T. J. Kowalski (Ed.), *Public relations in schools* (pp. 151–173). Upper Saddle River, NJ: Merrill, Prentice Hall.

Streitmatter, J. (1994). *Toward gender equity in the classroom: Everyday teachers' beliefs and practices.* Albany: State University of New York Press.

Thomas, G. (1996). Keys to effective public engagement in school reform. *Thrust for Educational Leadership, 25*(2), 16–17.

Thompson, D. R. (1996). Locking horns vs. linking arms the choice is ours. *School Administrator, 53*(5), 8.

Thompson, J. D. (1967). *Organization in action.* New York: McGraw-Hill.

Tomal, D. R. (1997). Collaborative process intervention: An alternative approach for school improvement. *American Secondary Education, 26*, 17–20.

Trimble, K. (1996). Building a learning community. *Equity and Excellence in Education, 29*(1), 37–40.

Uline, C. L., Tschannen-Moran, M., & Perez, L. (2003). Constructive conflict: How controversy can contribute to school improvement. *Teachers College Record, 105*(5), 782–816.

Valenzuela, A., & Dornbush, S. (1994). Familism and social capital in the academic achievement of Mexican origin and Anglo adolescents. *Social Science Quarterly, 75*, 18–36.

Verstegen, D. A., & Wagoner, J. L. (1989). Strategic planning for policy development: An evolving model. *Planning and Changing, 20*(1), 33–49.

Walker, G. (1997). Communication in leadership. *Communication Management, 1*(4), 22–27.

Weiler, H. N. (1990). Comparative perspectives on educational decentralization: An exercise in contradiction? *Educational Evaluation and Policy Analysis, 12*(4), 433–448.

Wert-Gray, S., Center, C., Brashers, D. E., & Meyers, R. A. (1991). Research topics and methodological orientations in organizational communication: A decade of review. *Communication Studies, 42*(2), 141–154.

Williamson, R. D., & Johnston, J. H. (1998). Responding to parent and public concerns about middle level schools. *NASSP Bulletin v, 82*(599), 73–82.

Winter, P. A. (1995). Vision in school planning. A tool for crafting a creative future. *School Business Affairs, 61*(6), 46–50.

5

Communicative Competence
in School Administration

As explained in the previous chapter, school restructuring is unlikely to occur unless administrators deploy culture change strategies. Properly diagnosing existing culture, building a collaborative vision, and interfacing existing culture with that vision require school leaders to be effective communicators. Although the topic of communication has received increased attention in school leadership literature (e.g., Bredeson, 1988; Hunt, Simonds, & Cooper, 2002), and although a growing number of authors (e.g., Geddes, 1993; Kowalski, 2005; Lester, 1993; Osterman, 1994) recommend the integration of communication into preparation curricula for administrators, the treatment of communicative competency within the profession has remained superficial (Kowalski, 2005; 2006). More specifically, there is no universally accepted definition of communicative competence in school administration, nor are there accepted criteria for assessing competency.

This chapter examines the meaning of communication competence with specific reference to school administration. First, the evolution of communication from a role-related skill to a role characterization is explained. Then, preparation/licensing communication criteria are analyzed to demonstrate their insufficiency in relation to current expectations for practitioners. Last, recommendations are made for developing a cogent definition of communication competence within the school administration profession.

COMMUNICATION AS A ROLE CHARACTERIZATION

As discussed in chapter 1, the context of practice for superintendents and principals began changing about 25 years ago, largely because of the convergence of school reform policies and rapid development of information technology. After 1980, the pursuit for meaningful improvement evolved from mandating students and educators to do more of what they were already doing to much more complex initiatives intended to restructure both school governance and school climate (Wirt & Kirst, 2001). Incrementally, new expectations were imposed on superintendents and principals, most notably that they function as change agents. For most experienced practitioners, the new expectations were unwelcomed, both because they were not socialized to be change agents and because their knowledge and skills in this area were limited (Kowalski, 2005).

Relationships between organizational structure and communication are highly relevant to building learning cultures (Fullan, 2001; Kowalski, 1998b). As explained in the previous chapter, the process of school restructuring is nested in the belief that public school districts will meet local community needs more fully if they are less hierarchical and more heterarchical or holographic (systemic) (Razik & Swanson, 2001). Put another way, schools are more successful when they maintain organizational equilibrium (i.e., meeting the community's needs), and achieving equilibrium requires school administrators to engage in inclusive and continuous communication processes.

Transitions in Normative Behavior

Normative communicative behavior refers to acceptable standards for communication behavior. Such standards vary depending on social environments. As an example, expectations for your behavior at home or at church may be different from those that exist at work. The argument is made here that standards for school administrator communication have been transformed in the recent past. Most notably, communication has evolved from a role-related skill to a separate and distinct role characterization.

Viewing Communication as a Skill

Historically, communication in school administration was treated as a role-related skill meaning that using specific communicative behaviors helped to determine if a person successfully met role expectations (Kowalski, 2005). More directly, a skill refers "to the ability to do something in an effective manner" (Yukl, 2002, p. 176), and a communication skill has been defined as "the ability of an individual to perform appropriate communicative behavior in a given situation" (McCroskey, 1982, p. 3).

Theory and craft knowledge traditionally taught in business schools reinforce the conclusion that normative communication standards have been set contextually in the past, most often in relation to two variables: *organizational character* and *executive function* (Henderson, 1987). Each merits explanation.

1. *Organizational character.* Mintzberg (1973) observes that different structures encourage and produce different communicative behaviors. As an example, administrative communication processes used in a professional bureaucracy (e.g., a hospital or school) and those used in a mechanical bureaucracy (e.g., a factory producing transformers) almost always are dissimilar. Administrators learn communicative norms based on organizational character during their induction into a specific organization—a process entailing institutional socialization.

2. *Executive function.* Although there are many administrative tasks, they are commonly divided into the two general categories of management and leadership. This categorization is not only prevalent in business administration (e.g., Yukl, 2006; Zaleznik, 1989) but also used widely in the literature on school administration (e.g., Kowalski, 2003; Razik & Swanson, 2001). Management functions concentrate on *how* to do things, and they focus on control, supervision, and subordinate relationships. Leadership functions concentrate on *what* needs to be done and they focus on inclusiveness, shared meaning, and collective visions (Duke, 2004; Kowalski, 2003). Executives often have learned to adjust their communicative behavior as they transition from a management role to a leadership role (Zaleznik, 1989). School administrators learn communicative norms based on executive functions during their induction into their profession (e.g., graduate study, internships, and contact with experienced practitioners)—a process entailing professional socialization.

Both the character of public schools and variations in general roles led administrators to believe that it was appropriate to adjust their communicative behavior depending on the function they were performing at any given time. For example, a principal would communicate one way when dealing with building maintenance issues and another way when providing clinical supervision to a teacher.

During most of the last century, management science advocated and organizational socialization reinforced a classical communication model. This paradigm, common in traditional bureaucracies, encouraged managers to communicate by issuing instructions and commands down a chain of command and only from them to the person or persons below (Luthans, 1981). In a book on administrative communication published in the early 1960s, for instance, Thayer (1961) identifies only four communication functions: informing, instructing (or directing), evaluating, and influencing. Within this conceptualization, communication effectiveness is determined solely by the quality of messages composed and transmitted downward by administrators (Clampitt, 1991). This narrow perspective ignored the fact that the communicative behavior of executives often influenced subordinate commitment and job satisfaction (e.g., Guzley, 1992; Trombetta & Rogers, 1988). School administrators, historically prone to emulate private sector managers, typically adopted this classical communication model; that is, they usually communicated with subordinates, and especially with teachers, impersonally and unilaterally (Achilles & Lintz, 1983).

The classical communication model promotes one-way, directive, coercive exchanges designed to reduce opportunities for mutual influence and information sharing (McGregor, 1967). It is a *complementary form of communication* that results in parties maximizing power and dominance differences (Burgoon & Hale, 1984). Although considered efficient, it seriously hampers the extent to which administrators engage stakeholders in meaningful discourse (Hoy & Miskel, 2005). Superintendents and principals who use complementary communication emphasize the detached nature of management in order to achieve efficiency but they also ignore both the moral dimension of dealing with people (Sergiovanni, 2001) and the negative consequences of their actions on organizational productivity (Razik & Swanson, 2001). Table 5.1 summarizes an elementary school principal's motives and behavior using a classical communication model.

In modern institutions, complementary communication can be especially disadvantageous for administrators because communicative behavior shapes perceptions of executive effectiveness (Richmond, McCroskey, Davis, & Koontz, 1980; Snavely & Walters, 1983). In an information age,

Table 5.1. Communication Characteristics in an Elementary School Using a Classical Model

Characteristic	Norm	Principal's Motive and Behavior
Flow	One-way, top-down	In an effort to control the use of information, the principal establishes unidirectional channels that do not permit information exchanges (e.g., sending memoranda to teachers).
Status	Formal	In an effort to maintain an impersonal relationship with teachers, he communicates only in his capacity as their superior and uses only established organizational channels.
Action	Sending	In an effort to reinforce the notion that teachers have no knowledge to offer him, he disseminates but does not exchange or receive information.
Nature	Directive	In an effort to reinforce his authority, he uses communication to issue commands, instructions, reprimands, criticism, and so forth.
Intent	Coercion	In an effort to fulfill his responsibility to ensure that teachers follow policy and rules, he uses communication to bully teachers.
Power/dominance	Maximize differences	In an effort to reinforce his power and dominance, he structures communication in a manner that maximizes role differences between administrators and teachers.
Symmetry	Asymmetrical	In an effort to protect his own interests, he deploys one-sided messages that are indifferent toward teacher interests.

restricting information, refusing to exchange information, and disregarding the needs of others are almost always viewed as unacceptable behavior. Not having studied communication formally, novice administrators typically shape their communicative behavior by accepting the beliefs of other administrators and by emulating their behavior (Kowalski, 1998a).

Viewing Communication as a Role

An *organizational role* is commonly defined as a set of expected behaviors associated with a particular position (Hanson, 2003). These expectations are seldom absolute or comprehensive (Yukl, 2002), but in the case of school administration, they commonly involve functions such as management, leadership, facilitation, and political advocacy. For example, historical analysis of school district superintendents has revealed that four distinct role conceptualizations emerged incrementally for this position between 1880 and 1965; chronologically, they included teacher of teachers (a scholarly leader role), business manager (traditional management role), statesman (political role), and applied social scientist (problem solving role) (Callahan, 1966). Subsequent studies of superintendents (Blumberg, 1985; Cuban, 1976; Kowalski, 1995) revealed that as each new role emerged, existing ones did not become irrelevant. Instead, the priority of each role depended on an intricate mix of general social conditions and prevailing needs in a specific school system (Kowalski, 2006).

More recently, Kowalski (2001; 2005) has argued that being an effective communicator has become a fifth distinctive role characterization. The rationale for this argument is based on the fact that situation-based behavior (i.e., shifting between leadership and managerial communicative behaviors) is no longer prudent. Relatively recent studies of the performance evaluation (e.g., Beverage, 2003; Peterson, 1999) and of dismissals (e.g., Davis, 1998) found that penalties administrators incur for inconsistent and incompetent communicative behavior have often been severe. Recognizing that administrators must continue to assume both leadership and management functions, complementary communication arguably is unacceptable behavior in an information-based society, even when it is deployed in conjunction with management functions (Kowalski, 2005).

Professionally and politically, *relational communication* has become normative for modern organizations. The paradigm prescribes interpersonal and symmetrical communication and focuses on participant perceptions of exchanges (Littlejohn, 1992). Its purposes are to erect and maintain positive relationships between an organization and the organization's stakeholder publics (Bruning & Ledingham, 2000). Interpersonal communication involves two-way exchanges in which persons influence one another's behavior over and above their organizational role, rank, and status (Cappella, 1987). Symmetrical communication benefits all interactants (Grunig, 1989), meaning that the interactants behave similarly, thus minimizing their formal authority and actual power differences (Burgoon & Hale, 1984). In essence, communication produces mutual understandings, mutual influence, negotiation, openness, credibility, and trust. When these characteristics are present, positive organizational development and equilibrium are more probable (Toth, 2000) for at least two reasons. First, administrators who communicate interpersonally and symmetrically are better able to identify and address unmet needs (Conrad, 1994). Second, communities satisfied with their public schools are more likely to treat these institutions as assets rather than liabilities (Bruning & Ledingham, 2000). Table 5.2 summarizes an elementary school principal's motives and behavior using a relational communication model, and a comparison of the classical model and the relational model is illustrated in Figure 5.1.

Table 5.2.   Communication Characteristics in an Elementary School Using a Relational Model

Characteristic	Norm	Principal's Motive and Behavior
Flow	Two-way, multidirectional	In an effort to improve the quantity and quality of information, he encourages information exchanges that are top-down, lateral, and bottom-up.
Status	Formal and informal	In an effort to build personal relationships, he communicates with teachers formally and informally, using both formal and informal channels.
Action	Sending and receiving	In an effort to build professional collegiality, he promotes information exchanges and invites teachers to send information to him.
Nature	Constructive	In an effort to attain organizational equilibrium, he encourages open and continuous communication as a means for using information to identify and solve problems.
Intent	Positive relationships	In an effort to build a learning community, he encourages exchanges of professional knowledge that empowers teachers and allows them to function as change leaders.
Power/dominance	Minimize differences	In an effort to create a sense of shared leadership, he uses communication to cast himself as a professional colleague rather than as an organizational boss.
Symmetry	Symmetrical	In an effort to build and maintain trust and confidence, he structures communication to be uniformly beneficial to the interactants and to the school.

Characteristic	Classical Model	Relational Model
Flow of information	One-way, top-down	Two-way, multidirectional
Status	Formal	Formal and informal
Primary action	Sending	Exchanging (sending and receiving)
Nature of communication	Directive	Constructive
Intent of communication	Coercing compliance	Building positive relationships
Power and dominance	Differences are maximized	Differences are minimized
Symmetry	Asymmetrical	Symmetrical

Figure 5.1. Comparison of the Classical and Relational Communication Models

COMMUNICATIVE COMPETENCE

Many educators, including school administration professors, believe that communication has received considerable attention within the profession since the 1970s. To some extent, they are correct. For instance, standards developed during the 1990s allude to communication. Mentioning communication and even stating its importance to effective practice, however, has not produced behavioral changes. To understand why it is challenging to prepare administrators to be effective communicators, we must define communicative competence in the context of the school administration profession and then establish criteria for acquiring and measuring competence.

Existing Standards in Educational Administration

Two standards documents clearly show that communication has been identified as an issue for school administrator preparation and licensing. Closer inspection, however, suggests that the treatment of this topic has been and remains largely superficial. The first document is *The Professional Standards for the Superintendency* published in 1993 by the American Association of School Administrators (AASA) (Hoyle, 1994). Standard 3, *Communications and Community Relations*, contains the following passage:

> The superintendent will articulate district purpose and priorities to the community and mass media; request and respond to community feedback; demonstrate consensus building and conflict mediation; identify, track, and deal with issues; formulate and carry out plans for internal/external communication; exhibit an understanding of school districts as political systems by applying communication skills to strengthen community support; align

constituencies in support of district priorities; build coalitions to gain financial and programmatic support; formulate democratic strategies for refer-
enda; and relate political initiatives to the welfare of children. (Hoyle,
Björk, Collier, & Glass, 2005, p. 65)

Eighteen indicators (described as what superintendents should know
and be able to do) are identified for this standard. Only the following six
specifically mention or directly pertain to communication: articulate a district's vision, mission, and priorities to the community and mass media;
understand and be able to communicate with all cultural groups in the
community; demonstrate that good judgment and actions communicate as
well as words; communicate and project an articulate position for education; write and speak clearly and forcefully; develop and carry out internal and external communication plans. The remaining indicators address
functions such as conflict resolution, conflict mediation, environmental
scanning, and issues management. Missing in the AASA document are a
definition of communication competence, specific recommendations for
teaching communication, and assessment criteria that can be applied to
professional preparation and licensing.

The second standards document, developed by the Interstate School
Leaders Licensure Consortium (ISLLC), applies to all licensed administra-
trative positions including superintendents (Shipman, Topps, & Murphy,
1998). The document's six standards are described and knowledge, disposition, and performance indicators are provided (Council of Chief State
School Officers, 1996). Applicable to both principals and superintendents,
the ISLLC standards arguably have been more influential than the AASA
standards; approximately 80% of the states have integrated them into their
licensing requirements (Shipman et al., 1998). The word *communication*
appears in statements for two standards. Standard 1 states, "A school administrator is an educational leader who promotes the success of all students by facilitating the development, articulation, implementation, and
stewardship of a vision of learning that is shared and supported by the
school community" (Council of Chief State School Officers, 1996, p. 10).
The fifth and last knowledge indicator for this standard is "effective communication." None of the 7 disposition indicators and only 2 of the 15 performance indicators for Standard 1 even mention communication. The
two performance indicators specify that administrators will facilitate

processes and engage in activities ensuring that: "the vision and mission of the school are effectively communicated to staff, parents, students, and community members" (p. 11); "progress toward the vision and mission is communicated to all stakeholders" (p. 11).

Standard 4 states, "A school administrator is an educational leader who promotes the success of all students by collaborating with families and community members, responding to diverse community interests and needs, and mobilizing community resources" (Council of Chief State School Officers, 1996, p. 16). Collaboration and communication with families are mentioned in a disposition but not addressed in knowledge or performance criteria. More noteworthy, neither effective communication (the term used in standard 1) nor communication competence is defined, nor are recommendations for injecting communication into formal preparation and for assessing competence provided.

Given the lack of specificity concerning communication in both the AASA and ISLLC standards, professors and state licensing officials have considerable leeway to self-define communicative competence (Kowalski, 2005; Kowalski & Keedy, 2003). Though such standards have given the issue of communication competence in school administration more visibility, they are deficient in that they do not (a) define competence within a professional context, (b) prescribe a curriculum for professional preparation, and (c) identify assessment criteria. Even in states using IS-LLC standards, school administration professors have had considerable leeway to self-define communicative competence in relation to both preparation and licensing (Kowalski, 2005; Kowalski & Keedy, 2003).

A Better Alternative

The critical point in relation to this book is that administrators who are incompetent communicators are at a distinct disadvantage with respect to leading and facilitating school restructuring. Consequently, the success of reform depends partially on the willingness of preparation programs and state licensing agencies to demand competence in relational communication. In fairness to both professors and policymakers, this is no easy assignment; the literature across professions and disciplines demonstrates that there are a myriad of perspectives on the topic of communicative competence (Wilson & Sabee, 2003). Literally hundreds of definitions have been developed (e.g., McCroskey, 1982; 1984; McCroskey & McCroskey, 1988), with the most prevalent having a distinctive behavioral overtone suggesting that competence, role, and performance are entangled (Wilson & Sabee, 2003). Perhaps the best known example of such behavioral definitions was developed by Wiemann (1977). He provided a contingency perspective of communicative competence predicated on the belief that effectiveness depends on contextual variables (i.e., conditions at the time of communication). In the case of school administration, these variables could include position (e.g., superintendent or principal), role (e.g., leader or manager), environmental circumstances (e.g., socio-economic status of the community), the issue at hand, and the people involved (e.g., staff, parents, or students). As already argued, contextual perspectives of competence have become less acceptable in an information-based and democratic society.

Communicative competence has three levels: individual, group, and organizational; competence in one level does not ensure competence in all levels (Jablin & Sias, 2000). Moreover, the construct is thought to span three knowledge domains (McCroskey, 1982). Spitzberg and Cupach's (1984) competence paradigm, for instance, includes *knowledge*, *skill*, and *motivation*. These competency spheres are typically described in the following manner:

- *Cognitive domain.* This domain requires knowledge and understanding of communication science (Larson, Backlund, Redmond, & Barbour, 1978).
- P*sychomotor domain.* This domain requires the ability to apply knowledge and understanding (Wiemann, Takai, Ota, & Wiemann, 1997).
- *Affective domain.* This domain pertains to possessing attitudes and feelings about communication (McCroskey, 1982).

Definitions of communicative competence also have been hindered by underlying assumptions and problematic premises that have influenced research on this topic. Jablin and Sias (2000) identify the most cogent suppositions.

- *Viewing competence as being discrete.* Individuals are classified as being competent or incompetent as if there were no variations between these extremes.

- *Viewing competence as being static.* The construct is treated as a constant rather than a dynamic and evolving condition.
- *Viewing competence as rational and objective behavior.* Communicative behavior is treated as a product of conscious thought; in truth, individuals often behave instinctively, emotionally, and politically.
- *Viewing motivation as a constant.* Judgments about communicative behavior fail to examine the effects of motivation on behavior at any given time.
- *Viewing competence outside of ideology.* Administrative behavior can be influenced by organizational and disciplinary ideologies. As an example, a principal may adopt a classical communication style even though the behavior conflicts with his understanding of effective communicative behavior.
- *Viewing competence outside of ethics.* Most research has failed to account for the effects of ethical standards on communicative behavior.
- *Viewing competence solely at the individual level.* As previously noted, competence should be addressed at the individual, group, and organizational levels. Often judgments about competence are made solely at the individual level.

Recognizing problems associated with definitional diversity, Wilson and Sabee (2003) address this topic by melding theory and behavior. Hypothesizing that definitional problems and the absence of theoretical applications to definitions are closely related concerns, they frame their analysis using Kaplan's (1964) dichotomy of constructs and theoretical terms. Asserting that most definitions have been shaped as constructs, they advocate a paradigm shift to using theoretical approaches. They contend the transition would allow scholars to reframe definitional obstacles so they could view competence in the context of various process, message production, and social theories. They caution, nonetheless, that their recommendation "will not lead to a single, final, and consensually agreed on understanding of competence" (p. 41)—a less than comforting conclusion, especially for those yearning for a simple, universally acceptable conception of competence for school administrators. More directly, they propose that competence must be explored in relation to professions and even to roles within professions. To frame competence within school administration, therefore, education policymakers and professors must meld the cognitive domain of communication, the social and cultural contexts of practice, and the profession's normative and ethical standards. This approach is likely to produce similar but not identical standards for principals and superintendents because practice in these two positions has become increasingly dissimilar (Glass, Björk, & Brunner, 2000).

Faculty in school administration, in collaboration with state policymakers and professional organization leaders, could outline a curriculum for defining and assessing communicative competence for school administrators (Kowalski, 2005). The following recommendations consider the ISLLC categories of knowledge, skills, and dispositions:

- At the knowledge level, school administrators should first study basic communication and then *situated communication pedagogy*. According to Dannels (2001), the former provides context-driven, disciplinary instruction, and the latter prescribes a process in which understanding and learning are based on social, interactive processes inseparable from the contexts in which they occur. In essence, practitioners would be required to complete a basic course in a communication department (most will have done this at the undergraduate level) and then a course or units of instruction that cover communication concepts applied specifically to school administration. This integrative approach to acquiring knowledge about communication already is being used in some professional schools preparing business executives and health care providers (Street, 2003).

- Communication application skills should be developed through a mix of activities in administration courses (e.g., work with case studies and simulations), out-of-class group activities (e.g., chairing a district or school committee), work-based assignments (e.g., developing a format for communicating with parents), and internships. The intent of these experiences is to demonstrate that administrators can effectively apply the communication knowledge.

- To nurture acceptable dispositions, students should have opportunities to interface and analyze complementary and relational forms of communication in the context of administrative practice in districts and schools. They should be exposed to positive role models who can demonstrate the power of interpersonal communication to change

people and organizational cultures. Interpersonal communication dispositions could be assessed and evaluated in traditional courses (e.g.,
having students write position papers or critiques on case studies) and
in school-based activities (e.g., documenting internship experiences
or evaluating the communicative behavior of superintendents they
shadow).

Since many practitioners have not experienced such a curriculum, parallel efforts to provide staff development, either through universities or professional
associations, are equally essential to improving professional preparation.

CONCLUDING COMMENTS

Unfortunately, the treatment of communication within school administration has been framed primarily by two inaccurate assumptions. The first is
that principals and superintendents learn to communicate effectively simply
by being exposed to the realities of practice (Dilenschneider, 1996; Walker,
1997). Research across all types of organizations refutes this conclusion.
Studies of chief executive officers in business, for example, have found that
communicative incompetence was the major reason why chief executive officers got dismissed (Perina, 2002). The second erroneous belief is that an
administrator communicates effectively when he or she adopts a contingency approach to communication that treats communicative behavior as a
role-related skill rather than as a pervasive role (Kowalski, 2005). As noted
earlier in the chapter, both incompetence and inconsistency are factors that
shape negative perceptions of administrative behavior.

Collectively, the chapters in the first part of this book provided a nexus
between school restructuring and communication competence. To improve our schools, we must be willing and able to alter change-resistant
and negative institutional cultures. That task is communication-intensive
and requires skilled leaders who are capable of engaging in relational
communication consistently. Though some progressive principals and superintendents have developed the knowledge, skills, and dispositions essential for this communicative behavior, most others have not. This is why
it is incumbent upon professors preparing administrators and policymakers controlling licensing to define communicative competence, to set rel-

evant preparation standards and licensing requirements, and to identify criteria to be used in assessing competence.

REFERENCES

Achilles, C. M., & Lintz, M. N. (1983, November). *Public confidence in public education: A growing concern in the 80s.* Paper presented at the Annual Meeting of the Mid-South Educational Research Association, Nashville, TN.

Beverage, L. H. (2003). *Inhibiting factors to effectiveness and the adaptability of new superintendents in Virginia.* Unpublished doctoral dissertation, University of Virginia, Charlottesville.

Blumberg, A. (1985). *The school superintendent: Living with conflict.* New York: Teachers College Press.

Bredeson, P. V. (1988). Communications as a measure of leadership in schools: A portraiture of school principals. *High School Journal, 71,* 178–186.

Bruning, S. D., & Ledingham, J. A. (2000). Organization and key relationships: Testing the influence of relationship dimensions in a business to business context. In J. Ledingham & S. Bruning (Eds.), *Public relations as relationship management: A relational approach to the study and practice of public relations* (pp. 159–174). Mahwah, NJ: Erlbaum.

Burgoon, J. K., & Hale, J. L. (1984). The fundamental topoi of relational communication. *Communication Monographs, 51,* 193–214.

Callahan, R. E. (1966). *The superintendent of schools: A historical analysis.* (ERIC Document Reproduction Service No. ED 0104410)

Cappella, J. N. (1987). Interpersonal communication: Definitions and fundamental questions. In C. R. Berger & S. H. Chaffee (Eds.), *Handbook of communication science* (pp. 184–238). Newbury Park, CA: Sage.

Clampitt, P. G. (1991). *Communicating for managerial effectiveness.* Newbury Park, CA: Sage.

Conrad, C. (1994). *Strategic organizational communication: Toward the twenty-first century* (3rd ed.). Fort Worth, TX: Harcourt Brace.

Council of Chief State School Officers. (1996). *Interstate School Leaders Licensure Consortium: Standards for school leaders.* Washington, DC: Author.

Cuban, L. (1976). *The urban school superintendent: A century and a half of change.* Bloomington, IN: Phi Delta Kappa Educational Foundation.

Dannels, D. P. (2001). Time to speak up: A theoretical framework of situated pedagogy and practice for communication across the curriculum. *Communication Education, 50*(2), 144–158.

Davis, S. H. (1998). Why do principals get fired? *Principal, 28*(2), 34–39.

Dilenschneider, R. L. (1996). Social IQ and MBAs: Recognizing the importance of communication. *Vital Speeches, 62*, 404–405.

Duke, D. (2004). *The challenge of educational change*. Boston: Allyn & Bacon.

Fullan, M. (2001). *Leading in a culture of change*. San Francisco: Jossey-Bass.

Geddes, D. S. (1993). Empowerment through communication: Key people-to-people and organizational success. *People and Education, 1*, 76–104.

Glass, T. E., Björk, L. G., & Brunner, C. C. (2000). *The American school superintendent: 2000*. Arlington, VA: American Association of School Administrators.

Grunig, J. E. (1989). Symmetrical presuppositions as a framework for public relations theory. In C. H. Botan (Ed.), *Public relations theory* (pp. 17–44). Hillsdale, NJ: Erlbaum.

Guzley, R. (1992). Organizational climate and communication climate: Predictors of commitment to the organization. *Management Communication Quarterly, 5*(4), 379–402.

Hanson, E. M. (2003). *Educational administration and organizational behavior* (5th ed.). Boston: Allyn & Bacon.

Henderson, L. S. (1987). The contextual nature of interpersonal communication in management theory and research. *Management Communication Quarterly, 1*(1), 7–31.

Hoy, W. K., & Miskel, C. G. (2005). *Educational administration: Theory, research, and practice* (8th ed.). New York: McGraw-Hill.

Hoyle, J. R. (1994). What standards for the superintendency promise. *School Administrator, 51*(7), 22–23, 26.

Hoyle, J., Björk, L. G., Collier, V., & Glass, T. (2005). *The superintendent as CEO: Standards-based performance*. Thousand Oaks, CA: Corwin.

Hunt, S. K., Simonds, C. J., & Cooper, P. J. (2002). Communication and teacher education: Exploring a communication course for all teachers. *Communication Education, 51*(1), 81–94.

Jablin, F. M., & Sias, P. M. (2000). Communication competence. In F. Jablin & L. Putnam (Eds.), *The new handbook of organizational communication* (pp. 819–864). Thousand Oaks, CA: Sage.

Kaplan, A. (1964). *The conduct of inquiry: Methodology for behavioral science*. New York: Harper & Row.

Kowalski, T. J. (1995). *Keepers of the flame: Contemporary urban superintendents*. Thousand Oaks, CA: Corwin Press.

Kowalski, T. J. (1998a). Communication in the principalship: Preparation, work experience, and expectation. *Journal of Educational Relations, 19*(2), 4–12.

Kowalski, T. J. (1998b). The role of communication in providing leadership for school reform. *Mid-Western Educational Researcher, 11*(1), 32–40.

Kowalski, T. J. (2001). The future of local school governance: Implications for board members and superintendents. In C. Brunner & L. G. Björk (Eds.), *The new superintendency* (pp. 183–201). Oxford, UK: JAI, Elsevier Science.

Kowalski, T. J. (2003). *Contemporary school administration: An introduction* (2nd ed.). Boston: Allyn & Bacon.

Kowalski, T. J. (2005). Evolution of the school superintendent as communicator. *Communication Education, 54*(2), 101–117.

Kowalski, T. J. (2006). *The school superintendent: Theory, practice, and cases* (2nd ed.). Thousand Oaks, CA: Sage.

Kowalski, T. J., & Keedy, J. (2003, November). *Superintendent as communicator: Implications for professional preparation and licensing.* Paper presented at the Annual Conference of the University Council for Educational Administration, Portland, OR.

Larson, C. E., Backlund, P. M., Redmond, M. K., & Barbour, A. (1978). *Assessing communicative competence.* Falls Church, VA: Speech Communication Association and ERIC.

Lester, P. E. (1993). *Preparing administrators for the 21st century.* Paper presented at the Annual Meeting of the New England Educational Research Organization, Portsmouth, NH.

Littlejohn, S. W. (1992). *Theories of human communication* (4th ed.). Belmont, CA: Wadsworth.

Luthans, F. (1981). *Organizational behavior* (3rd ed.). New York: McGraw-Hill.

McCroskey, J. C. (1982). Communication competence and performance: A research and pedagogical perspective. *Communication Education, 31*(1), 1–7.

McCroskey, J. C. (1984). Communication competence: The elusive construct. In R. N. Bostrom (Ed.), *Competence in communication: A multidisciplinary approach* (pp. 259–268). Beverly Hills, CA: Sage.

McCroskey, J. C., & McCroskey, L. L. (1988). Self-report as an approach to measuring communication competence. *Communication Research Reports, 5*(2), 108–113.

McGregor, D. (1967). *The professional manager.* New York: McGraw-Hill.

Mintzberg, H. (1973). *The nature of managerial work.* New York: Harper & Row.

Osterman, K. F. (1994). Communication skills: A key to collaboration and change. *Journal of School Leadership, 4*(4), 382–398.

Perina, K. (2002). When CEOs self-destruct. *Psychology Today, 35*(5), 16.

Peterson, M. R. (1999). *Superintendent competencies for continued employment as perceived by Louisiana public school superintendents and board presidents.* Unpublished doctoral dissertation, University of Southern Mississippi, Hattiesburg.

Razik, T. A., & Swanson, A. D. (2001). *Fundamental concepts of educational leadership* (2nd ed.). Upper Saddle River, NJ: Merrill, Prentice Hall.

Richmond, V. P., McCroskey, J. C., Davis, L. M., & Koontz, K. A. (1980). Perceived power as a mediator of management communication style and employee satisfaction: A preliminary investigation. *Communication Quarterly, 28*(41), 37–46.

Sergiovanni, T. J. (2001). *The principalship: A reflective practice perspective* (4th ed.). Boston: Allyn & Bacon.

Shipman, N. J., Topps, B. W., & Murphy, J. (1998, April). *Linking the ISLLC standards to professional development and relicensure.* Paper presented at the Annual Meeting of the American Educational Research Association, San Diego, CA.

Snavely, W. B., & Walters, E. V. (1983). Differences in communication competence among administrative social styles. *Journal of Applied Communication Research, 11*(2), 120–135.

Spitzberg, B. H., & Cupach, W. R. (1984). *Interpersonal communication competence*. Beverly Hills, CA: Sage.

Street, R. L. (2003). Interpersonal communication skills in health care. In J. O. Greene & B. R. Burleson (Eds.), *Handbook of communication and social interaction* (pp. 909–934). Hillsdale, NJ: Erlbaum.

Thayer, L. O. (1961). *Administrative communication*. Homewood, IL: Irwin.

Toth, E. L. (2000). From personal influence to interpersonal influence: A model for relationship management. In J. A. Ledingham & S. D. Bruning (Eds.), *Public relations as relationship management* (pp. 205–220). Mahwah, NJ: Erlbaum.

Trombetta, J. J., & Rogers, D. P. (1988). Communication climate, job satisfaction, and organizational commitment: The effects of information adequacy, communication openness, and decision participation. *Management Communication Quarterly, 1*(4), 494–514.

Walker, G. (1997). Communication in leadership. *Communication Management, 1*(4), 22–27.

Wiemann, J. M. (1977). Explication and test of a model of communication competence. *Human Communication Research, 3*, 195–213.

Wiemann, J. M., Takai, J., Ota, H., & Wiemann M. O. (1997). A relational model of communication competence. In. B. Kovacic (Ed.), *Emerging theories of human communication* (pp. 25–44). Buffalo: State University of New York Press.

Wilson, S. R., & Sabee, C. M. (2003). Explicating communicative competence as a theoretical term. In J. O. Greene & B. R. Burleson (Eds.), *Handbook of communication and social interaction* (pp. 3–50). Hillsdale, NJ: Erlbaum.

Wirt, F. M., & Kirst, M. W. (2001). *The political dynamics of American education* (2nd ed.). Berkeley, CA: McCutchan.

Yukl, G. (2002). *Leadership in organizations* (5th ed.). Upper Saddle River, NJ: Prentice Hall.

Yukl, G. (2006). *Leadership in organizations* (6th ed.). Upper Saddle River, NJ: Prentice Hall.

Zaleznik, A. (1989). *The managerial mystique: Restoring leadership in business.* New York: Harper & Row.

II

APPLICATIONS

6

Communication and the Learning Organization

Demands for reforming education have existed since public schools were first created in this country. Many education historians (e.g., Fink, 2000; Tyack & Cuban, 1995) have chronicled the fact that there have been a myriad of reform periods, each of which dissolved within a decade or so after beginning. These authors attribute recurring patterns of dissatisfaction to a politicization of schooling; that is, public education has been expected to respond to social needs and aspirations, but often these expectations have been impractical. Timar and Kirp (1987) conclude that education has not been appreciated for its intrinsic value but rather for what the institution could provide for society. They note that this instrumental view partially explains the waxing and waning of episodic waves of public concern. When society faced a crisis, public schools were expected to alleviate discomfort. The crises, nonetheless, did not lead to major structural changes in schooling. The reason is quite clear. As a crisis dissipated, usually because of governmental or societal interventions, the corresponding pressures for reform vanished.

The aftermath of *Sputnik* in 1957 provides a perfect example of why this instrumental view of schooling has failed to produce fundamental changes. Fearful that the nation was at risk of being dominated militarily by communist countries, politicians pointed the finger of blame at educators. The United States Congress then enacted the National Defense Education Act. School and state policymakers enthusiastically used the federal law to force selected curricular changes in local school districts. Most notably, they used intensification mandates in an effort to increase academic achievement in mathematics and science. In less than a decade, however, the country's main focus shifted from academic excellence and national defense to equality and racial harmony. After Congress passed the Elementary and Secondary Education Act in 1965, school administrators found themselves in a perplexing situation in which they were ordered to move schools in two arguably different directions (Kowalski, 1981).

This chapter first examines why past reform efforts have failed to change either the personality or underlying philosophy of public schools. Given the critical nature of these two characteristics to organizational development (OD), the argument is made that authentic and productive restructuring are more likely to occur in schools that engage in a process known as *organizational learning*. The chapter then concludes with a discussion of the role of administrator communication in this type of organizational culture.

NEED FOR IMPROVED CLIMATES AND CULTURE

Organizational development was described in chapter 4. In the past, public school administrators paid less attention to OD than did their counterparts in business, industry, and private schools. Two explanations are cogent to this condition. First, education historians (e.g., Spring, 1994) point out that public schools were established as institutions of stability; their purpose has been to protect society's values and standards by teaching them to young children. Consequently, public school administrators have tended to insulate themselves from individuals and groups proposing change, and they have supported values and beliefs that public schools are not supposed to change. Second, contemporary critics of public education (e.g., Chubb & Moe, 1990) argue that indifference toward OD is caused by a lack of market competition; that is, public schools are essentially monopolies. The existence of these institutions rarely has been threatened, even when performance and productivity are poor. In light of these circumstances, analysts have argued that restructuring requires fundamental transitions in school climate and culture (Kowalski, 2003).

Approximately 40 years ago, Sargeant (1967) likened organizational climate to individual personality—in essence an organization's climate is its personality. Using the four components of climate discussed in chapter 4, a comparison of individual personality and the organizational climate of a school is provided in Table 6.1. Personality is a collection of emotion, thought, and behavior patterns. Just as individual personality affects how we feel toward others, school climate affects how we feel toward a particular institution. When individuals try to alter their personality, they almost always do so by changing some aspect of their personal appearance. Why? Because modifying personal appearance is the easiest way to change your image—but the effects on personality are often slight and temporary. On the other hand, the greatest effect on personality is likely to be produced by modifying values and beliefs that shape emotions and drive behavior. This level of change, however, is almost always the most difficult. The same conditions apply to organizations. Changing a school's ecology (e.g., remodeling the building or adding new equipment) can increase institutional flexibility and enhance opportunities for greater productivity, but unless they are accompanied by other climatic changes, their potential value is attenuated (Kowalski, 2003).

Table 6.1. Comparison of Individual Personality and a School's Organizational Climate

Factor	Individual Personality	Organizational Climate
Ecology	Physical characteristics (personal appearance—e.g., clothing, jewelry, personal hygiene)	Physical characteristics (the school's physical environment—e.g., building, equipment, technology, instructional materials)
Milieu	Social behavior (how the person feels, treats and interacts with others)	Social atmosphere (how school employees and students feel, treat, and interact with others, including persons outside the school)
Organization	Structural behavior (how the person organizes information, solves problems, deals with competing demands)	Organizational structure (how the school is organized via calendars, schedules, curriculum, departments, or grade levels)
Culture	Symbolic behavior (assumptions based on values and beliefs that determine emotions and behavior)	Behavioral norms (standards based on shared values and beliefs that constitute organizational knowledge, especially in relation to dealing with threats, problems, and other challenges)

Clearly, then, culture is the least visible element of climate and thus the element most difficult to diagnose—especially when its overt (e.g., espoused beliefs) and covert (e.g., subconscious beliefs) assumptions are dissimilar (Schein, 1996). In part, the difficulty inherent in describing school culture stems from the fact that persons who are part of it learn to take it for granted; that is, they live with it daily and grow accustomed to its effects (Schwan & Spady, 1998). In addition, organizational members often do not recognize how their shared values and beliefs shape routine behaviors, especially in relation to dealing with common organizational problems (Schein, 1992). In the case of schools, teachers may not recognize that their instructional behavior and grading practices are influenced by school culture. As an example, a teacher who believes 30% of her students are predestined to fail may never admit to this conviction, but the conviction is manifested in her teaching and grading practices.

School culture is undeniably a major barrier to restructuring; for example, educators often have rejected the necessity for change or have concluded that the benefits of change would be negligible on student learning (Fullan, 2001; Hall & Hord, 2001). Even so, other factors contribute to failed reforms. Consider several that are commonly cited in the literature:

- Would-be reformers often underestimated the complexity of organizational change in general and school change specifically (DuFour & Eaker, 1998; Fullan, 2001).
- Change initiatives often lacked clarity (DuFour & Eaker, 1998).
- Initiatives were often discarded before they had a reasonable chance to succeed (Schlechty, 1990, 2001).
- The capacity of educators to scuttle change, even when mandated from the federal or state levels, was seriously underestimated (Sarason, 1996).

Since the early 1980s, policymakers and administration scholars have concluded that authentic reform cannot be achieved unless schools are restructured. More specifically, they now believe that this reorganization must begin by replacing closed climates (i.e., a negative disposition toward interacting with the external environment) with open climates (i.e., a positive disposition toward interacting with the external environment) and replacing change-resistant/negative cultures with change-friendly/positive cultures. Only then will educators accept and use organizational learning as a primary asset to refashion schools and personal practice.

BUILDING THE LEARNING ORGANIZATION

In his seminal book on the learning organization, *The Fifth Discipline*, Peter Senge (1990) advised that to be highly effective leaders had to replace change-resistant cultures with *learning cultures*. Unfortunately, terms like *learning culture* and *learning organization* have often been defined in various ways. In addition, authors have often disagreed in setting qualification criteria for a learning organization. As examples, some believe that behavioral change is essential; others insist that new ways of thinking are sufficient. Some cite information processing as the medium for learning; others propose that it is shared insights. And some think that the process of organizational learning is common, while others argue flawed, self-serving interpretations are the norm (Garvin, 1993).

Organizational Learning

Noted author Steven Covey (1996) predicts, "Only organizations that have a passion for learning will have an enduring influence" (p. 149). Descriptions of organizational learning have not been uniform, primarily because they have evolved over time. An early perspective, developed by English and English (1958), suggests that it occurs when organization members are able to respond differently to an identical stimulus over time. Several decades later, Weiss (1990) defines this concept as a permanent knowledge or skill change attributable to experience. While both descriptions are adequate, however, neither portrays "learning in a way that incorporates communication as a core determinant" (Weick & Ashford, 2000, p. 706). Normann (1985) recognizes that organizational culture and communication are connected in two important ways. First, past learning is stored in culture and culture provides the primary instrument for communicating accumulated knowledge to organization members. Consequently, organizational culture is a source of acquired knowledge and a framework for interaction that refines existing knowledge or produces new knowledge.

Organizational learning also is categorized in terms of time frames. Evolutionary learning is predicated primarily on the following convictions: (a) that the organization's knowledge and practices need to adjust periodically; (b) that minor modifications are more acceptable than major modifications because they pose less threat and cause less disruption; and (c) that routines, roles, and culture do not necessarily have to be challenged. Revolutionary learning is predicated on different convictions: (a) that the organization's knowledge and practices must change radically; (b) that change must occur quickly; and (c) that routines, roles, and culture need to be challenged (Belasen, 2000). Historically, public schools have engaged in subtle evolutionary change (Duke, 2004; Hall & Hord, 2001) and this pattern largely explains why school cultures have not been affected and why educators often respond negatively to revolutionary change proposals.

Learning Culture

The term *learning culture* is envisioned here as the intellectual characteristic of a learning organization. Weick and Ashford (2000) summarize the utility of culture in relation to learning.

> When people have experiences with the artifacts of an organization's environment, they learn. They strengthen responses, they reaffirm the ways in which the artifacts fit together, they confront and temporarily resolve competing interpretations that arise from new coalitions or unsocialized newcomers, they wrestle with whether to exploit what they already know or to explore new possibilities. They undertake trials of new behaviors. (p. 709)

Therefore, culture plays a critical role in storing, interpreting, and transmitting shared beliefs within the organization. According to Fullan (1999), a collaborative culture in a school is associated with the following conditions:

- *Diversity is fostered in a context of trust building.* On the one hand, teachers are encouraged to challenge highly complex problems by stating their views, especially when their viewpoints are dissimilar from administrator and peer views. On the other hand, teachers are unlikely to behave in this manner unless they feel that they can trust administrators and fellow teachers.

- *Anxiety is provoked and contained.* On the one hand, administrators seek to produce anxiety through dialogue because anxiety reduces comfort with current practices. On the other hand, administrators need to create safeguards that the level of anxiety generated is not counterproductive (i.e., excessive to the point that discourages teachers from challenging complex problems).
- *Teachers and administrators engage in knowledge building.* Educators first share tacit knowledge (individual knowledge) and then convert it to explicit knowledge (shared knowledge). They also seek new knowledge both among themselves and from outside sources. In essence, the educators function as a community of learners seeking pedagogical synergy by merging and expanding the school's professional knowledge base.
- *Connectedness and openness are combined.* The typical school is fragmented and inundated with unwanted and uncoordinated mandates. On the one hand, the principal pursues collaboration as a means for dealing with these problems. Teachers are encouraged to connect with other teachers so that they collectively develop better practices. On the other hand, the principal also wants teachers to be connected to the external environment (i.e., what is occurring outside the school).
- *Spiritual, political, and intellectual issues are fused.* Moral purpose (the spiritual dimension), power (the political dimension), and ideas and best practices (the intellectual dimension) are melded to respond to realities of school climates.

A collaborative culture is the nucleus of a learning organization for three important reasons:

1. *Change is not only tolerated; it is encouraged* (i.e., teachers and administrators have a professional and moral commitment to continuous growth).
2. *Collaborative cultures are strong* (i.e., the culture's underlying assumptions are shared by all or virtually all teachers and administrators).
3. *Collaborative cultures are positive* (i.e., the culture's underlying assumptions are congruous with the profession's knowledge base) (Kowalski, 2006).

Learning Organization

Senge (1990) describes a learning organization as "a place where people continually expand their capacity to create results they truly desire, where new and expansive patterns of thinking are nurtured, where collective aspiration is set free and where people are continually learning how to learn" (p. 3). Garvin (1993) defines it as "an organization skilled at creating, acquiring, and transferring knowledge, and at modifying its behavior to reflect new knowledge and insights" (p. 79). For Garvin, new ideas are essential to organizational learning regardless of whether they are initiated in or out of the organization itself; but by themselves, new ideas do not ensure a learning organization.

The most widely used image of a learning organization is Senge's (1990) five core disciplines. He describes a discipline as a series of principles and practices that can be studied, mastered, and integrated into an organization via its members. The five disciplines include the following:

1. *Systems thinking.* Systems theory is predicated on several beliefs: (a) an organization, like the human body; is composed of an intricate network of subsystems; (b) organizational outputs rarely are attributable to a single cause (Hanson, 2003); and (c) to survive, organizations must be open to their ecosystem (Morgan, 1987). By applying systems theory, organizational members are more likely to avoid erroneous or fatalistic attitudes about the probability of OD.

2. *Personal mastery.* Learning in organizations occurs at both the individual and group levels. Individual learning does not ensure organizational learning—but without it, organizational learning cannot occur. In order for organization members to achieve personal mastery, they must engage in continuous learning that focuses on subject matter pertinent to the organization's mission, vision, and development.

3. *Mental models.* Mental models are viewed as assumptions, generalizations, and images of life, the world around us, and of the organization in that world. The construction of these models begins at the individual level and requires a form of introspection called *reflection*, a process detailed by Schön (1987) and widely described in textbooks on teaching and school administration. Reflection is a process through which professionals use practice-based experiences to integrate theoretical and craft knowledge; it can occur at three stages: (1) preactive (reflection prior to acting), (2) interactive (reflection while acting), and

(3) postactive (reflection after acting) (Kowalski, 2003; Reitzug & Cornett, 1991).

4. *Building shared vision.* This discipline, now widely discussed in relation to school reform, entails building a mental image of what the organization should look like at some designated point in the future. Visions are instrumental because they provide a framework for long-term action, a symbolic statement that gives meaning to action for both organization members and for stakeholders (Conger, 1989). The process begins with individual visions; therefore, it relies on mental models. By having opportunities to state and test their views, organizational members work toward a consensus vision that is attainable, politically acceptable, and advantageous to the organization's mission (Kowalski, 2006). Senge (1990) describes this process as the capacity to hold a shared picture of the future that the organizational members want to create.

5. *Team learning.* This discipline is arguably the most communication-intensive. It begins with dialogue and entails "aligning and developing the capacities of a team to create the results its members truly desire" (Senge, 1990, p. 236). Personal mastery, shared vision, and collective action are essential. As group members work together, they learn together and the group becomes synergistic.

According to Senge, connecting dialogue to systems thinking facilitates a deep understanding of organizational complexity and of structural issues that often prevent visions from being reached. In this vein, both communication and systems thinking are foundational pillars of the learning organization. Garvin (1993) posits that the foundation also includes four building blocks that involve using (1) systemic problem-solving paradigms, (2) the scientific method rather than trial and error, (3) data rather than assumption to make important decisions, and (4) simple statistical techniques to organize data. The last two building blocks have become focal points in education over the past 2 years. Joyce and Calhoun (1996), for example, observe that schools are simultaneously information-rich and information-impoverished; principals and teachers collect a prodigious amount of student information but rarely use these data to shape change initiatives.

In summary, a learning organization is characterized by the capability to continuously acquire knowledge in relation to maintaining equilibrium. That knowledge is used in varying ways by organization leaders, but most notably to engage in OD. The learning organization maintains a symbiotic relationship with its environment (open climate) and behavior is guided by a change-supportive, strong, and positive culture.

SCHOOLS AS LEARNING ORGANIZATIONS

Restructuring obviously involves substantial changes. According to Schwahn and Spady (1998), productive change is framed by five conditions: (1) issues that are really important (meeting needs in relation to the vision) actually change, (2) changes lead to higher levels of productivity, (3) changes result in improved operational procedures, (4) both individuals and the school benefit, and (5) changes endure. Scholars studying school reform (e.g., Duke, 2004; Fullan, 2001; Hall & Hord, 2001) agree that productive change is most likely in schools that adopt the primary characteristics of a learning organization. Such schools operate more as a professional community than as a bureaucracy (Lashway, 1998). Teachers and administrators first make commitments to each other and then collectively make commitments to students, parents, and other stakeholders. They erect an environment of trust and mutual support in which they practice as true professionals.

Suggested applications of the learning organization in public schools became increasingly common during the 1990s. Leithwood, Leonard, and Sharratt (1998), for example, describe a "learning school" by using descriptors such as group activity, individual and common purposes, collective commitment to identified purposes, and continuously developing more effective and efficient ways of accomplishing those purposes. Lashway (1998), however, contends that most schools did not meet these idyllic criteria, largely because they had been unable to overcome obstructions such as teacher isolation, insufficient time for collaboration/group learning, and the complexity of teaching. Other observers (e.g., Sarason, 1996) conclude that schools were inert rather than dynamic organizations because most educators, including administrators, had neither the knowledge nor convictions necessary to facilitate restructuring. Even in schools where teachers appeared to have an open mind toward learning and applying proposed initiatives, change often was pursued in superficial or inconsistent ways producing only temporary effects (Elmore, Peterson, &

McCarthey, 1996). Often educators, recognizing the need to present an illusion of change, complied with mandates spitefully, and once the pressure for change subsided, they reverted to their traditional practices (Fullan, 2001).

Though a single description of a school as a learning organization may have limited utility because of contextual variables and less than constant needs, we can visualize that such an institution would be identifiable by certain recurring characteristics. The argument is made here that relational communication is a core characteristic that facilitates all other characteristics. This conceptualization is presented in Figure 6.1. The following are brief explanations of the components.

- *Relational communication.* Open, multidirectional communication is essential to all the critical characteristics of a learning organization. When deployed, information is shared upwardly (i.e., teacher to principal), downwardly (i.e., principal to teacher), and laterally (i.e., teacher to teacher). Relational communication produces interpersonal

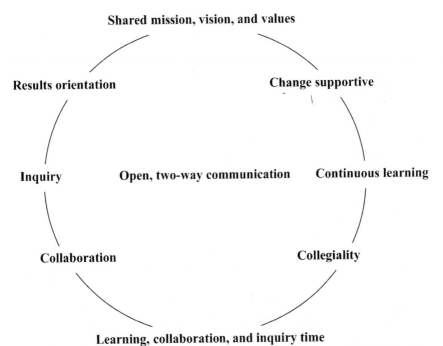

Figure 6.1. Common Characteristics of a School Functioning as a Learning Organization

exchanges necessary for questioning the status quo and for responding to known deficiencies (Kowalski, 1998). Thus, educators learn from each other in ways that facilitate school improvement (Hall & Hord, 2001).

- *Shared mission, vision, and values.* The member educators share basic assumptions about effective practice and integrate these values into a school's mission and deploy them to shape a collective vision (DuFour & Eaker, 1998).

- *Change supportive culture.* The member educators not only share assumptions about best practice but also believe that the need for change is constant. Correspondingly, they deem risk taking, innovation, critique, and quality to be essential for making successful adaptations to changing needs (Schwahn & Spady, 1998).

- *Continuous learning.* The member educators dedicate themselves to continuing education. Learning activities can be personal (e.g., reading a book or journals, enrolling in a graduate course) or collective (e.g., staff development workshops). In addition, there is evidence that the organization encourages, facilitates, and funds learning opportunities (Leithwood et al., 1998).

- *Collegiality.* The member educators express mutual respect and support, share a common commitment to serve students and the broader community, and share responsibility for engaging in OD (Hall & Hord, 2001).

- *Collaboration.* The member educators develop a collaborative culture. They cooperate rather than compete, especially when dealing with tensions and conflict pervasive in all organizations. Fullan (1999) writes, "Collaborative cultures are innovative not just because they provide support, but also because they recognize the value of dissonance inside and outside the organization" (p. 27).

- *Inquiry.* Educators focus on lessons learned from both effective and ineffective practice (Lashway, 1998). Individually and collectively they engage in a form of action research and findings and conclusions are shared and critiqued in an environment of collegiality (DuFour & Eaker, 1998).

- *Adequate time for learning, collaboration, and inquiry.* Educators are provided time to grow professionally and to engage in action research (Duke, 2004).

- *Best practices.* Administrators and teachers study best practices as defined in the professional knowledge base and, with appropriate adaptations, apply them to their practice (Duke, 2004; Hall & Hord, 2001).
- *Results orientation.* Administrators and teachers recognize that evaluation should focus on what is accomplished rather than on what is intended (DuFour & Eaker, 1998).

LEADERSHIP IN A LEARNING ORGANIZATION

The traditional perspective of organizational leadership is centered on three functions: giving direction, making key decisions, and energizing subordinates. Senge (1990) notes that this perspective is rooted in the assumptions that (a) most employees are powerless, (b) they lack personal vision, (c) they are capable of executing change on their own, and (d) they require control and direction. A learning organization requires a different leadership style that is rooted in the convictions that organization members can be change agents and they are willing and able to act on the structures and systems in their work environment. Senge describes effective leadership in a learning organization in relation to three roles:

1. *Designer.* This role begins with ensuring that mission (purpose), vision, and core values (culture) are identified, known, and accepted. It also involves (a) developing appropriate policies, strategies, and (b) integrating the five component technologies into OD.
2. *Steward.* This role involves commitment to and responsibility for pursuing the shared vision. As stewards, leaders function as storytellers, linking the learning culture to change initiatives. Communication is used to reinforce improvement efforts and to remind organization members of how specific initiatives relate to the ultimate goal—achieving the shared vision. Thus, stewardship is symbolic, spiritual, and inspirational.
3. *Teacher.* This role is not necessarily about teaching others how to change. Actually it involves defining reality, first at a personal level and then at an interpersonal level. The intent is to aid others to apply systems thinking to problems and to proposed solutions. The leader's

purpose is to avoid the common pitfall of having organization members developing simplistic conclusions about highly complex problems.

In the case of districts and schools, superintendents and principals are not the only persons who can or should lead. A more productive view is to have all professional staff view themselves as leaders and change agents (Fullan, 2001; Hall & Hord, 2001). Learning leaders are capacity builders, visionaries, facilitators, and role models. They present school improvement as a set of hypotheses to be tested rather than mandated solutions, they address problems that prevent collaboration, and they embrace a democratic leadership style (Lashway, 1998).

Schwan and Spady (1998) contend that organizational learning and restructuring require "total leaders." They described these individuals in the context of four domains:

1. *Authentic domain*—entails establishing and embodying purpose, values, and meaning for members of the organization and external stakeholders
2. *Visionary domain*—facilitating the process of building a reachable collective image of what a school should look like at some point in the future
3. *Cultural domain*—entails developing shared assumptions that promote risk taking, experimentation, and continuous learning
4. *Quality domain*—entails building the capacity for continuous OD and creating feedback loops that improve performance in relation to current and future performance standards

Conflict in open climate organizations is viewed positively because it is deemed to be a catalyst for needed change (Hanson, 2003). Therefore, administrators are expected to create and manage creative tensions that engage organization members in dialogue about gaps between the shared vision and realities of current conditions.

COMMUNICATION IN THE LEARNING ORGANIZATION

Many of the popular books on learning organizations provide a practical road map for applying the concept to changing schools. Though they clearly provide insightful ideas about subjects such as developing visions, leadership, and collegiality, many have either ignored the role of communication or have treated the topic superficially. This is indeed unfortunate since the communicative behavior of superintendents, principals, and other administrators is known to influence organizational learning through language and process (Weick & Ashford, 2000). Language entails interpretations, descriptions, definitions, and concepts that influence relationships, individual behavior, group behavior, and ultimately organizational outcomes. Process refers to communicative procedures, the manner in which information is transmitted, and the channels used for transmission.

The content of communication between and among educators either enhances or deters organizational learning. For example, principals who only talk to teachers about politics (e.g., community pressures, factionalism among the faculty) and finances (e.g., inadequate resources, program costs) neither challenge ineffective practice nor encourage teachers to do so. By comparison, a principal who engages other educators in discussions of student needs, curricular relevance, and instructional effectiveness is doing the opposite. By focusing on cogent topics, the second principal is using language to influence organizational learning.

Communication networks play a major role in process. These channels exist in districts and schools and they are the primary sources of information for organization members (Belasen, 2000). Both formal networks (i.e., those established by organization officials) and informal networks (i.e., those formed by employees to serve their interests) were discussed in detail in chapter 3. Formal networks usually have been vertical; informal (or emergent) networks usually have been horizontal. In the past, school administrators typically were socialized to control formal networks and to oppose informal networks (Kowalski, 2006). Organizational learning, however, requires a shift from a hierarchical communicative structure to horizontal communicative structure. Belasen (2000) explains why this is true: "Horizontal organizations increase their learning by obtaining information externally through formal scanning processes and boundary spanning activities, as well as through the dissemination of information through nondirectional communication relationships between organizational members" (p. 301). This activity refines or expands organizational knowledge and guides decision making in the organization's idiosyncratic communication processes (West & Meyer, 1997). Consequently, schools that function as learning organizations take advantage of both formal and informal networks, and administrators use both channels to open and increase communication between the school and the community and among organization members. To do this, principals need to be competent at the individual, group, and organizational levels of communication (Kowalski, 2005).

Administrators also assume tasks essential to organizational learning and OD and each requires interpersonal communication. The following are the more noteworthy assignments:

- Conducting a climate audit (i.e., determining the extent to which the climate is closed or open)
- Analyzing the current culture (i.e., determining the strength and quality of the school's culture)
- Building a shared vision (i.e., facilitating a process in which individuals develop visions and then reach consensus for a single school vision)
- Identifying needs (i.e., determining gaps between the status quo and vision)
- Identifying problems or barriers that prevent needs from being met (i.e., determining the obstacles that stand in the way of reaching the vision, including those related to school culture)
- Developing a strategic plan to meet the vision
- Promoting the vision in and out of the organization
- Facilitating risk taking and experimentation
- Evaluating progress toward the vision

Though all these assignments are integral to school restructuring, facilitating risk taking and experimentation is especially essential for organizational learning. Analyzing problems and seeking solutions through collaborative teams requires intense interaction (Fullan, 1999). Consequently, dialogue intended to provoke discussion, to learn from experience, and to change individual and collective convictions is essential (Stacey, 1996).

Research on relational communication and discourse analysis provide insights into the conversational practices of organization leaders. Outcomes of these explorations demonstrate that how administrators and constituents speak to each other reveals their relationship. Addressing this issue, Fairhurst (2000) notes that the relationship is "synonymous with communication because redundancies in patterns of communicating define the form of relationship" (p. 384). Therefore, leadership is overtly observed and interpreted as a communicative process manifested through relationships (Drecksel, 1991).

Finally, the nexus between culture and communication was described in chapter 4, but at this point, it is important to reiterate that culture change is a communication-intensive activity. A school's culture is at the core of restructuring because it is simultaneously the embodiment of past learning and the framework for future learning (Weick & Ashford, 2000). Consequently, how superintendents and principals convey and challenge culture through dialogue and nonverbal behavior influence teacher dispositions toward risk taking, experimentation, and their own communicative behavior.

CONCLUDING COMMENTS

Linkages among school climate, culture, and restructuring were restated in the beginning of this chapter. The argument is made that climate and culture change require organizational learning; that is, administrators and teachers must challenge assumptions that guide their behavior (especially when the assumptions have a negative effect) and, through shared experiences and dialogue, develop more effective practices. Throughout this pursuit for school improvement, administrators are expected to lead, facilitate, encourage, and interpret collective actions. Studies of learning organizations make it abundantly clear that leaders succeed in these difficult assignments by establishing trust, collegiality, and other characteristics of positive professional relationships—and these relationships are shaped by communicative behavior (Weick & Ashford, 2000).

Consider an elementary school principal who convinced her faculty as part of a school improvement grant to meet with her for 1 hour every Wednesday after school. The purpose was to discuss instructional practices. Teachers were asked to write notes about their personal classroom experiences over the past week. The notes focused on both negative and positive outcomes and included personal observations regarding possible reasons for the outcomes. During the meetings, teachers exchanged written notes, and each teacher had 3 to 5 minutes to comment on his or her notes. After several months of meetings, an external consultant monitoring the improvement grant visited the school and interviewed teachers. When he asked them to identify the most useful element of the grant, they uniformly replied, "I've learned a great deal from the Wednesday notes." The consultant also discovered that teachers were extending discussions of the Wednesday meetings voluntarily during their preparation periods and during lunch.

This vignette summarizes the content of this chapter. School improvement is more than new paradigms and mandates. When educators recognize their potential to improve schools through collective learning, they are likely to alter their basic assumptions about personal practice and school improvement. Unfortunately, progress toward organizational learning requires more than good intent. In the vast majority of schools, teachers are not given opportunities for collaborative learning and principals contend that they are mired in management and political problems. Nevertheless, we now have a better perspective of organizational learning and its potential to change negative cultures and produce badly needed restructuring.

REFERENCES

Belasen, A. T. (2000). *Leading the learning organization: Communication and competencies for managing change.* Albany: State University of New York Press.

Chubb, J. E., & Moe, T. M. (1990). *Politics, markets, and America's schools.* Washington, DC: Brookings Institution.

Conger, J. A. (1989). *The charismatic leader.* San Francisco: Jossey-Bass.

Covey, S. (1996). Three roles of the leader in the new paradigm. In F. Hesselbein, M. Goldsmith, & R. Beckhard (Eds.), *The leader of the future* (pp. 149–160). San Francisco: Jossey-Bass.

Drecksel, G. L. (1991). Leadership research: Some issues. In J. Anderson (Ed.), *Communication yearbook 14* (pp. 535–546). Newbury Park, CA: Sage.

DuFour, R., & Eaker, R. (1998). *Professional learning communities at work: Best practices for enhancing student achievement.* Alexandria, VA: Association for Supervision and Curriculum Development.

Duke, D. (2004). *The challenge of educational change.* Boston: Allyn & Bacon.

Elmore, R. F., Peterson, P. L., & McCarthey, S. J. (1996). *Restructuring in the classroom: Teaching, learning, and school organization.* San Francisco: Jossey-Bass.

English, H. B., & English, A. C. (1958). *A comprehensive dictionary of psychological and psychoanalytical terms.* New York: Longman.

Fairhurst, G. T. (2000). Dualism in leadership research. In F. Jablin & L. Putnam (Eds.), *The new handbook of organizational communication* (pp. 379–389). Thousand Oaks, CA: Sage.

Fink, D. (2000). *Good schools/real schools: Why school reform doesn't last.* New York: Teachers College Press.

Fullan, M. (1999). *Change forces: The sequel.* Philadelphia: Falmer.

Fullan, M. (2001). *Leading in a culture of change.* San Francisco: Jossey-Bass.

Garvin, D. A. (1993). Building a learning organization. *Harvard Business Review, 71*(4), 78–91.

Hall, G. E., & Hord, S. M. (2001). *Implementing change: Patterns, principles, and potholes.* Boston: Allyn & Bacon.

Hanson, E. M. (2003). *Educational administration and organizational behavior* (5th ed.). Boston: Allyn & Bacon.

Joyce, B., & Calhoun, E. (1996). School renewal: An inquiry, not a prescription. In B. Joyce & E. Calhoun (Eds.), *Learning experiences in school renewal: An exploration of five successful programs* (pp. 175–190). Eugene, OR: ERIC Clearinghouse on Educational Management.

Kowalski, T. J. (1981). Organizational patterns for secondary school curriculum. *NASSP Bulletin, 65*(443), 1–8.

Kowalski, T. J. (1998). The role of communication in providing leadership for school reform. *Mid-Western Educational Researcher, 11*(1), 32–40.

Kowalski, T. J. (2003). *Contemporary school administration: An introduction* (2nd ed.). Boston: Allyn & Bacon.

Kowalski, T. J. (2005). Evolution of the school superintendent as communicator. *Communication Education, 54*(2), 101–117.

Kowalski, T. J. (2006). *The school superintendent: Theory, practice, and cases* (2nd ed.). Thousand Oaks, CA: Sage.

Lashway, L. (1998). *Creating a learning organization.* (ERIC Document Reproduction Service No. ED420897)

Leithwood, K. A., Leonard, L. J., & Sharratt, L. (1998). Conditions fostering organizational learning in schools. *Educational Administration Quarterly, 34*(2), 243–276.

Morgan, G., (1987). *Images of the organization.* Newbury Park, CA: Sage.

Normann, R. (1985). Developing capabilities for organizational learning. In J. Pennings (Ed.), *Organizational strategy and change* (pp. 217–248). San Francisco: Jossey-Bass.

Reitzug, U. C., & Cornett, J. W. (1991). Teacher and administrator thought: Implications for administrator training. *Planning and Changing, 21*(3), 181–192.

Sarason, S. B. (1996). *Revisiting the culture of the school and the problem of change.* New York: Teachers College Press.

Sargeant, J. C. (1967). *Organizational climate in high schools.* Danville, IL: Interstate.

Schein, E. H. (1992). *Organizational culture and leadership* (2nd ed.). San Francisco: Jossey-Bass.

Schein, E. H. (1996). Culture: The missing concept in organization studies. *Administrative Science Quarterly, 41*(2), 229–240.

Schlechty, P. C. (1990). *Schools for the twenty-first century: Leadership imperatives for educational reform.* San Francisco: Jossey-Bass.

Schlechty, P. C. (2001). *Shaking up the schoolhouse: How to support and sustain educational innovation.* San Francisco: Jossey-Bass.

Schön, D. (1987). *Educating the reflective practitioner.* San Francisco: Jossey-Bass.

Schwan, C. J., & Spady, W. G. (1998). *Total leaders: Applying the best future-focused change strategies in education.* Arlington, VA: American Association of School Administrators.

Senge, P. M. (1990). *The fifth discipline: The art and practice of the learning organization.* New York: Doubleday/Currency.

Spring, J. (1994). *The American school: 1642–1993* (3rd ed.). New York: Mc-Graw-Hill.

Stacey, R. (1996). *Complexity and creativity in organizations.* San Francisco: Berrett-Koehler.

Timar, T. B., & Kirp, D. L. (1987). Education reform and institutional competence. *Harvard Educational Review, 57*(3), 308–330.

Tyack, D., & Cuban, L. (1995). *Tinkering toward utopia.* Cambridge, MA: Harvard University Press.

Weick, K. E., & Ashford, S. J. (2000). Learning in organizations. In F. Jablin & L. Putnam (Eds.), *The new handbook of organizational communication* (pp. 704–731). Thousand Oaks, CA: Sage.

Weiss, H. M. (1990). Learning theory and industrial and organizational psychology. In M. Dunnette & L. Hough (Eds.), *Handbook of industrial and organizational psychology* (Vol. 1, pp. 171–222). Palo Alto, CA: Consulting Psychologists Press.

West, P. G., & Meyer, D. G. (1997). Communicated knowledge as a learning foundation. *The International Journal of Organizational Analysis, 5*(1), 25–58.

7

Democratic Leadership and Communication

Districts and schools nationwide are under attack from critics who offer a variety of proposed solutions to "fix" the system. Initiatives such as charter schools, vouchers, and increased student testing are clear examples. The No Child Left Behind Act (NCLB), in particular, reflects a deep federal distrust of the ability of public education to reform itself. In several significant ways, this law represents the deepest, most intensive federal intrusion ever into local school governance and operations.

As a result of persistent criticism, America's "faith in the ability of educational institutions to inculcate its citizenry with knowledge, democratic virtues, and skills required for prosperous participation in the economy and civic polity has diminished in the past several years" (Rorrer & Fusarelli, 2000, p. 2). One needs to look no further than the dramatic growth of the home schooling movement as evidence of public education's seemingly tenuous place in society. School boards and school administrators across the nation are now scrutinized to a degree unheard of in previous times. As Kolderie (1996) observes, school systems, particularly those in urban areas, have had to struggle for legitimacy amid public dissension and conflicting agendas for education. Increasingly, citizens feel no collective sense of ownership of public education (Mathews, 2006).

The struggle for legitimacy arguably is not the product of meddlesome parents or intrusive school boards; rather, it is the result of parents, students, and other community members feeling alienated from their schools. In large measure, such feelings have been fueled by a perceived erosion of local control and citizen involvement. Increased centralized controls in the form of intrusive state and federal policy has increasingly disconnected the public from schools and made many citizens unresponsive to improving and supporting them. A recent report released by the Kettering Foundation concluded that alienation is tied to the public's belief that citizens have no sense of ownership with respect to public education (Mathews, 2006). Estrangement is particularly troublesome in a democratic society where liberty remains a driving force for public policy; for instance, school officials in many states require taxpayer approval for local rates. The steady erosion of public confidence coupled with feelings of alienation have produced a social environment that is counterproductive to school improvement (Mathews, 2006).

DRIFT FROM DEMOCRATIC GOVERNANCE

Scholars from a variety of disciplines have become concerned about the increasingly antidemocratic character of institutions in society. Wolin (1989) observes that even Republicans, who promote liberty and espouse local control and decentralization, have not scaled down government or returned power to the people; rather, they have expanded the reach of government. Ronald Reagan, for example, vowed to disband the U.S. Department of Education when he was campaigning to be president. Once he was elected, however, this newly created department actually expanded. Furthermore, the size and scope of the department under subsequent presidents from both major political parties continued to get larger and more politically powerful.

Citizens have long reacted negatively to their public institutions, and especially schools, being controlled by government bureaucrats far removed from local operations. This problem is exacerbated when policymakers and the public have competing philosophies (Berger & Neuhaus, 1977). In part, alienation explains why voter turnout in local school board elections is often low, especially among younger voters; studies of voting behavior have linked the fact that the nation's youth have lower levels of civic obligation than all other age groups with a serious decline in democratic processes (Bennett & Bennett, 1990).

Many state and federal policymakers seem obsessed with centralization, standardization, and narrowly defined views of an educated citizen. As a result, there was a declining emphasis on preparing students to live in a democracy for much of the last half of the 20th century (Callahan, 1962; Fusarelli, 1999; Katz, 1987; Wood, 1992). As early as the late 1970s, some scholars (e.g., Wise, 1979) recognized that centralized governmental control of public education was producing a policy environment in which learning would be legislated.

Many educators and citizens continue to ask, "How did we lose control of our schools?" The erosion of local control, according to many historians (e.g., Callahan, 1962; Hansot & Tyack, 1982; Tyack, 1974; Tyack & Hansot, 1982), began circa 1910 after ambitious superintendents and school boards attempted to run schools like businesses. Their efficiency-driven efforts were guided by classical theory and the tenets of industrial management. School administrators, and especially superintendents, were recast as managerial experts who would function best if protected from the political realities of democracy. By reframing public education as nonpartisan, efficiency advocates weakened local control and removed key areas of decision making from popular pressure (Katznelson & Weir, 1985). In the aftermath, generations of school administrators were socialized to equate citizen involvement with politics, politics with conflict, and conflict with organizational inefficiency (Hanson, 2003). In essence, citizen control over education was gradually eroded by school officials pressured to place a higher priority on technical efficiency and a lower priority on citizen involvement (Kowalski, 2006).

From approximately 1930 to 1960, the concept of democratic school administration enjoyed a revival, led by a mix of progressive educators, such as George Sylvester Counts (a social reconstructionist), and forward-thinking academics, such as Ernest Melby (dean of education at Northwestern University) (Kowalski, 2005). These enlightened scholars argued that the community was public education's greatest resource. Melby (1955), in particular, urged administrators to "release the creative capacities of individuals" and "mobilize the educational resources of communities" (p. 250). But by 1960, the concept again fell into disfavor, being described as a quaint and idealistic concept that ignored the complex nature of contemporary social and political problems (Kowalski, 2003).

The weakening of local control over public elementary and secondary education is remarkable given the strong, local participatory norms and values pervasive in the United States. The loss of citizen control reflected a distrust of laypeople and a disdain for conflict. Moreover, centralization was abetted by legal interventions such as those requiring states to ensure all students reasonably equal educational opportunities. Ironically, many of the concerns about centralization being voiced today echo the concerns voiced between 1930 and 1960. Wood (1992), for example, astutely observes that many modern school reform initiatives are corporatist in character, tied to economic productivity, and seemingly unconcerned with the development of independent-minded citizens.

The loss of citizen control is antithetical to the ideals on which America's public school system was founded. The common school movement, the driving force behind the development of schools in the late 1800s and early 1900s, had the purpose of taking disparate peoples and inculcating in them democratic values to protect and preserve America's democratic heritage (Skocpol, 1992). As such, schools were supposed to play a crucial role in supporting and maintaining society's ideological foundations. In his seminal work on the relationship between democracy and education, Dewey (1916) explains the role that education plays in the maintenance and continued creation of democratic culture and institutions.

Education is simply the means by which society prepares, in its children, the essential conditions of its own existence (Giddens, 1972). A truly democratic form of public education, according to Maxcy (1995), is nested in three core beliefs:

1. A belief in the worth and importance of individuals participating in decision making
2. A belief in intelligence and inquiry
3. A belief that individuals, working together within communities of learning, are capable of engaging in strategic planning and problem solving

Accordingly, Wood (1992) asserts that if we expand our vision of the purpose of education and think of the educational system differently, we will produce a very different reform agenda—one whose core purpose is the preparation of active, participatory, democratic citizens. The communitarian model of school governance detailed in this chapter is one model by which we can begin this endeavor.

CASE FOR DEMOCRATIC LEADERSHIP

Concept of Community

How can schools become more democratic and more responsive? One suggested solution is communitarianism, a democratic model of school governance in which participatory communities of decision makers "recognize and accept both the obligation and the right to participate in the educational decisions which most affect their lives" and gather together to improve schooling for all children (Fusarelli, 1999, p. 98). Citizenship is a shared initiative and responsibility among persons committed to mutual care (Sullivan, 1986). By adopting this model, administrators can recapture the democratic essence of education and preserve the nation's democratic heritage.

Communitarianism emphasizes social responsibility, democracy, and collective commitment to the common good. Communitarians favor a strong democracy—that is, a democracy that is more responsive, more representative, and more participatory than our governing institutions seem to permit (Etzioni, 1993; Mason, 1982). According to Wood (1992), to live and fully participate in a democratic society requires the development of traits such as a commitment to community, a desire to participate, and values such as justice, equality, and liberty.

Student Involvement

Schools must educate liberal democratic citizens in a liberal democratic way through modeling behavior (Strike, 1991). Strike's rationale is that participatory systems become self-sustaining insofar as the more deeply citizens participate, the better they are able to do so. Extending Strike's argument, students' character may be more influenced by the structure and practices of educational institutions than by its curriculum and instructional methods. Thus, the primary question is whether public schools reflect democratic principles. The answer appears to be that they once did but no longer do—a response that has led some scholars to assert that direct political participation is a prerequisite for civic education in a democracy (Barber, 1984).

If youth, particularly those most recently completing high school, are the citizens least likely to participate in a democratic society, then it is difficult to argue that public schools are succeeding in molding good citizens. As in any organization, individuals quickly discern what is important and valued.

In this vein, the behavior of school administrators is critically influential, both directly and symbolically (Kowalski, 2006). Therefore, teaching citizenship begins with democratic leadership, and students learn to accept responsibility when they are given an opportunity to participate in meaningful ways. Participation in governing is best learned through practice (Mill, 1963). Critical theorists, such as Aronowitz and Giroux (1985), believe that it is a contradiction to envision a democratic society when its inheritors, our children, are forced to live under conditions of unrelieved subordination. In the real world of school administration, allowing students to control schools is clearly unrealistic, but involving them in governance in meaningful ways is not. Unfortunately, public schools typically have not been havens of democracy (Wood, 1992).

If any organization should reflect democratic ideals, it is the school; yet students are rarely invited to become active participants in their own education (Clark & Meloy, 1989; Goodlad, 1984; McNeil, 1986; Silberman, 1970). Kohn (1993) is correct in his observation that schooling is typically about doing things to children, not working with them. Aside from school council or student government, students are basically excluded from involvement in significant decisions. Rarely are they given, even in high schools, any real voice in shaping policies that most affect them. Schools have been more likely to dictate behavior than to encourage responsibility, self-discipline, and citizenship.

Democratic schools offer opportunities for students to gain real, firsthand knowledge and participatory experience with democratic governance. This is not an unrealistic objective. For example, Raywid (1992) found that in effective schools, teachers and students have a significant amount of autonomy and responsibility, are encouraged to cooperate with their peers, are treated as important and valued contributors to the school, and are controlled more by a shared set of common values and guiding principles than by rules and regulations. Repeated examples of genuine participation must be provided for both teachers and students if democracy is to be a vital, live possibility (Beyer, 1992). Only when young people in school experience over and over again, in thousands of individual incidents, the ways in which democracy works and feels do they learn to act democratically (Grambs & Carr, 1979). As Kohn (1993) passionately argues, students should not only be educated to live in a democracy when they become adults; they should have the chance to live in a democracy while they are students. To make this happen, school administrators must share power—which is not easy, if only because the results of doing so are less predictable than in situations where superintendents and principals have complete or nearly complete control.

Educator and Citizen Involvement

Schools are often authoritarian in nature, consisting of countless rules, regulations, and sharply defined procedures that constrain behavior. Such an organizational context makes it more difficult for administrators to ensure the equal right of employees and citizens to participate in deliberations about collective decisions that affect them and the right of all to have their interests fairly considered (Strike, 1989). Authoritarian administrators usually communicate using memoranda, and they discourage, in their words and actions, others from participating in school governance. Their approach to practice is guided by two misconceptions: that teachers are merely subordinates and that parents are merely clients. In truth, teachers are colleagues and peer professionals, and parents are both clients and stakeholders. Recent political pressure to involve teachers and parents expectedly have made autocratic administrators uncomfortable, and those who just pretend to be democratic "usually revert to their former behavior once those forces dissipate" (Petersen & Kowalski, 2005, p. 13).

Reversion can be avoided if administrators are philosophically committed to democratic leadership. By practicing democratic, communitarian leadership, they can make schools more open, participatory, and inclusive. How? As an example, they can incorporate Dahl's (1956, 1989) five criteria for democracy into school operations:

1. Voting equality
2. Effective participation
3. Enlightened understanding
4. Control of the agenda
5. Inclusion

Most schools meet none of these criteria—not with faculty, staff, or the community. Democratic or communitarian leadership requires a school culture that operates from the principle of the consent of the governed (Clark & Meloy, 1989).

Gradually across the nation, a growing reliance on deregulation and decentralization (Kowalski, 2006) is helping ensure that parents and members of the community are more involved in open debates about key educational issues and decisions (Baker, 1997). The challenge is sustaining this trend. For schools to remain democratic, they must have climates in which practical arguments are made, all relevant considerations are aired, and all competent speakers are heard on important school issues (Habermas, 1984; 1990; Young, 1989). Such a climate is characterized by Fishkin's (1991) conceptualization of political equality—a system that grants equal consideration to everyone's preferences and that grants everyone appropriately equal opportunities to formulate preferences on the issues under consideration. Under a communitarian model of school governance, a democratic decision would occur after full and fair discussion in which all sides of the question are examined, and everyone with anything to contribute has been allowed to have his or her say (Lucas, 1976). Such speech is as open and free as possible. Decisions result from the stronger argument, rather than a concession to majority rule.

Learning Communities and Cultural Citizenship

Obviously, bringing participatory democracy back into school governance is not an easy task, since the scope of potential conflict is widened, parameters of authority change and may become unclear, and governance is less linear and directed (Zeichner, 1991). School administrators pursuing this goal must be diligent to ensure that power and authority are distributed in such a way as to encourage people to participate in decision making (Pateman, 1970). To create true learning communities, schools must offer students and families cultural citizenship—that is, the right to be different and to belong in a democratic sense (Reyes, 1994; Rosaldo, 1993). Cultural citizenship requires full membership in a group and the ability to influence one's destiny by having a significant voice in fundamental decisions (Rosaldo, 1993).

In learning communities, the goal of reaching consensus becomes more important than either the efficiency of administrative rule or the convenience of voting (a process that results in winners and losers). Participation in consensual goal formation is not something administrators or others learn naturally (Clegg & Higgins, 1987). Moreover, the deployment of requisite knowledge and skills depends on effective communication, philosophical commitment, and patience. Yet, principals, teachers, parents, and others are often asked to participate in collaborative decisions on an ad hoc basis, and they come to the process with no previous experience in building consensus (Stone, 1988). Predictably, the process fails, and when it does, the participants come to believe that *they* have failed or that the process is unworkable. Consequently, preparing individuals to collaborate is an essential step in democratic administration (Kowalski, 2005).

DEMOCRATIC LEADERSHIP AND COMMUNICATION

The communication implications for democratic leadership are rather obvious. Administrators who view themselves as controlling managers or scientific experts have little concern for sharing power and for exchanging information. They tend to protect information and to distribute it selectively (Kowalski, 2005). Democratic leadership, by comparison, involves galvanizing support for public schools (Howlett, 1993), a change requiring superintendents and principals to engage in politics—not as traditional politicians but rather as professional educators seeking to gain scarce resources for schools.

Consequently, a transition to a democratic leadership style demands more than conviction and good intent; it also requires relational communication as defined earlier in this book. That is, administrators must be committed to and capable of open, symmetrical, and ongoing information exchanges with multiple publics. Regrettably, this important point has been overlooked by policymakers and school administration professors who advocate democratic administration but fail to require the study of communication (Kowalski & Keedy, 2003). In an information-based society, the nexus between effective communication and effective leadership has become axiomatic, both in politics and in business. Unfortunately, this connection has received far less attention in the realm of education.

All too often, practitioners think about becoming more democratic without thinking about why and how they must change their communicative behavior. The manner in which superintendents and principals communicate affects (a) how they are perceived, (b) their ability to pursue change, and (c) the attitudes and feelings of those with whom they have contact (Kowalski, 2005). All three of the conditions are integral to re-shaping schools as democratic institutions.

CONCLUDING COMMENTS

Equality, autonomy, and democracy can be said to make up the central moral principles that should guide education (Wood, 1992). In the rush to embrace a corporatist model of schooling, with its overriding emphasis on testing and accountability, the educative and ethical purposes of schooling often have been lost. To recapture them, school administrators, teachers, and communities must communicate more effectively, not only with each other but also with state and federal policymakers who have pursued centralized, top-down reforms.

Though democratic schools are debatably messy and idealistic places, they are essential to preserving a democratic society. Such schools (a) inculcate civic responsibility, (b) preserve our democratic heritage, (c) build goodwill and political support, and (d) foster symbiotic relationships between public education and local communities. Involving employees, students, and other stakeholders is the most prudent way to put the public back in public education—and when they are back in public education, they become accountable for school improvement and student success (Mathews, 2006).

Life in an information age and global economy already has produced many demands for schooling to be different and more effective. Recognizing this fact, most states have adopted reform strategies requiring local district administrators and school boards to chart a reform agenda and to be accountable for its success. As a result, democratic leadership already has become a normative standard for practice in the superintendency (Petersen & Kowalski, 2005), and it is rapidly becoming the normative standard for principals.

REFERENCES

Aronowitz, S., & Giroux, H. (1985). *Education under siege: The conservative, liberal, and radical debate over schooling.* Hadley, MA: Bergin & Garvey.

Baker, B. (1997). Public relations in government. In C. L. Caywood (Ed.), *The handbook of strategic public relations and integrated communication* (pp. 453–480). New York: McGraw-Hill.

Barber, B. R. (1984). *Strong democracy: Participatory politics for a new age.* Los Angeles: University of California Press.

Bennett, L. M., & Bennett, S. E. (1990). *Living with leviathan: Americans coming to terms with big government.* Lawrence: University of Kansas Press.

Berger, P. L., & Neuhaus, R. J. (1977). *To empower people: The role of mediating structures in public policy.* Washington, DC: American Enterprise Institute.

Beyer, L. E. (1992). Can schools further democratic practices? *Theory into Practice, 27*(4), 262–269.

Callahan, R. E. (1962). *Education and the cult of efficiency.* Chicago: University of Chicago Press.

Clark, D. L., & Meloy, J. M. (1989). Renouncing bureaucracy: A democratic structure for leadership in schools. In T. J. Sergiovanni & J. H. Moore (Eds.), *Schooling for tomorrow: Directing reforms to issues that count.* Boston: Allyn & Bacon.

Clegg, S. R., & Higgins, W. (1987). Against the current: Sociology, socialism and organizations. *Organizational Studies, 8*(3), 201–221.

Dahl, R. A. (1956). *A preface to democratic theory.* Chicago: University of Chicago Press.

Dahl, R. A. (1989). *Democracy and its critics.* New Haven, CT: Yale University Press.

Dewey, J. (1916). *Democracy and education.* New York: The Free Press.

Etzioni, A. (1993). *The spirit of community: The reinvention of American society.* New York: Simon & Schuster.

Fishkin, J. S. (1991). *Democracy and deliberation: New directions for democratic reform.* New Haven, CT: Yale University Press.

Fusarelli, L. D. (1999). Education is more than numbers: Communitarian leadership of schools for the new millennium. In L. T. Fenwick (Ed.), *School leadership: Expanding horizons of the mind and spirit* (pp. 97–107). Lancaster, PA: Technomic.

Giddens, A. (Ed.). (1972). *Emile Durkheim: Selected writings.* Cambridge, UK: Cambridge University Press.

Goodlad, J. I. (1984). *A place called school: Prospects for the future.* New York: McGraw-Hill.

Grambs, G., & Carr, L. (1979). *Modern methods in secondary education.* New York: Holt.

Habermas, J. (1984). *Theory of communicative action.* (T. McCarthy, Trans.). Boston: Beacon.

Habermas, J. (1990). *Moral consciousness and communicative action.* Cambridge, MA: MIT Press.

Hanson, E. M. (2003). *Educational administration and organizational behavior* (5th ed.). Boston: Allyn & Bacon.

Hansot, E., & Tyack, D. B. (1982). A usable past: Using history in educational policy. In A. Lieberman & M. W. McLaughlin, (Eds.), *81st yearbook of the national society for the study of education. Part I: Policy making in education* (pp. 5–10). Chicago: University of Chicago Press.

Howlett, P. (1993). The politics of school leaders, past and future. *Education Digest, 58*(9), 18–21.

Katz, M. B. (1987). *Reconstructing American education.* Cambridge, MA: Harvard University Press.

Katznelson, I., & Weir, M. (1985). *Schooling for all: Class, race, and the decline of the democratic ideal.* New York: Basic Books.

Kohn, A. (1993). Choices for children: Why and how to let students decide. *Phi Delta Kappan, 75*(1), 9–20.

Kolderie, T. (1996). How the state should 'break up' the big-city district. In R. Crowson, W. L. Boyd, & H. Mawhinney (Eds.), *The politics of education and the new institutionalism: Reinventing the American school* (pp. 127–134). Washington, DC: Falmer.

Kowalski, T. J. (2003). *Contemporary school administration: An introduction* (2nd ed.). Boston: Allyn & Bacon.

Kowalski, T. J. (2005). Evolution of the school superintendent as communicator. *Communication Education, 54*(2), 101–117.

Kowalski, T. J. (2006). *The school superintendent: Theory, practice, and cases* (2nd ed.). Thousand Oaks, CA: Sage.

Kowalski, T. J., & Keedy, J. (2003, November). *Superintendent as communicator: Implications for professional preparation and licensing.* Paper presented at the Annual Conference of the University Council for Educational Administration, Portland, OR.

Lucas, J. R. (1976). *Democracy and participation.* Baltimore: Penguin.

Mason, R. M. (1982). *Participatory and workplace democracy.* Carbondale: Southern Illinois University Press.

Mathews, D. (2006, April 12). Putting the public back in public education. *Education Week, 25*(31), 39, 48.

Maxcy, S. J. (1995). *Democracy, chaos, and the new school order.* Thousand Oaks, CA: Corwin.

McNeil, L. (1986). *Contradictions of control: School structure and school knowledge.* New York: Routledge & Kegan Paul.

Melby, E. O. (1955). *Administering community education*. Englewood Cliffs, NJ: Prentice Hall.

Mill, J. S. (1963). *Collected works*. Toronto, Canada: University of Toronto Press.

Pateman, C. (1970). *Participation and democratic theory*. London: Cambridge University Press.

Petersen, G. J., & Kowalski, T. J. (2005, November). *School reform strategies and normative expectations for democratic leadership in the superintendency*. Paper presented at the Annual Meeting of the University Council for Educational Administration, Nashville, TN.

Raywid, M. A. (1992). Why do these kids love school? *Phi Delta Kappan, 73*(8), 631–633.

Reyes, P. (1994). *Cultural citizenship and social responsibility: A call for change in educational administration*. UCEA presidential address. Presented at the Annual Conference of the University Council for Educational Administration (UCEA), Houston, TX.

Rorrer, A., & Fusarelli, L. D. (2000, November). *Institutional responses to the needs of at-risk students: District and campus perspectives*. Paper presented at the Annual Meeting of the University Council for Educational Administration, Albuquerque, NM.

Rosaldo, R. (1993). *Cultural citizenship and educational democracy*. The America Paredes Lecture. The University of Texas at Austin.

Silberman, C. E. (1970). *Crisis in the classroom: The remaking of American education*. New York: Random House.

Skocpol, T. (1992). *Protecting mothers and soldiers: The political origins of social policy in the United States*. Cambridge, MA: Belknap.

Stone, D. A. (1988). *Policy paradox and political reason*. New York: HarperCollins.

Strike, K. A. (1989). *Liberal justice and the Marxist critique of education*. New York: Routledge.

Strike, K. A. (1991). The moral role of schooling in a liberal democratic society. *Review of Research in Education, 17*, 413–483.

Sullivan, W. M. (1986). *Reconstructing public philosophy*. Berkeley: University of California Press.

Tyack, D. B. (1974). *The one best system: A history of American urban education*. Cambridge, MA: Harvard University Press.

Tyack, D. B., & Hansot, E. (1982). *Managers of virtue*. New York: Basic Books.

Wise, A. E. (1979). *Legislated learning: The bureaucratization of the American classroom*. Berkeley: University of California Press.

Wolin, S. S. (1989). *The presence of the past: Essays on the state and the constitution*. Baltimore: Johns Hopkins University Press.

Wood, G. H. (1992). *Schools that work: America's most innovative public education programs.* New York: Dutton.

Young, R. E. (1989). *A critical theory of education: Habermas and our children's future.* New York: Harvester Wheatsheaf.

Zeichner, K. M. (1991). Contradictions and tensions in the professionalization of teaching and the democratization of schools. *Teachers College Record, 92*(3), 363–379.

Communication Networks

As board president Sharon O'Hara prepared to open the Jackson Township school board meeting, she whispered to Superintendent Mark Kyle, "Why are all these teachers here?" All 100 seats provided for visitors were filled, and at least 30 more people were standing around the perimeter of the room. The board president estimated that teachers comprised about 70% of the audience. The superintendent shrugged his shoulders and said, "Your guess is as good as mine."

The teachers sat silently until the agenda reached an item pertaining to student field trips. After being recognized, Superintendent Kyle told the school board members that he wanted their approval to appoint a committee to evaluate current field trip policy and regulations and to possibly recommend revisions.

Albert Preston, president of the teachers' union, asked to be recognized so he could state an opposing view. Mrs. O'Hara then inquired, "You are opposed to having a committee study this issue?"

"Yes. The teachers' association opposes Mr. Kyle's recommendation because his real intent is to discontinue most field trips."

Looking at the superintendent, the board president inquired, "Is that true?"

"My recommendation is as stated. It is to form a committee to look at this issue. With rising fuel costs, I and my staff believe that we need to revamp policy. I have never indicated to anyone an intention to discontinue field trips," the superintendent answered.

Mrs. O'Hara permitted Mr. Preston to respond to the superintendent's comment.

"For the past few months, Mr. Kyle has been asking the principals questions about field trips. He wanted to know whether they were necessary and productive. On several occasions he told principals that he questioned the cost-benefit relationships of these trips. Several of our members also learned that the superintendent has mapped out a strategy for eliminating field trips. It involves getting you to approve this committee and then handpicking the members to ensure that his view is recommended. And as you can see by tonight's attendance, teachers don't support his idea or his tactic. We are upset."

The superintendent responded immediately. "I have asked questions about field trips because one of my responsibilities is to keep this district fiscally solvent. The cost of field trips has been rising steadily for at least the last 3 years. However, at no time did I conclude, or even suggest, that field trips should be discontinued. As to the suggestion that I intend to stack the deck in my favor, I am comfortable having the board select the committee members. My intention was to have a five member committee that would be chaired by the assistant superintendent for curriculum and include the transportation director. I'm sure that both of these individuals will verify that I have never stated an intention to discontinue field trips to them."

Mr. Preston then responded to the superintendent. "Costs go up for everything. That's no reason to get rid of something or even to change it. I am not at liberty to disclose how we learned of the superintendent's intention but we are convinced the information is accurate. This committee is not necessary, and I and the teachers present urge you to defeat the superintendent's recommendation."

After additional discussion, the board voted unanimously to table the superintendent's recommendation.

INTRODUCTION

Rumors can be destructive in organizations, because they have the potential both to reduce efficiency (time and money are often needed to deal with them) and to influence employee morale negatively. In this situation, incompatible information has produced conflict. The union president admits that he has alternative sources of information and that he relies on them, but he refuses to reveal what they are.

In districts and schools, information is disseminated, received, and exchanged through communication networks. These conduits are shaped by school administrators and by employees. This chapter examines the nature of these networks and the factors that contribute to their development. The argument is then made that administrators need to engage in network analysis as a means of determining how they can improve communication.

ORGANIZATIONAL THEORIES AND COMMUNICATION

Administrator perspectives on communication in schools and between schools and external publics are shaped primarily by knowledge of how organizations should and actually do function. This knowledge was "built slowly, piece by piece, as preceding models were proposed, tested, modified, and retained" (Conrad, 1990, p. 95). To demonstrate the influence of organizational theories, the communication ramifications of three primary theory approaches are summarized here.

Classical Theory

Classical theory provides a normative structural approach to shaping organizations. A combination of Max Weber's structure of authority and Frederick Taylor's principles of scientific management (Hanson, 2003), the bureaucracy became the icon of technical efficiency that was adopted first by business and industry and subsequently by public education (Callahan, 1962). The primary foci of the "ideal organization" were formal hierarchies, managerial functions, worker efficiency, and managerial control (Hoy & Miskel, 2005). From approximately 1900 to 1930, formal-structural communication became the dominant paradigm and an integral component of the traditional organizational model (Conrad, 1990).

Contrary to popular belief, not all classical theorists held identical views of organizational communication. For example, Taylor believed that upward communication could serve a purpose, whereas Weber restricted information exchanges to downwardly directed messages, most of which were to provide interpretations of policy and rules to subordinates (Tompkins, 1987). Despite such differences, classical theorists consistently concentrated on transmission processes and formal channels; in this regard, they all embraced a mechanistic view of organizational communication (Euske & Roberts, 1987).

Human Relations Theory

The human relations movement was generally guided by the principle that a happy worker is a productive worker (Hanson, 2003). This theoretical perspective "centered on the social and psychological features of the individual and the work group rather than on formal roles and macro-structures" (Euske & Roberts, 1987, pp. 44–45). For many supporters, improving relationships among workers and between supervisors and subordinates became essential. To achieve this goal, they promoted open organizational climates, power sharing, and open communication.

Though classical theorists and human relations theorists shared an interest in formal structures, they differed in their perspectives regarding behavior and ways for achieving productivity. Human relations proponents pointed out that classical theory failed to account for individual interests, group interests, and social interaction. Whereas classical theories concentrated on scientific management, rules, and managerial controls, the human relations movement focused on job satisfaction, worker involvement, and motivation. These differing focal points had implications for their interests regarding organizational communication. The classical theorists emphasized formal channels, downward information flow, and written documents; the human relations theorists emphasized informal networks, relational communication, and participatory decision making (Euske & Roberts, 1987).

Systems Theory

While classical theory tends to be one-dimensional, views organizations as static, and embraces simplistic assumptions about organizational relationships, systems theory is multidimensional, includes complex assumptions about organizational relationships, and views organizations as having a continuous need for change (Chance & Björk, 2004). Conrad (1990) explains that systems theory is erected on three key concepts:

1. *Wholeness.* Organizations are composed of smaller interdependent subsystems that act in ways that influence every other subsystem. In a high school, for example, academic departments are subsystems. A change in requirements in the English Department could have consequences for scheduling and enrollment in all other departments.
2. *Boundaries.* A boundary is a system limitation. In the case of education, this concept defines the extent to which schools maintain open dialogue with their environments (e.g., the local community).
3. *Process.* This concept entails ways in which organizational members analyze and adapt to information and changing conditions. In highly closed schools (those with rigid boundaries), little or no effort is made to respond to changing societal conditions.

Systems theory, as developed by Katz and Kahn (1978), views organizational operations as a linear chain of activities categorized as *inputs*, *throughputs*, and *outputs*. The following information provides examples of the theory applied to a school:

- *Inputs.* This activity entails extracting human and material resources from the environment. Students, faculty, buildings, books, and budgets are examples.
- *Throughputs.* This activity entails processing inputs; that is, it specifies how inputs are treated in the organization. Curriculum, extracurricular activities, and discipline programs are examples.
- *Outputs.* This activity entails releasing products back into the environment after they have been processed. Graduates, social services, and research are examples.

Social systems theory also recognizes that organizations do not always function as intended. For example, schools usually look like bureaucracies on paper (e.g., line and staff charts) but actually function more like organized anarchies (Hoy & Miskel, 2005). This is because teachers and other employees have considerable independence, largely because schools cannot afford to employ enough administrators to ensure close supervision.

Organizations also are political entities. In the case of public schools, their organizational boundaries are easily penetrated by external forces (e.g., government agencies and political pressure groups), and power is distributed among individuals and groups (e.g., individual teachers or employee groups). As a result, administrators face continuous political interventions—that is, efforts to influence important decisions. Political activity occurs because schools do not have sufficient resources to satisfy all employee and public needs and wants. Consequently, individuals form groups and groups form coalitions in order to amass and exercise power as they pursue their interests (Hanson, 2003).

With respect to communication, systems theories have concentrated on issues such as the development and impact of information generated in the environment (community), what channels would be most effective given the social and political realities, and how the organization managed, interpreted, and used information. Katz and Kahn (1978) cast communication primarily as a feedback and evaluation activity—a sharply different perspective than the one found in classical theory.

Synthesis

More than two decades ago, Lysaught (1984) advised school administrators that "failures in communication lie at the heart of problems in organization, goal setting, productivity, and evaluation" (p. 102). Since he shared this insightful observation, literally hundreds of articles have been published about applications of organizational theory to school administration, but, regrettably, few of them have addressed communication. In light of the literature published in other disciplines, this oversight is inexcusable. No single organizational theory is superior in relation to communication and each offers insights into how administrators view the purpose of and best ways to structure their communicative behavior. (See Table 8.1 regarding a comparison of relevant characteristics from the three theory categories discussed in this chapter.) Supporters of classical, human relations, and systems theories clearly provided different views of effective communication; however, they uniformly treated communication as a product of rather than as a determinant of organizational design (Cummings, Long, & Lewis, 1987). This is the primary reason why the study of organizational theory without a concentration on communication has been disappointing.

Organizational theory has provided two essential perspectives relative to understanding and structurally analyzing communication. First, it gave scholars information about values and beliefs that guided choices adminis-

Table 8.1. Comparison of Selected Characteristics Relevant to Communication in Schools

Factor	Classical	Theory Category Human Relations	Social Systems
Relationships	Unimportant except for supervisor-subordinate	Important	Variable depending on organizational climate/culture
Individual needs/ interests	Unimportant	Important	Variable depending on organizational climate/culture
Authority/power	Centralized and concentrated at the upper management levels	Dispersed among individuals and groups, especially in areas affecting job satisfaction	Dispersed among individuals and groups as a result of social and political realities
Decision making	Managerial task focuses exclusively on organizational goals	Shared task focused on both the organization and individuals	Variable depending on organizational climate/culture
Conflict	Counterproductive	Potentially productive	Potentially productive
Organizational change	Disruptive and pursued autocratically when absolutely necessary	Essential and pursued collaboratively by organizational members	Essential and pursued collectively by organizational members and external stakeholders
Communication networks	Formal	Formal and informal	Formal and informal
Communication direction	Vertical, almost always downward	Multidirectional	Multidirectional
Communication flow	Predominately one-way	Two-way	Predominately two-way depending on organizational climate/culture
Communication mode	Predominately written	Predominately oral	Variable depending on organizational climate/culture

trators made as they erected formal communication networks (Monge & Eisenberg, 1987). Second, it revealed the importance of social networks— a variable that was instrumental both to the development and use of informal networks and to broadening structural analysis (Mitchell, 1972). The three theories summarized here provide a foundation for understanding three traditions of communication research in organizations as explained by Monge and Eisenberg (1987).

1. *Positional tradition.* Studies conducted in this tradition examined relations among positions. The two major foci were to determine prescribed communication direction (who should talk to whom) and prescribed communication content (legitimate topics).
2. *Relational tradition.* Studies conducted in this tradition examined emergent interactions among organizational members. Researchers typically sought to determine the extent to which people behaved in accordance with their prescribed roles when they communicated collectively, and the extent to which they followed the organization's prescribed communication structure.
3. *Cultural tradition.* Studies conducted in this tradition arguably extended the relational tradition. Researchers typically sought to determine the importance of symbols, meanings, and their use in social systems.

Over time, we have come to understand that actual communicative behavior in schools is shaped by an intricate combination of what is prescribed and responses to those prescriptions. In every organization, administrators face the challenge of dealing with both formal and informal networks.

FORMAL AND INFORMAL NETWORKS

Defining Networks

Communication networks (or channels) are conduits for distributing, receiving, and exchanging information. As previously discussed in chapter 3, they are either formal or informal; the former being created and sanctioned by the formal organization (i.e., district or school) and the latter being created by organizational members through social contact. In communication literature, informal networks are often called "emergent networks." Collectively, a district's or school's networks constitute a "tapestry of communicative relationships, a complex, interwoven, symbolic fabric" (Stohl, 1995, p. 22). As such, they play a central role in determining collective, interactive processes for generating, receiving, exchanging, and interpreting information.

Formal networks typically address critical questions about communication:

- What is the accepted direction(s) for communication (e.g., one-way, two-way)?
- Who should communicate with whom?
- In what ways should communication occur (e.g., verbal, nonverbal)?
- What is the intended purpose of communication?
- In what context may communication occur?

Very often, school administrators have simply deployed organizational charts (delineating a chain of command) to answer these questions (Dow, 1988). School district networks for announcing school closings due to inclement weather are prime examples. Following a traditional command chain, communication flows in one direction, and contact responsibilities and required points of information are specified.

Informal networks consist of "employees linked together by consistent patterns of communicating with one another" (Conrad, 1990, p. 169). They form through social interaction but for a variety of reasons. One motive is simply to satisfy social needs—that is, to provide a means for employees to exchange information with other employees (Fulk, 1993). Dissatisfaction with or distrust of established formal networks is another prevalent cause (Shockley-Zalabak, 1988). For example, teachers may believe that information received through the formal network is unreliable, self-serving, incorrect, or irrelevant. Poor timing also may be a reason. For example, employees react negatively when they receive late or outdated messages. Recognizing the importance of immediacy in today's information society, employees predictably bypass formal networks that fail to provide information in a timely manner. In comparison with formal networks, grapevines almost always are faster and more likely to answer questions (though at times incorrectly) posed by connected persons (Wells & Spinks, 1994). A schematic comparison of a formal and informal network in a school district is provided in Figure 8.1.

Though informal networks exist across all districts and schools, their influence and consequences are not constant. In some organizations, informal networks are primarily destructive—the source of rumors and misinformation. In other organizations, they contribute to job satisfaction, efficiency,

Formal Network
Developed and Controlled by the Superintendent

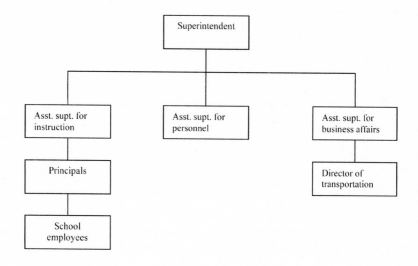

Informal Network
Developed and Controlled by Involved Employees

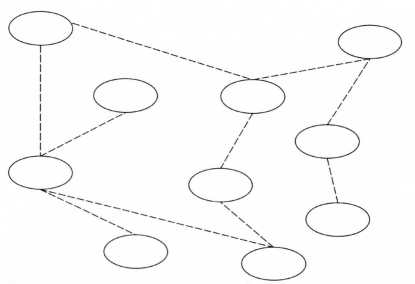

Figure 8.1. Formal and Informal Networks in a 2,000-Student School District

and productivity. In many ways, informal networks are like organizational conflict; they are inevitable and are neither inherently constructive nor destructive. Their value ultimately depends on how they are deployed and managed. Concepts such as learning communities and strategies such as culture change have made informal networks increasingly important to schools for at least three reasons:

1. Teachers traditionally have not had access to a wealth of information; much of their communication occurs via informal networks.
2. Teachers are increasingly being involved in decision making. Informal networks help them to identify and evaluate decision options.
3. Teachers are being asked to experiment and take risks. Informal networks make it possible for them to challenge the status quo and to propose and test new ideas.

March and Simon (1958) conclude that formal and informal networks were intricately intertwined in organizational behavior, and therefore organizational communication was not reducible to either. Consequently, school administrators should not ignore, condemn, or suppress informal networks; rather, they should strive to apply them productively.

Critical Network Properties

Both formal and informal networks are characterized by three general properties: symmetry, strength, and reciprocity (Farace, Monge, & Russell, 1977). Symmetry in communication has two dimensions. The first relates to participation. In this vein, a network is symmetrical when participants have reasonably equal participation (Shockley-Zalabak, 1988). Symmetry also pertains to intended benefit; that is, a network is symmetrical when it is intended to benefit all participants (Kowalski, 2004). A traditional chain of command, for instance, is almost always considered asymmetrical because its intended purpose is to benefit only the organization (or its top administrators), and communication typically is distributed by but not received by top administrators. Generally, symmetry contributes to communication effectiveness.

The property of strength is characterized by the frequency with which employees use networks and the length of their participation when they gain access. If a school has a weak network, it is used infrequently and employees spend little time communicating via this conduit. Generally, strength contributes to communication effectiveness. More noteworthy, strong communication networks increase the probability that linked individuals will influence each other's behavior (Shockley-Zalabak, 1988).

Reciprocity refers to the extent to which linked members agree about the nature of the networks (Farace et al., 1977). For examples, do all members agree about the purposes and effectiveness of their networks? Generally, networks that have high levels of reciprocity are the most effective conduits, regardless of whether they are formal or informal.

Effective networks are typically characterized by the following criteria:

- *Inclusiveness*—the extent to which all employees are part of the network
- *Transmission*—conduits for communication are reliable and accessible to network members
- *Feedback capacity*—the network encourages and facilitates two-way communication
- *Efficiency*—the cost of creating and maintaining the network is reasonable in relation to the benefits derived from it
- *Organizational fit*—the network is appropriate given the size and nature of the district or school

Factors Shaping Formal Networks

Historically, most organizations, including schools, structured communication channels on the basis of formal (or legitimate) authority as discussed previously in relation to classical theories. Accordingly, communication was intended to parallel lines of authority; supervisors passed information to subordinates basically on a "need to know" basis, in writing, and typically in relation to providing directives or policy/rule interpretations. Subordinates were neither encouraged to respond nor provided easy access to do so (Hanson, 2003). This perspective of communication is intended to establish control and coordination in organizations where work tasks are discretely separated (Dow, 1988; Jablin, 1987). Principals and superintendents guided by the classical approach tend to see teachers as subordinates and not as peer professionals.

In addition to philosophical convictions expressed through normative theory, administrator choices in relation to formal networks and media selection for them can be determined by several other variables. The most notable include the following:

- *Efficiency.* This variable is based on the ratio of cost to benefits. Typically, it guides administrators to identify an adequate (or minimum) level of communication and then to select procedures, hardware, and software that provide that level at minimum cost.
- *Social interactions.* Social interaction always has been an issue of interest to organizational theorists. The human relations movement that gained popularity in the mid-1930s characterized a productive worker as a happy worker and social interaction was associated with job satisfaction (Hanson, 2003). Today, school administrators also are encouraged to heighten social interaction to nurture teacher professionalism and collegiality. Superintendents and principals who view social interaction as being important are likely to shape formal networks on the basis of this goal.
- *Actual or intended decision making.* Decision making is a core organizational activity that entails making choices, often in relation to problem solving. Communication is a key factor that facilitates actual or intended procedures (Kowalski, Lasley, & Mahoney, in press). For example, shared decision making requires more inclusive and effective networks than does autocratic decision making.
- *School culture.* Culture is composed of fundamental values and beliefs shared by organizational members, especially in relation to identifying preferred behavior. Consequently, culture informs teachers and administrators, both directly and symbolically, as to how they should interact with each other. In strong cultures (i.e., in schools where values and beliefs are shared by all or most organizational members), formal networks are expected to conform to shared convictions. Communication scholars (e.g., Conrad, 1994; Hall, 1997) conclude that the nexus between organizational culture and communication is reciprocal—a deduction that was discussed in more detail in chapter 4.

In summary, school administrators have made important choices about formal communication networks, but the factors influencing those choices have not been constant across districts and schools. In the past, education institutions typically had communication networks that conformed to a chain of command, and most superintendents and principals gave little thought to changing them (Kowalski, 2005). After the United States became an information-based society and after demands for school reform swelled, this indifference toward communication became increasingly problematic. The following three conditions help us to understand this fact.

1. Mounting research demonstrates that culture plays an essential role in school effectiveness (e.g., Fullan, 2001; Sarason, 1996). Traditional communication channels have been an obstacle to culture change (primarily because they limit or at least discourage two-way communication) and perpetuate practices that restrict the ability of teachers to be change agents (Hall & Hord, 2001).

2. There is increasing research indicating that schools functioning as learning communities are more effective than schools that do not (DuFour & Eaker, 1998). Sergiovanni (2000), for instance, describes highly effective schools as "a community of relationships" (p. 66). In essence, relational communication is essential to organizational learning and organizational learning is essential to school effectiveness. This association between organizational learning and communication is demonstrated by four of the learning organization's prevalent characteristics: peer dialogue (Kline & Saunders, 1998), collective inquiry, experimentation, and collaboration (DuFour & Eaker, 1998).

3. Researchers have long recognized that classical communication does not satisfy employee needs and wants. Consequently, networks based on this philosophy actually induce employees to develop their own communication channels—informal networks that are exclusive and the source of rumors and misinformation (Hanson, 2003).

In highly effective schools, formal and informal communication networks complement rather than compete with each other. Recognizing that they cannot prevent or eradicate grapevines, forward-thinking administrators seek to monitor and utilize these networks to enhance school improvement.

Network Analysis

As articulated earlier in chapter 5, contemporary administrators must be competent communicators. However, they also must possess the knowledge, skills, and will to envision, plan, and facilitate communicative competent organizations. Both the content and delivery of education are rapidly changing, and in this dynamic environment effective practice is being defined primarily by the ability to access, communicate, and deploy information rapidly (Kowalski, 2006). Effective schools have personnel who continuously adjust to their environments by improving curriculum, instruction, organizational structure, and institutional culture. These modifications are highly dependent on formal and informal communication networks.

Unfortunately, conditions in highly effective schools are not pervasive. In the typical school, principals face the extremely difficult challenge of producing change with scarce resources. Lacking sufficient resources to satisfy competing needs and wants, their efforts to engage in reform are often thwarted by political action. Most notably, employees in organizations with scarce resources predictably build coalitions to pursue or protect their interests (Bacharach & Lawler, 1980). Once created, these coalitions compete rather than cooperate with each other. The presence of political coalitions makes network analysis a powerful administrative tool because the process is a proven alternative for identifying and managing internal coalitions (Karathanos, 1994).

Network analysis is intended to provide rich and accurate accounts of how people communicate in schools and the outcomes of their interactions. Examples include descriptions of who communicates to whom and in what frequency. The process also looks for patterns and connections revealing how people disseminate, receive, and exchange information. The process, however, goes beyond identifying the flow and direction of communication; it also is intended to determine how information is accessed, shared, and used to (a) reduce uncertainty, (b) challenge the status quo, (c) acquire, distribute, and use power, and (d) experiment with new ideas (Heath, 1994).

One reason why network analysis is difficult relates to the layers of organizational communication. Heath (1994) identifies four:

1. *Personal networks*—linkages that administrators, teachers, and other employees have with each other

2. *Group networks*—linkages among group members, such as the members of an academic department or curriculum committee
3. *Organizational networks*—linkages that span entire districts or schools
4. *Interorganizational networks*—linkages between and among districts and schools

Equally important, there are different types of networks. According to Stohl (1995), there are three:

1. *Task networks.* These are rooted in positions but extending beyond minimal job requirements (e.g., a network that is used by a group of teachers who are attempting to revise a portion of the curriculum).
2. *Social networks.* These are linkages and communication practices rooted in personal relationships (e.g., a network used by a group of teachers who play bridge together twice a month).
3. *Occupational networks.* These are linkages and communication practices rooted in one's work but they transcend organizational boundaries and reinforce shared education, values, or political dispositions (e.g., a national coalition of mathematics teachers).

In summary, communication networks can identify both structural and functional relationships among school employees. In the context of school reform, the value of this type of assessment and evaluation is axiomatic. The validity of this claim is demonstrated by examining two pervasive facets of organizational behavior: decision making and conflict management.

NETWORKS AND DECISION MAKING

School administrators make literally hundreds of decisions daily. Most are rather inconsequential, requiring little forethought because their potential consequences are rather insignificant. For example, a principal may decide to approve a teacher's request to attend a conference. Decisions of this type typically cause few problems. On the other hand, superintendents and principals encounter problems that threaten the welfare of people, the school, or even the community. Making decisions in relation to these situations is far more difficult and dangerous, largely for three reasons:

1. The administrator has limited information regarding alternative decisions.
2. Known alternative decisions are shrouded in uncertainty.
3. Because outcomes cannot be predicted with a high degree of accuracy, the risk of selecting any alternative is relatively high. (Kowalski et al., in press).

Both the quantity of decisions in this category and expectations that they will be made effectively have increased in recent years. Consider just a few reasons underlying this condition.

- Society and schools have become more diverse and as a result, they have evolved into increasingly complex social systems (Hoy & Miskel, 2005) and become more political as individuals and groups compete to protect their interests (Wirt & Kirst, 2001).
- The quantity and quality of information available to educators are much greater now than they were just 25 years ago (Popham, 2006). This fact is known by the public and understandably has influenced their expectation that administrators make better decisions.
- School reform has heightened expectations that district and school administrators will be democratic and accurate in making consequential decisions (Henkin & Dee, 2001).

These and other factors appear to have influenced portions of the No Child Left Behind Act (NCLB)—a federal law requiring the use of quantitative or qualitative information sources in decisions affecting curriculum and instruction (Picciano, 2006). Explaining this mandate for data-driven decision making, Doyle (2002) writes:

> Today's education leader, whether the leader of the school district, the school building or the classroom, must change data into knowledge, transform knowledge into wisdom and use wisdom as a guide to action. But if data-driven decision making and scientifically based research are the necessary preconditions to wise decision making, they are not sufficient. True, without data and solid evidence the modern decision maker is helpless, but simply possessing data and evidence is no guarantee of success. (p. 30)

Doyle's comment reminds us that our rapidly increasing reservoir of information will only benefit schools staffed by individuals who know how to use data and who are committed to deploying data in decision making. Unfortunately, many education practitioners are opposed to or ambivalent about data-driven decision making and the following factors have contributed to this problem:

- Educators traditionally have not been prepared adequately to engage in assessment; therefore, they have difficulty linking assessment data to their decisions (Popham, 2006).
- Educators who study research methodology and statistics often find the subject matter abstract and unrelated to practice (Kowalski, Petersen, & Fusarelli, 2005).
- Educators often see data as the enemy; they note that information such as student test scores has been used historically to point the finger of blame at them (Doyle, 2003).
- The process is viewed as burdensome and time-consuming (Doyle, 2003).
- Schools are social and political institutions and therefore, values and biases have become institutionalized in decision making (Hoy & Miskel, 2005).
- Unlike practitioners in most other professions, educators have not typically engaged in collaborative assessment, analysis, and decision making (Popham, 2006).

Excuses aside, NCLB requires administrators and teachers to develop and use information systems, especially in relation to decisions that directly affect student achievement. Meeting this mandate depends on four organizational characteristics:

1. *Proficiency generating data*—the degree to which principals, teachers, and support staff are prepared to conduct assessment and related research
2. *Proficiency using data*—the degree to which principals, teachers, and support staff are prepared to apply assessment outcomes to important decisions
3. *Resource adequacy*—the degree to which principals, teachers, and support staff have access to data, time, equipment, and technical assistance

4. *Cultural acceptance*—the degree to which principals, teachers, and support staff share values and beliefs supportive of data-driven decision making (Kowalski et al., in press)

Increasingly, scholars and policymakers are coming to believe that the development of these conditions requires communication networks that support structural and cultural change. In the context of school reform, examples of structural change have included decentralizing authority (e.g., Wohlstetter, Chau, & Malloy, 2003) and group decision making (e.g., Malen, 1999); examples of cultural change have included teacher professionalism (e.g., Darling-Hammond, 1994) and organizational learning (e.g., Silins, Mulford, & Zarins, 2002).

Research on organizational behavior has established that communication affects the quantity and quality of information used to make decisions and that quality is at least as important as quantity (O'Reilly, Chatman, & Anderson, 1987). Two types of information are used in decisions: information to make decisions and information to support decisions (Meltsner, 1976). Studies reveal two common predispositions that shape decisions. First, bias is expressed in relation to how information is collected: access is usually more important than reliability. Second, bias is expressed in relation to the type of information people seek: a person often seeks data that supports his or her preference rather than data to conduct an objective analysis of known options (O'Reilly et al., 1987). Consequently, a school may be flooded with information, but it is either not used or not used appropriately. Network analysis in relation to decision making requires administrators to ask and answer the following three questions:

1. Does current communication facilitate the pursuit of our vision?
2. What barriers prevent meaningful reform?
3. What changes are necessary to eradicate the barriers?

NETWORKS AND CONFLICT MANAGEMENT

Conflict, a topic that is discussed in great detail in the next chapter, occurs when there are at least two competing and usually incompatible positions (Cummings et al., 1987). Common in all organizations, it is ubiquitous in public institutions where philosophical and political differences are usually substantial (Wirt & Kirst, 2001), especially in relation to school reform (Bauman, 1996). It can occur between and among individuals, groups, and even organizations (Spaulding & O'Hair, 2004).

Though conflict management has long been recognized as a school administration responsibility, few textbooks in this discipline have focused directly on the role communication plays in this process. Communication scholars, on the other hand, have written extensively on this topic. For example, Putnam and Poole (1987) write:

> Communication constitutes the essence of conflict in that it undergirds the formation of opposing issues, frames perceptions of the felt conflict, translates emotions and perceptions into conflict behaviors, and sets the stage for future conflicts. Thus communication is instrumental in every aspect of conflict, including conflict avoidance and suppression, the open opposition, and the evolution of issues. Conflict strategies and tactics are also manifested through communication. (p. 552)

In the past, administrators were socialized to accept a classical theory perspective that cast conflict as being consistently counterproductive, largely because it reduces technical efficiency. As a result, avoidance and accommodation became preferred behaviors even though neither provides an acceptable managerial response (Hanson, 2003). A disdain for conflict was most evident in collective bargaining decisions made during the 1960s and 1970s; school boards and superintendents usually yielded to demands rather than analyze and resolve the tensions that produced them (Kowalski, 2006). In other words, eliminating conflict became more important than improving the organization. This precarious disposition largely ignored the destructive by-products of unmanaged or poorly managed conflict—problems such as increasing employee/group isolation, lowering participation in problem solving, reducing information exchanges, and lowering job satisfaction (Cummings et al., 1987).

For many superintendents and principals who face competing demands daily, it is difficult to understand that conflict actually can be productive. Research reveals that it can motivate individuals, facilitate organizational learning, and be a catalyst for necessary change—but only if it is managed appropriately in the context of a positive school climate. That is, constructive outcomes are more probable in schools in which administrators promote and engage in (a) organizational learning (DuFour & Eaker, 1998),

(b) open and continuous communication (Kowalski, 2005), and (c) ethical communication behaviors (Shockley-Zalabak, 1988).

Communication networks are pivotal to generating, managing, and eliminating conflict. In most schools, the quality and quantity of information available to and possessed by individuals varies considerably. As a result, the probability of information-driven conflict, defined as two or more parties having opposing information (Cummings et al., 1987), increases markedly; it is most prevalent in schools having multiple, unreliable information networks. Equally important, most conflict resolution strategies (e.g., collaboration, information sharing, and compromise) and tactics (e.g., framing the problem, describing behavior, and exhibiting concern) are communication-intensive.

Determining the extent to which organizational communication is an asset or liability would be a less complicated task if there was a consistent relationship between conflict and communication. But this is not the case. In some instances, communication reduces conflict and in others it exacerbates the situation. Actual effects are determined by a mix of issues and relationships (Putnam & Poole, 1987); therefore, communication in general, and networks specifically, need to be analyzed on a school by school basis.

CONCLUDING COMMENTS

Recognizing that school employees now have access to more information than ever before and that schools must become more effective, policymakers and education scholars promoting reform have focused considerable attention on organizational communication. As a result, they often have criticized the structure of schools and the inability or unwillingness of educators to make schools more productive (Sarason, 1996). The passage of NCLB a few years ago reflects a growing impatience among elementary and secondary education's critics.

In previous chapters, the argument was made that reform in an information-based society requires leadership and management from administrators who are effective communicators. This chapter presents a second and equally cogent claim: *meaningful reform will only occur in schools in which educators are able to access and deploy information rapidly to solve problems and to then use that information to adjust to changing needs and demands.* Since the 1980s, a number of authors have illuminated the importance of organizational learning and the role that personal communication and communication networks play in this process. Consequently, the contemporary challenge for school administrators is to shape school climates in which such learning can occur. One facet of this responsibility is to engage in network analysis, most notably to answer three key questions: What networks exist? To what extent do these networks facilitate or hinder achieving a collaborative vision? What changes are needed to make the networks more facilitative?

REFERENCES

Bacharach, S., & Lawler, E. (1980). *Power and politics in organizations.* San Francisco: Jossey-Bass.

Bauman, P. C. (1996). *Governing education: Public sector reform or privatization.* Boston: Allyn & Bacon.

Callahan, R. E. (1962). *Education and the cult of efficiency: A study of the social forces that have shaped the administration of public schools.* Chicago: University of Chicago Press.

Chance, P. L., & Björk, L. G. (2004). The social dimension of public relations. In T. J. Kowalski (Ed.), *Public relations in schools* (pp. 125–150). Upper Saddle River, NJ: Merrill, Prentice Hall.

Conrad, C. (1990). *Strategic organizational communication: An integrated approach* (2nd ed.). Fort Worth, TX: Harcourt Brace.

Conrad, C. (1994). *Strategic organizational communication: Toward the twenty-first century* (3rd ed.). Fort Worth, TX: Harcourt Brace.

Cummings, H. W., Long, L. W., & Lewis, M. L. (1987). *Managing communication in organizations: An introduction.* Scottsdale, AZ: Gorsuch Scarisbrick.

Darling-Hammond, L. (1994). Will 21st-century schools really be different? *Education Digest, 60*(9), 4–8.

Dow, G. K. (1988). Configurational and coactivational views of organizational structure. *Academy of Management Review, 13,* 53–64.

Doyle, D. P. (2002). Knowledge-based decision making. *School Administrator, 59*(11), 30–34.

Doyle, D. P. (2003). Data-driven decision-making. *T.H.E. Journal, 30*(10), S19–S21.

DuFour, R., & Eaker, R. (1998). *Professional learning communities at work: Best practices for enhancing student achievement.* Alexandria, VA: Association for Supervision and Curriculum Development.

Euske, N. A., & Roberts, K. H. (1987). Evolving perspectives in organizational theory: Communication implications. In F. Jablin, L. Putnam, K. Roberts, & L. Porter (Eds.), *Handbook of organizational communication: An interdisciplinary perspective* (pp. 41–69). Newbury Park, CA: Sage.

Farace, R., Monge, P., & Russell, H. (1977). *Communicating and organizing.* Reading, MA: Addison-Wesley.

Fulk, J. (1993). Social construction of communication technology. *Academy of Management Journal, 36*, 921–950.

Fullan, M. (2001). *Leading in a culture of change.* San Francisco: Jossey-Bass.

Hall, E. T. (1997). *The silent language.* New York: Doubleday.

Hall, G. E., & Hord, S. M. (2001). *Implementing change: Patterns, principles, and potholes.* Boston: Allyn & Bacon.

Hanson, E. M. (2003). *Educational administration and organizational behavior* (5th ed.). Boston: Allyn & Bacon.

Heath, R. L. (1994). *Management of corporate communication: From interpersonal contacts to external affairs.* Hillsdale, NJ: Erlbaum.

Henkin, A., & Dee, J. (2001). The power of trust: Teams and collective action in self-managed schools. *Journal of School Leadership, 11*(1), 48–62.

Hoy, W. K., & Miskel, C. G. (2005). *Educational administration: Theory, research, and practice* (8th ed.). New York: McGraw-Hill.

Jablin, F. M. (1987). Formal organization structure. In F. M. Jablin, L. L. Putnam, K. H. Roberts, & L. W. Porter (Eds.), *Handbook of organizational communication: An interdisciplinary perspective* (pp. 389–419). Newbury Park, CA: Sage.

Karathanos, P. H. (1994). Network analysis and dysfunctional organizational coalition. *Management Decision, 32*(9), 15–19.

Katz, D., & Kahn, R. L. (1978). *The social psychology of organizations* (2nd ed.). New York: Wiley.

Kline, P., & Saunders, B. (1998). *Ten steps to a learning organization* (2nd ed.). Arlington, VA: Great Ocean Publishers.

Kowalski, T. J. (2004). School public relations: A new agenda. In T. J. Kowalski (Ed.), *Public relations in schools* (pp. 3–29). Upper Saddle River, NJ: Merrill, Prentice Hall.

Kowalski, T. J. (2005). Evolution of the school superintendent as communicator. *Communication Education, 54*(2), 101–117.

Kowalski, T. J. (2006). *The school superintendent: Theory, practice, and cases* (2nd ed.). Thousand Oaks, CA: Sage.

Kowalski, T. J., Lasley, T. J., & Mahoney, J. (in press). *Data-driven decisions and school leadership: Best practices for school improvement.* Boston: Allyn & Bacon.

Kowalski, T. J., Petersen, G. J., & Fusarelli, L. (2005, November). *Facing an uncertain future: The preparation and readiness of first-time superintendents to lead in a democratic society.* Paper presented at the annual meeting of the University Council for Educational Administration, Nashville, TN.

Lysaught, J. P. (1984). Toward a comprehensive theory of communication: A review of selected contributions. *Educational Administration Quarterly, 20*(3), 101–127.

Malen, B. (1999). The promises and perils of participation on site-based councils. *Theory into Practice, 38*(4), 209–216.

March, J. G., & Simon, H. A. (1958). *Organizations.* New York: Wiley.

Meltsner, A. J. (1976). *Policy analysts in the bureaucracy.* Berkeley: University of California Press.

Mitchell, J. C. (1972). Networks, norms and institutions. In J. Boissevain & J. C. Mitchell (Eds.), *Network analysis studies in human interaction* (pp. 15–36). The Hague, The Netherlands: Mouton.

Monge, P. R., & Eisenberg, E. M. (1987). Emergent communication networks. In F. Jablin, L. Putnam, K. Roberts, & L. Porter (Eds.), *Handbook of organizational communication: An interdisciplinary perspective* (pp. 304–342). Newbury Park, CA: Sage.

O'Reilly, C. A., Chatman, J. A., & Anderson, J. C. (1987). Message flow and decision making. In F. M. Jablin, L. L. Putnam, K. H. Roberts, & L. W. Porter (Eds.), *Handbook of organizational communication: An interdisciplinary perspective* (pp. 600–623). Newbury Park, CA: Sage.

Picciano, A. G. (2006). *Data-driven decision making for effective school leaders.* Upper Saddle River, NJ: Merrill/Prentice Hall.

Popham, W. J. (2006). *Assessment for educational leaders.* Boston: Allyn & Bacon.

Putnam, L. L., & Poole, M. S. (1987). Conflict and negotiation. In F. Jablin, L. Putnam, K. Roberts, & L. Porter (Eds.), *Handbook of organizational communication: An interdisciplinary perspective* (pp. 549–599). Newbury Park, CA: Sage.

Sarason, S. B. (1996). *Revisiting the culture of the school and the problem of change.* New York: Teachers College Press.

Sergiovanni, T. J. (2000). *Leadership for the schoolhouse: How is it different? Why is it important?* San Francisco: Jossey-Bass.

Shockley-Zalabak, P. (1988). *Fundamentals of organizational communication.* New York: Longman.

Silins, H. C., Mulford, W. R., & Zarins, S. (2002). Organizational learning and school change. *Educational Administration Quarterly, 38*(5), 613–642.

Spaulding, A., & O'Hair, M. J. (2004). Public relations in a communication context: Listening, nonverbal, and conflict-resolution skills. In T. J. Kowalski (Ed.), *Public relations in schools* (pp. 96–122). Upper Saddle River, NJ: Merrill, Prentice Hall.

Stohl, C. (1995). *Organizational Communication: Connectedness in action.* Thousand Oaks, CA: Sage.

Tompkins, P. K. (1987). Translating organizational theory: Symbolism over substance. In F. M. Jablin, L. L. Putnam, K. H. Roberts, & L. W. Porter (Eds.), *Handbook of organizational communication: An interpretive approach.* (pp. 70–96). Newbury Park, CA: Sage.

Wells, B., & Spinks, N. (1994). Managing your grapevine: A key to quality productivity. *Executive Development, 7*(2), 24–27.

Wirt, F. M., & Kirst, M. W. (2001). *The political dynamics of American education* (2nd ed.). Berkeley, CA: McCutchan.

Wohlstetter, P., Chau, D., & Malloy, C. L. (2003). Improving schools through networks: A new approach to urban school reform. *Educational Policy, 17*(4), 399–430.

9

Managing Conflict

The difficulty with conflict lies in the fact that it is subject to interpretation in the minds and hearts of those who are at odds.

Don't be afraid of opposition. Remember, a kite rises against; not with; the wind.

—Hamilton W. Mabie, American essayist

Dr. Juan Bautista was completing his first semester as principal of San Miguel Elementary School. San Miguel is one of two small K–6 schools, located in the Ceilo Hermoso School District (CHSD). The surrounding community and student population are culturally and economically diverse. Of the 480 students attending San Miguel, 82% are of Hispanic origin; the other 18% represent American Indian, Asian, Filipino, Black, Pacific Islander, and Caucasian cultures. Roughly 65% of the students qualify for the federal government's school lunch program. Although CHSD serves a predominately rural and agricultural community, it is situated between two medium-sized cities that offer coastal recreation, tourism, and boast of some of the finest wineries in the state.

Dr. Bautista was appointed principal of San Miguel midyear. Prior to his appointment in January, Ms. Cynthia Doloroso had been the school's principal. Although a competent and well-liked teacher for many years, Ms. Doloroso was an ineffectual administrator and leader. She was frequently absent or unavailable to the faculty, students, and parents to address questions or concerns. While at odds with the district administration on several academic and business priorities for San Miguel, she never discussed or confronted these issues with the superintendent, but she instead attempted to undermine various initiatives through negative comments, paper work delays, marginal work, or procrastination. Ms. Doloroso's lack of performance left many school projects and initiatives uncompleted and the principal's office in general disarray.

The No Child Left Behind Act (NCLB) had brought to bear some changes and challenges in the academic expectations and outcomes of San Miguel. One of the district's priorities was the establishment of a more rigorous science and math curriculum at all schools in the Ceilo Hermoso district. The superintendent had decided to dedicate monies to hire two *"high-quality"* full-time resource teachers that would work with students and faculty specifically in math and science at each of the elementary schools. Ms. Doloroso had been repeatedly asked by the district superintendent to hire a teacher for San Miguel in order to fulfill this new district initiative. In meetings at the district office, Ms. Doloroso would agree with the superintendent and tout the importance of the plan to improve the math and science curriculum; yet, while in meetings with teachers at San Miguel, she dismissed the superintendent and indicated that she saw his request as interfering with her ability to decide what was "best for her students and staff," as well as an "insult to her teachers' ability to effectively teach math and science." Needless to say, a teacher was never hired, and the results from the state test revealed San Miguel's stagnation and slight decline in these subject areas. When Dr. Bautista became principal, the superintendent directed him to make this math and science initiative a top priority.

In his first meeting with the faculty, Dr. Bautista put the district's math and science program on the agenda and spoke with the faculty, detailing its importance and asking for teacher input. All of the teachers seemed to agree and indicated their support of the program for San Miguel. When seeking volunteers to serve on the search committee, Ms. Doloroso agreed to serve and chair the committee with two other teachers. The position was advertised; applications were received at the district office and qualified applications were sent onto San Miguel for final screening and to establish interviews with the top candidates. One afternoon, Dr. Bautista asked Ms. Doloroso about the candidate pool. She indicated that there were several candidates and that interviews were being scheduled. Dr. Bautista felt that he had made progress on two fronts, one with this district initiative and the other with Ms. Doloroso by involving her in this search for a math and science teacher.

The following week, Dr. Bautista spoke with Ms. Doloroso regarding the applicant pool and expressed interest in meeting the finalists and hiring the best candidate. Ms. Doloroso replied that the committee was interviewing the final candidate on Friday and after that meeting they would forward a recommendation to him on Monday. The next week was a wild one at San Miguel. A broken water pipe in the cafeteria, vandalism of the media center, firecrackers in the boy's bathroom, and several other incidents took Dr. Bautista's attention away from the search for a new teacher. By week's end, things were calming down and he wondered about the recommendation from Doloroso's committee. Checking his voice mail, e-mail, school mailbox, and asking his secretary for any messages, he found nothing from the committee. After school he went to Ms. Doloroso's classroom, but she had left for the day. On his way home, Dr. Bautista left notes for each of the teachers who participated on the search committee and asked them to meet in his office during the first recess the following day. At recess time, Ms. Doloroso phoned the principal's secretary and instructed her to tell Dr. Bautista to check his e-mail for the committee's recommendation. The message read:

> After meeting and interviewing the teachers sent to us by the district, it was clear that none of the applicants are as qualified as the current faculty of San Miguel and therefore we have voted unanimously not to forward any of the candidates for consideration. We feel that this entire process is demeaning and harmful to the efficacy of the dedicated faculty and\staff at San Miguel. I am sure that if you reflect on this issue honestly and objectively, and don't let your male ego get in the way, you will agree with us and this decision.

After opening and reading the message, he found himself staring blankly at his computer screen and wondering what this was all about. He realized that this action by Doloroso and the committee would only create more problems for the students and teachers at San Miguel.

Dr. Bautista went to Ms. Doloroso's classroom and asked for the candidate files and notes from the committee. He indicated that this initiative was a priority for the school and district and that a teacher would be hired. As he sat in his office poring over the applicant files, he began to hear the murmur of several voices outside his office. His secretary came in and said that about 10 teachers wanted to talk to him . . . now! When he stepped out to meet with the teachers, he was greeted by intense looks and angry words. Before he could say anything, one of the teachers said that she was shocked that the school principal didn't think she was able to teach math to her second graders! Another said, "I can't believe you think we are unable to teach the science curriculum! I guess they're right, you are just a pawn for the district superintendent and his pet projects!" A third teacher said, "How can we have confidence in you since you don't have any confidence in us?!" Dr. Bautista was taken aback by these comments. As calmly as he could, he said that he valued the teachers' input and assured them that he had never expressed any reservations about their ability to be effective teachers, but clearly this was not the time or place to discuss this. He indicated that he would call a special faculty meeting after school tomorrow so that the issue of hiring a math and science teacher could be discussed by everyone. After that he went back in his office and sat in his chair, knowing that the resistance to hiring a math and science teacher was only a symptom of a larger issue, but what? As he thought about the meeting for tomorrow, he asked himself, "Where do I start?"

INTRODUCTION

This chapter addresses fundamental aspects of organizational conflict faced by successful school administrators. It is divided into four parts. The first part provides an overview of organizational conflict, its definition, as well as an examination of the underlying conditions that lead to conflict. A discussion of conflict as an inescapable phenomenon is examined next. The chapter then provides a detailed overview of the various types and examples of organizational conflict. Finally, evidence of the successful conflict resolution strategies are outlined and provided. The strategies are offered as a means for school leaders to identify and effectively manage the inevitable conflict experienced by all organizations.

ORGANIZATIONAL CONFLICT

The term *conflict* has no single or clearly defined meaning. Evidently much of the confusion had been created by scholars from a variety of disciplines who are interested in the topic and its influence on individuals and organizations (Rahim, 2001). For example, March and Simon

(1958) consider conflict a "breakdown in the standard mechanisms of decision making, so that an individual or group experiences difficulty in selecting an alternative" (p. 12). Other scholars view conflict as "an interactive state in which the behaviors or goals of one actor are to some degree incompatible with the behaviors or goals of some other actor or actors" (Tedeschi, Schlenker, & Bonoma, 1973, p. 232). Although, the word *conflict* apparently describes a range of phenomena from a simple difference of opinion to all-out-war (Daresh & Playko, 1993), there is a general concurrence that there are central elements to any conflict: (a) Conflict includes *opposing interests* between individuals or groups; (b) such opposed interests must be *recognized* for conflict to exist; (c) conflict involves *beliefs,* by each side, that the other will thwart (or has already thwarted) its interests; (d) conflict is a *process*; it develops out of existing relationships between individuals or groups and reflects their past interactions and the contexts in which these took place; and (e) *actions* by one or both sides do, in fact, produce thwarting of others' goals (Rahim, 2001, p. 18).

To rephrase a well-known bumper sticker idiom, "Conflict happens!" It seems to be a natural part of the collective human experience. Disputes can and do arise between employees, between partners or collaborators, between a company and a client, between students and a teacher, or between a superintendent and a principal.

> Conflict runs the gamut of social experience–between individuals, between groups, and between whole societies and cultures. Conflict can occur *within* persons or social units; it is *intrapersonal* or *intragroup* (or, of course, *intranational*). Conflict can also be experienced *between* two or more people or social units: so called *intergroup* or *international* conflict. (Owens & Valesky, 2006, p. 337)

Defining Conflict

Conflict is generally portrayed as a struggle between at least two interdependent parties who perceive incompatible goals, scarce resources and rewards, and potential interference from the other party in achieving their goals (Uline, Tschannen-Moran, & Perez, 2003). With this in mind, conflict is defined as *a social condition in which two or more interdependent parties cannot have the same thing at the same time.* "Organizational conflict occurs when members engage in activities that are incompatible with those of colleagues within their network, members of other collectivities, or unaffiliated individuals who utilize the services or products of the organization" (Roloff, 1987, p. 496).

Some scholars have conceived of organizational conflict as a pathology to be diagnosed and treated (De Dreu & De Vries, 1997). "People in organizations often avoid or suppress conflict because they fear uncontrollable consequences resulting from a lack of self-efficacy and skills to manage the conflict constructively. They may also fear retaliation. They may be hesitant to break the general norm of behaving peacefully, feeling the need to protect their reputations and save face" (Uline et al., 2003, p. 785).

Pervasive Nature of Conflict

Classical theory posits a negative view of conflict, largely because it is known to produce inefficiencies. Therefore, managers traditionally have been socialized to eliminate conflict as quickly as possible; accommodating or ignoring the situation become predictable responses (Hanson, 2003). Conflict in organizations, however, is now seen as inevitable, endemic, and, in many cases, legitimate and desirable (Hoy & Miskel, 2005). Principal causes range from communication failure, personality conflict and the lack of cooperation to noncompliance of rules, perceptions of authority, and competition over resources. Although the causes of conflict are abundant, research in this area makes clear that in order for conflict to transpire, it must exceed what organizational members perceive as an acceptable threshold of intensity. This is coupled with the fact that organizational conflict and responses to it are embedded within the existing organizational culture (e.g., attitudes, practices, and beliefs of the system and its members). Put another way, before individuals or groups experience conflict, the incompatibilities, disagreements, or differences must be serious and intense enough to breach organizational practices, rules, and expectations, and must be experienced by all parties involved (Costantino & Merchant, 1996; Rahim, 2001).

One significant reason for the unavoidability of conflict in organizations lies in the fact that individuals and groups within a human social system are interdependent and constantly engaged in the dynamic process of defining and redefining the nature and extent of their interdependence (Owens & Valesky, 2006). For example, in complex organizations like schools, leaders are responsible for the acquisition and allocation of resources (e.g., time, money, facilities, materials, recognition, etc.) designed to achieve the goals of the organization. The naturally interdependent work of schools results in members (e.g., teachers, aids, students, office staff, etc.) being forced to share available resources. Provided that in all organizations, especially schools, resources are limited and finite, this leads to competing ideas and opinions of how resources should be allocated and employed.

While conflict may be viewed as natural and unavoidable, occurrences cannot be expected to disappear of their own accord. Instead, disputes should be brought out into the open and managed by means of channels or occasions through which adversaries can introduce their conflicting claims into the business of the educational organization (Schmuck & Runkel, 1995). As seen in the case involving Dr. Bautista at the beginning of this chapter, interdependence among members has the potential to create *intrapersonal* or *intragroup* conflict. The point here is simple: it is not the issue of whether conflict is present nor the degree to which it is present; the central issue boils down to how well conflict is managed by the leaders of the organization (Owens & Valesky, 2006).

Effects of Conflict in Schools

Although conflict may be a natural part of social life, if the opposing interests, beliefs, and actions that generate conflict are not addressed serious consequences may follow. For example, highly effective employees may resign; valuable relationships dissolve; teachers psychologically and emotionally withdraw. Great schools, divisions, departments, and even entire companies can become unproductive. Because organizations are reliant on the cooperative efforts of their members in order to achieve goals that cannot be achieved individually, successful schools typically foster environments that emphasize cooperation, collaboration, and consensus.

There are two general results of organizational conflict; one is good, the other is not. When disagreements occur, they actually can serve as catalysts for positive change (Hanson, 2003). For example, faculty divided by a proposal to change an existing discipline rule may engage in discussions that result in a deeper understanding of all rules or that result in needed revisions to several other rules. In this instance, conflict produced a positive outcome. Conversely, disagreements that are not openly addressed and communicated may result in a heightened level of incompatibility and polarization of viewpoints. Over time, this divergence of positions and beliefs fosters an environment where open and meaningful communication is absent, resulting in greater degrees of personal animosity and distrust among members of the organization (Daresh & Playko, 1995). Clearly a "bad" thing.

UNDERSTANDING CONFLICT

Types of Conflict

Though research on organizational conflict is vast, two broad categories are used to classify this condition here. The first involves conflict that occurs *within* a person, group, or organization; it is called *intrapersonal*. The second involves conflict that occurs *between* people, groups, or organizations; it is called *interorganizational* (Owens, 2004). In some situations, the two categories overlap. For example, conflict existing between two or more people working at the same school may be simultaneously interpersonal and intraorganizational. This cross-categorization simply allows one to view conflict from a wider perspective.

Every choice that we make as human beings involves some degree of intrapersonal conflict. Should I do this or that? What are the consequences of my actions? This option seems more appealing to me now, but which choice will be better in the long run? As a school administrator, one's career may be rife with intrapersonal conflict. Personal views and beliefs may run counter to school policies. Rules and regulations may make it difficult, if not impossible, to use one's judgment in determining the best course of action. As Owens (2004) points out, when a person is torn between two or more incompatible choices, this intrapersonal conflict can lead to feelings of stress and manifest itself in other physical symptoms.

Intraorganizational conflict is probably a more pervasive concern for school administrators. Think again of Dr. Bautista and the simmering emotions surrounding the hiring of an additional science and math teacher. What seemed a favorable situation—utilizing Ms. Doloroso's skills and experience to assist with the recruitment, in an effort to *minimize* potential conflict between him and the former principal—quickly escalated into an uproar involving several more teachers and eventually the entire school. In this case, Ms. Doloroso's personal views and narrow agenda interfered with Dr. Bautista's attempts to effectively run and enhance the curricular offerings of the school.

Sources of Conflict

Another way to view conflict is to identify the underlying causes. According to the Oregon Mediation Center (2006), there are five primary sources.

1. *Relationship conflicts.* These disputes occur between people as a result of "the presence of strong negative emotions, misperceptions or stereotypes, poor communication or miscommunication, or repetitive negative behaviors" (Oregon Mediation Center, 2006). When people get angry or fail to communicate clearly and effectively, negative emotions ensue. Things are said in the heat of the moment, at times causing irreparable damage to one or both parties involved. Although relationship conflicts are most common between friends, family, and romantic partners, they certainly can occur in the workplace as well. Colleagues are often friends outside work, and seeking the appropriate balance between work and one's personal life can certainly be challenging, especially for school administrators, who in many instances have assumed the position from the ranks of the teaching faculty. This being the case, the greater the attachment and emotion, the more damaging conflict may be.

2. *Data conflicts.* Another source of conflict in the workplace occurs when people "lack information necessary to make wise decisions, are misinformed, disagree on which data is relevant, interpret

information differently, or have competing assessment procedures" (Oregon Mediation Center, 2006). These disputes already
have become more common in school settings because of pressures to use data-driven decision making (Kowalski, Lasley, &
Mahoney, in press). How people choose to interpret data may
have profound effects on students' education and shape decisions
surrounding curriculum and instruction.

3. *Interest conflicts.* A third source of conflict is the seemingly incompatible needs of individuals and groups. These disputes occur when
"one or more of the parties believe that in order to satisfy his or her
needs, the needs and interests of an opponent must be sacrificed. According to the Oregon Mediation Center (2006), there are three typical categories of interest conflicts: (1) substantive issues, such as
concern about finances, time, and resources; (2) procedural issues,
such as the manner in which conflict should be addressed or resolved; and (3) psychological issues, such as conflict over perceived
levels of trust, equitability, and respect.

4. *Structural conflicts.* These disputes occur over tangible issues, physical constraints, organizational changes, and so forth. Changes to a
school's procedure for handling student absenteeism, for example,
may result in conflict as teachers' roles and responsibilities shift.
Some may find the new system cumbersome, whereas others respond positively to it.

5. *Philosophical conflicts.* This source of conflict centers on values
and beliefs. "Values are beliefs that people use to give meaning to
their lives . . . and explain what is 'good' or 'bad,' 'right' or
'wrong,' 'just' or 'unjust'" (Oregon Mediation Center, 2006).
However, having different value systems does not mean necessarily that people or groups cannot get along; it is how people choose
to manage their differences that matters. When people try to force
their values on others, conflict often ensues. In a school setting,
administrators and teachers may be prone to assign value to a rule
or policy (i.e., whether the rule is "right" or "wrong"). For example, if two teachers disagree on the value of the rule and try to con-
vince the other party that only one viewpoint is correct, then it is
likely that conflict will arise.

Process of Conflict

How does conflict come about? Does it occur overnight? Does it fester for days, weeks, or even months before erupting into a volatile situation? Thomas (as cited in Owens, 2004, p. 332) describes conflict as a *process*, beginning typically with feelings of frustration. As these feelings grow, people begin to conceptualize the problem, often imposing values or ideals on the situation. This subjectivity frequently focuses more on the person or persons involved, rather than on the issue at hand. Based on the conceptualization of the problem, certain steps or behaviors are implemented in an effort to handle the conflict. These actions necessarily require the participants to interact, which may either worsen or ameliorate the situation. All of this leads to the outcome, whether a satisfactory resolution to all, or increased frustrations, thereby beginning the process all over again. This cycle is illustrated below (see Figure 9.1).

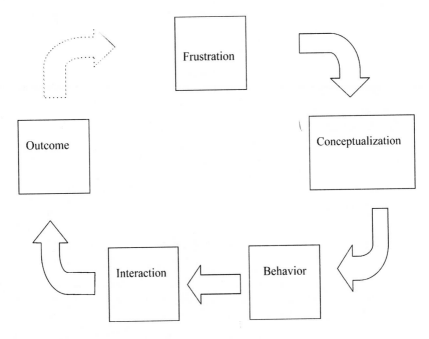

Note: Adapted from Thomas (1976).

Figure 9.1.   The Process of Conflict

CONFLICT MANAGEMENT AND RESOLUTION STRATEGIES

Conflict in the workplace is inevitable; therefore, the real goal for a leader is not trying to eliminate conflict but developing strategies in order to effectively manage it. As Cloke and Goldsmith (2000) note, few people, whether in schools or in the workplace, receive explicit training in how to deal with conflict; if training does occur, it may be a short workshop or one-hour lecture, but it is often insubstantial. Lipsky, Seeber, and Fincher (2003) recognize the rising need for conflict management systems in organizations today, largely due to an "increasingly litigious society" (p. 6).

Because conflict can result in feelings of hostility, school administrators need to recognize that it is usually hostile feelings or actions that result in destructive behavior, not simply the presence of conflict. Boulding (1962) identifies two types of hostility

1. *Malevolent hostility* focuses on people rather than issues and is characterized by hateful and emotional language and a reluctance or inability to listen to, or respond to, new ideas.
2. *Nonmalevolent hostility* focuses on ideas and not people and is characterized by rational or philosophical arguments.

Unfortunately, many disputes in schools involve malevolent hostility. "Any public education administrator needs to be sensitive to this problem and to be aware of the significant difference between attacks for the sake of destruction and vigorous expression of essentially constructive — though sharply divergent and perhaps unwelcome — views" (Owens, 2004, p. 332).

What can an administrator do to manage conflict and minimize, if not prevent, malevolent hostility? First, it is important to understand one's view toward conflict. Most people react to conflict by wanting to *win* (Owens, 2004, p. 337). By definition, then, if one party wins, the other must lose. This mind-set can be damaging to organizations, resulting in "a greater deepening of the original rift, which then reduces the chances of compromise" (Owens, 2004, p. 337). Win-lose situations can also cause employees to reject their leader and foster feelings of resentment and anger. If, however, leaders adopt a win-win approach to conflict, a satisfactory solution or outcome is much more likely. When the parties involved focus on collaboration and compromise, negative feelings and frustration are typically reduced.

Several researchers (Cloke & Goldsmith, 2000; Kowalski, 2004; Lipsky et al., 2003) recognize that there is not just one way to handle, manage, or resolve conflict. Because there are numerous choices, it is imperative to analyze the situation in an effort to determine the best course of action. Different types of conflict (i.e., over values, interests, tangible items, etc.) will have different, yet appropriate, strategies.

Rather than simply listing numerous resolution strategies, Lipsky et al. (2003) describe the components of an effective conflict management *system*—a system that attempts to channel conflict in productive directions. Five components are identified:

1. *Broad scope.* First, an organization's conflict management system should be broad in scope, not narrowly focused, able to manage conflict on any scale.
2. *Open culture.* The organizational culture should be open to agreement and disagreement, recognizing the inevitability of conflict in the workplace.
3. *Open communication.* There should be open lines of communication, allowing employees access to the right person at the right time.
4. *Integrated systems.* Integrated systems should produce several options for resolving conflict as opposed to relying on a single option.
5. *Support structures.* An organization should have sufficient support structures that are capable of "integrating effective conflict management into the organization's daily operations" (Lipsky et al., p. 13).

To have multiple options for resolving conflict, an administrator needs to be aware of common and effective strategies for minimizing, preventing, or ending conflict in schools. One key strategy is *using appropriate language*. The words we use can be our most powerful tool . . . or our most damaging weapon. Language that reflects a win-lose approach to conflict will further polarize the parties involved. Statements such as "I *won* that argument" or "We've been *battling* over this policy for months now" are indicative of a "conflict as war" view (Cloke & Goldsmith, 2000, p. 25). Even if this type of language is not used directly with the other party involved in the conflict, consistent use of "war" metaphors and descriptors will shape one's view—negatively—toward the situation, regardless of conscious intent. On the other hand, language that reflects a win-win approach, or that sees "conflict as an opportunity" (Cloke & Goldsmith, 2000, p. 27), is more likely to lead to an effective resolution. "We have a number of options for handling this issue" or "This is a good opportunity for us to come up with a better solution than we had before" are examples for expressing this viewpoint. Simply avoiding the use of the word *problem* by utilizing a more positive word such as *challenge* can have a profound effect on people's opinion of a matter. Cloke and Goldsmith (2000) also suggest using language that refers to "conflict as a journey" (p. 29). Examples of this include "We are getting somewhere" or "We are on a good path."

Another effective communication tactic for minimizing conflict is to avoid the use of "you" language, instead utilizing "I" language. Because "you" statements often are perceived as accusatory (e.g., "You did such and such" or "You upset me"), the use of "I" language can reduce friction between two parties. For example, saying, "I am feeling frustrated because of what happened" rather than "You really upset me" can neutralize a situation, thereby promoting a more likely environment for reaching a conflict resolution. Additional phrases to avoid include "You must . . ." (imperatives); "If you don't, then . . ." (ultimatums); and "You always . . ." (broad generalizations); among others (Cloke & Goldsmith, 2000).

Listening also is an effective strategy. When involved in a conflict, people often fail to truly listen to the other party. Real listening requires one to put aside any preconceived notions or opinions and open oneself up to the chance that there may be something to learn from the other person or group. In other words, it means running the risk that the other person is "right." As Benjamin Franklin said to the delegates at the U.S. constitutional convention in 1787, "Having lived long, I have experienced many instances of being obliged by better information, or fuller consideration, to change opinions even on important subjects, which I once thought right, but found to be otherwise. It is therefore that the older I grow, the more apt I am to doubt my own judgment, and to pay more respect to the judgment of others" (Rossiter, as cited in Bolman & Deal, 2003, p. 178).

Thus, if conflict is seen not as a win-lose situation but rather as a win-win opportunity, then listening to the other side is not only easier but also more productive. According to Cloke and Goldsmith (2000), effective listening involves (though is not limited to) encouraging the other speaker, asking for clarification, acknowledging what is said, empathizing with the other party, supplementing the conversation with the use of the phrase "Yes, *and* . . ." rather than "Yes, *but* . . ."; inviting elaboration; summarizing, and validating the other side's points. Furthermore, when people are able to truly listen to the other party, they are more likely to recognize the underlying issue(s) at hand.

Taking time to deal with conflict is a third proven strategy. Too often when people are involved in conflict, emotions run high and things are said in the heat of the moment. Sometimes, the best alternative is to simply take a break from the situation, even if it means saying, "I need to take a few minutes to collect my thoughts. Can we continue this discussion later?" Although avoidance and denial are typically ineffective, though common, ways to deal with conflict, giving one and the other party a chance to cool down when feeling angry can increase the chances of finding a resolution (Owens, 2004). In today's technological age, taking the time to reflect carefully on a response to an inflammatory e-mail can prove beneficial for one's career. Once an e-mail is sent, that written record exists indefinitely. Simply waiting an hour or two, or even until the next day, before hitting "send" can save jobs, in some cases, if not at least minimize further conflict.

Mediation also has been an effective approach to managing conflict. Sometimes it is necessary to bring in an outside, third party to help mediate during a conflict. A trained facilitator can provide immeasurable assistance when people or groups have reached an impasse. Often, a facilitator can lead those involved toward a compromise, thus providing a win-win situation. In schools, facilitators may be used during contract negotiations between unions and school boards, frequently tense and heated situations.

Changing the environment also can produce a desirable outcome. Moving to a neutral place like someone else's office, relocating to a café, or simply going outside are all ways to reduce tensions. When meeting with an employee about a potentially sensitive topic, a wise leader may avoid sitting directly across from the other person, choosing instead to sit next to him or her. This reduces the feeling of confrontation, promoting a calmer and more conducive environment for open discussion.

Commonality is yet another conflict management strategy, especially for intra-organizational conflict. Edgar Schein notes that "The basic strategy of reducing conflict . . . is to find goals upon which groups can agree and to reestablish valid communication between the groups" (Hersey, Blanchard, & Johnson, 1996, p. 493). In order to achieve shared goals, Hersey et al. (1996) recommend that leaders should incorporate three techniques:

1. Focus on the contributions made that benefit the larger group as a whole, not just those beneficial to smaller, subgroups.
2. Try to improve and increase communication between subgroups, including rewarding those groups that help others.
3. Expose all employees whenever possible to a variety of positions and roles within an organization in order to expand their knowledge and deepen their empathy.

CONNECTING CONFLICT MANAGEMENT AND COMMUNICATION

Both conflict and conflict management are interactive processes; therefore, they are communication-intensive activities (Putnam & Folger, 1988). The manner in which administrators communicate has a profound influence not only on individuals involved in a given incident but also on the overall culture of schools (Lincoln, 2002). Discourse is considered the primary medium by which individuals make sense of and construct social reality in organizations. In schools, teachers, other employees, and students determine what is real, what is important, and what is valued through interactions, and more specifically through discursive relations with each other. Noting this fact, many authors (e.g., Hanson, 2003; Hoy & Miskel, 2005; Reed, 1982) have pointed out that conflict resolution and communication are inextricably linked in the practice of school administration.

School reform has heightened the importance of understanding why and how communication is pivotal to shaping reality in organizations. Conflict is both a catalyst for and a product of organizational change in districts and schools (Hanson, 2003), and an administrator's communicative behavior during conflict management helps determine whether individual and group transformations occur and whether these transformations are positive (i.e., congruent with school improvement efforts) (Kowalski, 2005).

When managing conflict, administrators differ in the degree to which they are responsive and assertive (Merrill & Reid, 1999). Building on this fact, Darling and Walker (2001) identify four basic behavioral styles and noted that each had positive and negative attributes.

1. *Relators.* Administrators adopting this style are higher than average in responsiveness but below average in assertiveness. Whereas they may be praised for being sympathetic (to the needs of others), loyal, supportive, and easygoing, they also may be criticized for being conforming and permissive.
2. *Socializers.* Administrators adopting this style are relatively high in responsiveness and high in assertiveness. Whereas they may be praised for being enthusiastic and imaginative, they also may be criticized for being undisciplined and unrealistic.
3. *Analyzers.* Administrators adopting this style are relatively low in responsiveness and low in assertiveness. Whereas they may be praised for being precise and systematic, they may be criticized for being exacting and inflexible.
4. *Directors.* Administrators adopting this style are relatively low in responsiveness and relatively high in assertiveness. Whereas they may be praised for being determined and objective, they may be criticized for being dominating and insensitive.

Studying the effects of these styles in organizations, Darling and Walker conclude that successful conflict management depends primarily on two factors: flexibility and reducing the negative dimensions of a leadership style. Flexibility entails shifting among the styles as required by the contextual variables of a given conflict situation. Moving from one style to another, however, does not mean that a superintendent or principal should abandon relational communication (Kowalski, 2005). Reducing the negative dimensions entails diminishing criticism and dissatisfaction commonly associated with each behavior style. For example, analyzers may prolong conflict by collecting and analyzing data; they should compensate by trying to make decisions in a timely manner. Directors often are impatient and make quick decisions; they should compensate by slowing down and listening to others. Relators tend to be slow and indecisive; they should compensate by setting achievable goals and exhibiting self-direction. Socializers tend to make quick, impulsive decisions; they should compensate by being more introspective and by allowing others to express their positions.

As administrators alter behavior, they can pursue two-way, symmetrical dialogue and still make adjustments that can compensate for problems commonly associated with each behavioral style. Table 9.1 contains a summary of communicative adjustments that are advantageous.

In summary, the facets of effective communication described throughout this book are essential to conflict management. Though administrators can and arguably should adjust their behavior when trying to resolve disputes, they can meet this objective while retaining a consistent and predictable communicative pattern that allows information to flow in multiple directions in ways that are intended to benefit individuals and groups involved.

CONCLUDING COMMENTS

Conflict is inevitable in schools and its effects depend on the manner in which it is managed. In many instances, conflict can be a positive catalyst for needed change. More often, unfortunately, it is destructive and hinders schools from achieving their mission and vision. To effectively manage

Table 9.1. Maintaining Effective Communication During Conflict Management

Common Problems	Recommended Actions
Being slow to address conflict	Evaluate the negative effects of unresolved conflict and devote sufficient time to resolve the matter in a timely manner.
Prolonging conflict by engaging in fact finding and other types of data analysis	Set deadlines for reaching decisions and making interventions; be sensitive to anxiety created by unresolved conflict.
Being impatient	Focus on and listen to all parties and viewpoints before making a decision.
Making quick, impulsive decisions	Slow down and concentrate on listening to all parties; assess and evaluate opposing views before making decisions.
Being intolerant	Be sensitive to competing views, especially when those views are incongruent with your personal views.
Being indecisive	Exhibit self-direction and articulate objectives and goals when communicating.

conflict, administrators need to understand (a) types of conflict, (b) sources of conflict, (c) conflict's inevitability and potentialities, and (d) the nexus between conflict and communication.

Equally important, the contemporary practitioner must know that effective conflict management requires relational communication, a concept discussed extensively throughout this book. Efforts to improve schools require change and change fuels conflict. In this vein, communicative competence has come to be recognized as an essential leadership quality for both superintendents and principals.

REFERENCES

Bolman, L. G., & Deal, T. E. (2003). *Reframing organizations: Artistry, choice, and leadership.* San Francisco: Jossey-Bass.

Boulding, K. E. (1962). *Conflict and defense: A general theory.* New York: Harper.

Cloke, K., & Goldsmith, J., (2000). *Resolving conflicts at work: A complete guide for everyone on the job.* San Francisco: Jossey-Bass.

Costantino, C. A., & Merchant, C. S. (1996). *Designing conflict management systems: A guide to creating productive and healthy organizations.* San Francisco: Jossey-Bass.

Daresh, J. C., & Playko, M. A. (1993). *Supervision as a proactive process: Concepts and Cases* (2nd ed.). Long Grove, IL: Waveland.

Darling, J. R., & Walker, W. E. (2001). Effective conflict management: Use of behavioral style model. *Leadership & Organizational Development Journal, 22*(5), 230–242.

De Dreu, C. K. W., & De Vries, N. K. (1997). Minority dissent in organizations. In C. K. W. De Dreu & E. Van de Vlirt (Eds.), *Using conflict in organizations* (pp. 72–86). Thousand Oaks, CA: Sage.

Hanson, E. M., (2003). *Educational administration and organizational behavior* (5th ed.). Boston: Allyn & Bacon.

Hersey, P., Blanchard, K. H., & Johnson, D. E. (1996). *Management of organizational behavior: Utilizing human resources* (7th ed.). Upper Saddle River, NJ: Prentice Hall.

Hoy, W. K., & Miskel, C. G. (2005). *Educational administration: Theory, research, and practice* (8th ed.). New York: McGraw-Hill.

Kowalski, T. J. (2004). *Public relations in schools* (3rd ed.). Upper Saddle River, NJ: Merrill, Prentice Hall.

Kowalski, T. J. (2005). Evolution of the school superintendent as communicator. *Communication Education, 54*(2), 101–117.

Kowalski, T. J., Lasley, T. J., & Mahoney, J. (in press). *Data-driven decisions and school leadership: Best practices for school improvement*. Boston: Allyn & Bacon.

Lincoln, M. (2002). *Conflict resolution communication: Patterns promoting peaceful schools*. Lanham, MD: Scarecrow.

Lipsky, D. B., Seeber, R. L., & Fincher, R. D. (2003). *Emerging systems for managing workplace conflict: Lessons from American corporations for managers and dispute resolution professionals*. San Francisco: Jossey-Bass.

March, J. G., & Simon, H. A. (1958). *Organizations*. New York: Wiley.

Merrill, D. W., & Reid, R. H. (1999). *Personal styles and effective performance: Make your style work for you*. Boca Raton, FL: CRC Press.

Oregon Mediation Center. (2006). Conflict resolution theory and skills: Types of conflict. In *Mediation training manual*. Retrieved September 4, 2006, from www.internetmediator.com/medres/pg18.cfm.

Owens, R. G. (2004). *Organizational behavior in education: Adaptive leadership and school reform* (8th ed.). Boston: Allyn & Bacon.

Owens, R. G., & Valesky, T. C. (2006). *Organizational behavior in education: Adaptive leadership and school reform* (9th ed.). Boston: Allyn & Bacon.

Putnam, L. L., & Folger, J. P. (1988). Communication, conflict, and dispute resolution: The study of interaction and the development of conflict theory. *Communication Research, 15*(4), 349–359.

Rahim, M. A. (2001). *Managing conflict in organizations*. Westport, CT: Quorum Books.

Reed, R. J. (1982). Urban secondary school leadership: Contemporary challenges. *Education and Urban Society, 15*(1), 6–25.

Roloff, M. E. (1987). Communication and conflict. In C. R. Berger & S. H. Chaffee (Eds.), *Handbook of communication science* (pp. 484–534). Newbury Park, CA: Sage.

Schmuck, R. A. & Runkel, P. J. (1995). *The handbook of organizational development in schools and colleges* (4th ed.). Prospects Heights, IL: Waveland.

Tedeschi, J. T., Schlenker, B. R., & Bonoma, T. V. (1973). *Conflict, power and games: The experimental study of interpersonal relations*. Chicago: Aldine.

Uline, C. L., Tschannen-Moran, M., & Perez, L. (2003). Constructive conflict: How controversy can contribute to school improvement. *Teachers College Record, 105*, 782–816.

10

Maintaining Positive Relationships

Dr. Teresa Avila was settling into her first year as superintendent of the Ovada School District. Once a predominantly rural area, the district had rapidly evolved into a suburban hub for Metro City. Approximately 4,500 students attended the six elementary schools, two middle schools, and one high school in Ovada. The community was culturally diverse, and about 40% of the students qualified for the federal government's school lunch program. Since her arrival, Dr. Avila routinely met with various individuals and groups and actively worked in cultivating a positive working relationship with her board as well as several influential people in the community, including the editor of the local newspaper. Board members had explained to their new executive of the previous superintendent's often antagonistic relationship with local journalists and his failed efforts to "control the media."

One evening after leaving the office, Dr. Avila stopped by Easton High School to watch the girl's basketball team play Rawlings High School for the state championship. Easton and Rawlings had been friendly but highly competitive rivals for many years. These contests usually generated strong school pride and high attendance from both schools. Because of the importance of the night's game, members of the newspaper and television media from Ovada, Rawlings, and Metro City were present to cover the event. As the intensity between the two teams increased and the lead flip-flopped between the two rivals, students from Rawlings began seating themselves in the midst of the Easton cheering section and started heckling Easton players, fans, and

185

cheering for the Rawlings team. Heated words were exchanged between fans from each school, and threats were traded. Before any one could intervene, physical violence ensued, victimizing five band members not involved in the original altercation. That evening the television news broadcast footage of the fighting and chaos in the bleachers. Interviews with parents of the injured band members were featured in the report. The next morning the local headline read, "Fighting Injures Five at Easton High Basketball Game," and again the fighting video and parent interviews were used as the lead story on the Metro City news channels as well as some larger national outlets. The next morning Dr. Avila was in her office at 6:30 A.M. and had already been contacted by several news outlets, many of whom planned on visiting the campus that day to investigate the incidents of violence and injury at Easton.

INTRODUCTION

This chapter addresses three essential arenas of internal and external communication required of successful school administrators. First, an examination of school administrators' relationship with the media, the media's role in informing and influencing public opinion, and suggestions for school leaders in developing and fostering positive media relations. The means of fostering positive community relations is examined next. An overview of various methods and examples of information dissemination employed by schools to improve communication is addressed from both internal and external perspectives. Finally, evidence of the essential importance of organizational communication with school personnel is explored. The examination of administrator-employee communication and its influence on organizational culture, climate, and leadership is also detailed.

RELATIONS WITH THE MEDIA

Historical Context

A survey was conducted at the American Educational Research Association asking approximately 200 attendees at a presentation on education and the media about editorial policy and educational reporting in the newspapers read by participants. According to the investigators, about 95% of those queried believed that news reporting about public education was negatively biased and highly critical of schools; reporting on education was simple and incomplete and editorial policy was exceedingly unfavorable to schools and not particularly thoughtful (Berliner & Biddle, 1998). Other research focused on public confidence in democratic institutions has pointed to the fact that the negative media portrayal of public schools and public school leaders has become more pronounced in the last decade (Moy & Pfau, 2000). Although a *paradox* exists in the public's perception between "local and institutional" attitudes toward public schools, with nearly 40% of people giving high marks to their own local schools, the enduring element of a "generally" negative opinion toward the institution of public schools carries undeniable implications for school administrators and educational policy (Moy & Pfau, 2000).

Historically, school administrators approached media relations either wounded and bloody or naively optimistic. Over the past few decades, numerous books and professional publications have encouraged school administrators to rethink conventional wisdom about the media and its role and influence on public education. Most of the advice ardently encourages administrators to take full advantage of the media in order to enhance the public image of schools, and in the process garner public and political support. Yet, only a small number of school administrators recognize or are prepared to fully appreciate how the media works, the pressures and timelines faced by reporters, and how differing judgments about what constitutes *news* often creates adversarial relationships (Pinsdorf, 1999). However, like all associations, it is not just the ignorance or inflexibility of one party that contributes to friction or dysfunction. The often-tenuous relational dynamic between schools and the media is exacerbated by the stressful conditions under which reporters often seek information, particularly in times of conflict, serious problems, or controversy. Adding to the uneasiness is the fact that reporters, too, share a limited understanding of the professional and political dimensions of leading schools (Kowalski, 2004). "Misperceptions spring not from inaccuracy alone, but from genuine differences as well. As outsiders, journalists are . . . immune to the internal vested interests—the politics, history of a decision, especially the pressures on decision-makers" (Pinsdorf, 1999, p. 23).

Well-publicized and dramatic stories aside, there are compelling and newsworthy stories about educational reform successes in our schools and classrooms, and the media has the potential to be a valuable ally with their ability to widely disseminate information on important policies and accomplishments to the community at large. Unfortunately, news coverage often thrives on conflict, whether that conflict is an international crisis or a controversial decision at the local elementary school (Martin, 2000).

Importance of Media Relations

In a recent publication for superintendents, the National School Public Relations Association (NSPRA) put forth a short list of "newsworthy" issues for school leaders to keep in mind:

- If it's unusual, it's news.
- If it's a local twist on a national trend, it's news.
- Names make news.
- Innovation (real innovation) makes news.
- Evaluation makes news.
- Controversy makes news.
- Anticipation of consequences makes news.
- Money makes news.
- Kids make news.
- Mistakes (especially big mistakes) make news.

There is a public relations axiom that schools provide news for two things many people consider most important: their children and their money. Consequently, schools remain at the top of most reporters' high interest list (National School Public Relations Association, 2005a). Because public schools are open arenas, accessible to all members of the community, any notion of controlling the media is unrealistic and counterproductive. Yet, even with these very public and well-known points of contention and friction, common ground exists between schools and the media. Educational leaders share with reporters the goal of providing the most accurate public depictions of the school, its successes, contributions, and its role in the larger community. Consequently, cultivating *friends* among the media is of paramount importance for a school administrator. It is through this relationship that school administrators are able to get the word out on the important work and achievements of schools in a fair and regular basis. Keep in mind that no matter the success of the school, the brilliance of its students and faculty, or the innovativeness of its programs, the school will have a difficult time being viewed as successful if no one sees it, hears about it, or reads about it in the paper.

Having a Media Relations Plan

Even the best-designed media relations program cannot hide incompetence, a pattern of dishonesty, or a lack of organizational direction. Yet, in the absence of such a media plan, administrators find themselves in tenuous situations where they make spontaneous decisions about what to communicate, how it should be communicated and to whom, often resulting in arbitrary and capricious interactions that cast unfavorable or uninformed opinions of the schools in the minds of the public (Kowalski, 2004).

A district or school must have an internal plan before its media relations can be effective. Several authors have articulated the underlying components of successful media relations plans (e.g., Gonring, 1997; Kowalski, 2004; Leinemann & Baikaltseva, 2004; Marconi, 2004; Pinsdorf, 1999; Ridgway, 1996). Table 10.1 provides a list of critical questions that should be asked and answered in conjunction with developing such a plan. In addition, Gonring (1997) identifies four considerations that can guide administrators in planning:

1. *Organizational purpose.* Why does the organization exist?
2. *Ownership.* Is the school public or private?
3. *Media interest.* To what extent do the media seek to report on the district or school?
4. *Organizational expectations.* What does the district or school hope to gain by interacting with the media?

In addition a media relations plan should be characterized by the following attributes:

- *Clarity.* The plan is written in language readily understood by those affected.

Table 10.1. Central Questions in Developing a Media Relations Plan

Question	Relevance
What has been the history of media relations?	Journalists expect that the past practices will be perpetuated even when personnel change.
What media have a primary interest in schools?	Certain print and electronic media show much more interest in schools than others.
Who is assigned to cover the schools?	Identifying and meeting the reporters who cover education are essential tasks.
What are the interests and goals of targeted media?	Knowing why and how certain media outlets cover schools is also crucial. This information informs administrators of what the media deems newsworthy.
Who will manage the media plan?	Though many employees and all administrators should participate in planning, one individual should have the responsibility of overseeing the plan's development.
Who will receive or use the media relations plan?	Determining distribution and use is important because this information may affect the plan's content.
How often will the plan be revised?	Unless the plan is presented as a living document, it is unlikely to be revised periodically.

Note: Adapted from Kowalski (2004).

- *Direction.* The district or school has a policy that provides parameters for the plan's goals and strategies. The policy should provide a detailed outline regarding the exchange of information between the organization and its multiple publics.
- *Unity.* The plan is an extension of a more comprehensive public relations plan to ensure that interactions with media personnel are connected to more global communication and information management objectives.
- *Sponsorship.* The plan is supported and approved by the school board and superintendent. (Kowalski, 2004, p. 254)

Working Effectively With Journalists

Mark Twain advised that one should never make enemies with people who buy paper by the ton and ink by the barrel. Nevertheless, many school administrators view reporters as their enemies. On the surface, working with the media appears easy and uncomplicated, yet the opposite is often true, especially for the busy, harried, and unprepared school administrator. Often, superintendents and principals do not understand the work of journalists nor do they recognize the value of working with media in an information based society (Kowalski, 2004). As a result, contact with the media is typically viewed at best as an anxiety producing experience and at worst as a disaster. "Interviews with journalists are often high-anxiety situations in which countless numbers of intelligent, articulate, capable men and women report they were 'unhappy with how that went' and wait nervously to see how a writer or editor will represent what they said" (Marconi, 2004, p.180).

As used here, *media relations* refers to activities between school administrators and journalists. The term is defined as the patterns of communication that occur between organization members and media personnel (Ridgway, 1996). Regardless of past relationships and the factors that may have shaped them, every administrator should accept the responsibility of building positive relationships. This includes more than being cooperative. Astute practitioners are proactive; that is, they take the initiative to build and maintain these associations (Kowalski, 2004).

Because of intense interest in elementary and secondary education, school administrators must develop a professional capacity to get the district's message before the public through an exchange of information with print and electronic media outlets. Yet, creating a positive relationship is complex, intensive, and reliant on several factors. They include

- understanding the reporter's job, roles, and timelines;
- realizing that the media is a business with the goal of attracting viewers and readers;
- acknowledging that the school and media relationship is more of a marathon than a sprint;
- being proactive rather than reactive when it comes to media coverage; and
- being willing to take the bad news with the good.

A district's or school's reputation depends on positive media relationships. Administrators who put children first, admit mistakes, treat others with dignity, and tell the truth are much more likely to receive fair treatment from the media (National School Public Relations Association, 2005b). However, effective behavior is more likely when school employees are guided by a well-developed media plan that includes specific guidelines for media relations.

"Operating executives trained in an immediate, pragmatic, can-do attitude, find planning for amorphous contingencies a mind stretch. . . . They find it even more difficult when forced to accept surprise, disorderliness, lack of control and a good quick solution" (Pinsdorf, 1999, p. 73). The vignette at the beginning of this case demonstrates this point. No district or school is immune to tragedies or crises; however, exposure to risk can be reduced through effective planning.

In today's information society, citizens demand accurate, complete, and timely information about governmental agencies; and if their needs and wants are not satisfied by school officials, they will rely on the media or the Internet to obtain information (Kowalski, 2005). Yet, many superintendents and principals remain unprepared to communicate openly, with the public generally and with the media specifically. Moreover, relatively few public school districts are large enough to employ a full-time public relations or media director; 90% of school districts in the United States enroll less than 5,000 students (Kowalski, 2006). Regardless of district size, working with the media should be seen as a responsibility for all superintendents and principals because either regularly or intermittently, administrators will be spokespersons for their districts or schools. Table 10.2 offers lists of the professional competencies and responsibilities relevant to working with journalists.

Often administrators reflect negatively on their previous contact with reporters. They may lament the fact that they did not speak clearly or that they forgot to make an important point. Because administrators are never totally in control of media interviews, they need to take steps to prevent undesirable outcomes. Practitioners can use the following guidelines to prepare for interviews:

- Try to avoid saying anything negative about yourself, the staff, students, or the school.
- Don't interrupt the reporter. Listen to the entire question so that you can give the best and most appropriate answer.

Table 10.2. Selected Professional Competencies and Responsibilities Related to Working With the Media

Factor	Implications
Competency	
Knowledge of an issue or crisis	The administrator should have the knowledge necessary to respond to media inquiries or to redirect the inquiry to the most appropriate person.
Knowledge of policy	The administrator should know all relevant district policy concerning contact with journalists.
Information management	The administrator should be able to retrieve and interpret data in a timely manner.
Communicative competence	The administrator should be able to engage in relational communication and make adjustments based on contextual variables.
Relationship building	The administrator should know how to build and maintain credibility and trust with journalists.
Responsibilities	
Evaluating media relations	The administrator should periodically evaluate both institutional and personal performance relative to media relations.
Assisting employees in media relations	The administrator should provide information, direction, and consultation that assists employees to interact with the media.
Presenting positive information	The administrator has a responsibility to ensure that positive stories are provided to the media.

- Never agree to speak "off the record." Keep in mind that the rule of thumb is to never say anything you are unwilling to see in print.
- Never respond by saying "No comment." Such a response suggests that you have something to hide.
- Try to provide short, specific, and clear responses. Appearing focused and answering questions directly indicates that you are not trying to be evasive.
- Never lie. Though telling the truth can be painful at times, false or misleading answers can destroy credibility and trust.

RELATIONSHIPS WITH THE PUBLIC

Though the media play a pivotal role in informing the public, administrators should develop other information sources. These sources should be selected to ensure that information is exchanged and not just disseminated. Several of the most prominent options are described here. The purpose here is to identify their potentialities for improving communication and not to discuss them in great detail. Additional information on all of these processes is available from multiple sources.

District and School Web Pages

One method school leaders can utilize to provide and support two-way communication is through user-friendly Web pages. Today, the vast majority of districts and schools have such sites but they clearly differ in quality and purpose. For example, some websites do not even provide information essential for contacting school officials because they are designed solely to disseminate information.

Especially in smaller districts and schools, the responsibility for creating and operating websites falls on superintendents and principals. The following are useful guidelines for completing these tasks.

- Design the site so that it can be updated frequently. Good sites are updated at least weekly and sometimes even daily.
- Provide essential information that defines the sponsoring institution. For example, mission, vision, and philosophy statements provide context for site visitors.
- Supply contact information so that users know how they can communicate directly with school personnel.
- Include pertinent information that typically draws parents, students, and other visitors to the website. School calendars, lunch menus, and special announcements are examples.
- Provide updated and active links that will assist site visitors to obtain more detailed information. For example, a school site should contain links to the district's site and to the state department of education.

- Include information about school performance. In this age of accountability, many site visitors expect to find assessment data, state report cards, and so forth.
- Feature teachers, staff, and students as often as possible. The Web sites should not focus exclusively or primarily on administrators.
- Design the site for easy navigation. The user should not be confused about moving from one area of the site to another.
- Make sure that all information provided is correct. Not infrequently, principals have created school websites and then failed to update them for months or even years.
- Provide a mechanism that allows information to be exchanged by site visitors. An electronic bulletin board is a good example.

Maintaining a website is a time-consuming but necessary assignment. Fortunately, more and more school districts are employing technology directors, and these individuals often work closely with principals to develop and maintain school websites. Other options include contracting for this service or relying on volunteers (e.g., a parent who has the requisite expertise). Increasingly, however, principals are being expected to acquire the knowledge and skills necessary to administer websites.

Print Materials

Even in this electronic world, print material remains important to organizations. In the case of schools, this includes newsletters, school papers, brochures, student handbooks, policy manuals, and promotional material (e.g., for a tax referendum). Printed materials offer schools a simple and direct method to share the mission and goals, ideas, innovations, and successes to insiders, students, families, as well as the community at large. According to Hyde (2004), organizations require printed literature for two reasons:

1. *Establishing credibility.* People expect organizations to have printed literature. If you want to look professional, get your message out and look like you mean business, brochures and other forms of printed materials are essential.

2. *Providing convenience.* People usually prefer printed materials that they can take home and read at their leisure.

In developing print materials, an administrator should address three key queries:

1. *What* do you want the printed materials to accomplish? *What* are your objectives and goals with this brochure, report, bulletin, or newsletter?
2. *Who* are included in the target audiences?
3. *How* must you communicate to deliver the intended messages to the targeted audiences? (Hyde, 2004).

Once an administrator has answered the "what, who, and how" questions, he or she should follow several guidelines for preparing print material. Ferrari (2005) provides the following suggestions for producing professional-looking materials:

• Keep the look clean and simple; don't overload the reader visually.
• Avoid too much type; pages filled with writing are not appealing.
• Use headers and subheadings to lead the reader.
• Make sure everything is spelled correctly and avoid using professional jargon or terms readers are unlikely to comprehend.
• Do not use every inch of paper; doing so results in a cluttered appearance.
• Include captions for photographs.
• Using charts and graphs is preferable to using tables; most readers respond more favorably to items that are visually appealing.

Given the ability of citizens to access information rapidly and in many forms, administrators are relying less on student newspapers and printed newsletters as a primary communication medium. This does not mean that these items have disappeared; rather, their purpose has narrowed. Regardless of what other mediums may be available, newsletters and newspapers should provide a feedback capacity; that is, there should be a provision for readers to communicate with the publishers (Kowalski, 2004).

Focus Groups and Opinion Polls

Two additional methods for enhancing two-way communication are *focus groups* and *opinion polls*. These are "an excellent way to improve your understanding of the views, priorities, and concerns of your community" (Cambron-McCabe, Cunningham, Harvey, & Koff, 2005, p. 271). The former technique involves conducting discussions with a sample of the population. The purported advantage is that a focus group allows school officials to gain richer and deeper information about a subject through a face-to-face format. The latter technique involves surveying a population or sample, by telephone, via the Internet, or through a mail survey. The purported advantage is that general information can be obtained from a large group of people in a relatively short time.

When collecting information via focus groups or opinion polls, administrators should adhere to the following guidelines:

- These tools should be used to collect data. As such, they provide information that may illuminate confusion or a problem but they are not intended to resolve those situations (Cambron-McCabe et al., 2005).
- As explained with printed material, administrators should answer the what, who, and how questions before proceeding. That is, what information is needed; from whom is it needed; and how should it be collected?
- Collect and analyze data objectively.
- Determine how the results will be disseminated and used.

Public Forums

Open forums are one of the most common approaches to communicating with the public. Cambron-McCabe et al. (2005) offer several suggestions for these public meetings.

- Try to attract community members outside the typical circle of people who usually attend school board meetings or other functions. These individuals may provide viewpoints that school officials do not hear every day.

- Educators should not dominate the discourse in these sessions. Rather, they should facilitate the process and answer questions.
- Provide a social dimension, such as providing refreshments. Doing so often improves attendance.
- Focus on one or a few select topics. Not doing so presents the possibility that many subjects will be raised but none of them will be discussed in detail.
- If the forum is being held to discuss a controversial issue, it also is beneficial to select a neutral site and to have a person considered to be neutral serve as the moderator.

Public forums are not productive if they become chaotic or contentious. Consequently, administrators should develop rules that govern procedures. As an example, speakers should not be allowed to make personal attacks, to continue beyond a specified time limit, and to stray from designated topics (Kowalski, 2006). Attendees always have the option of extending their remarks in a letter to school officials.

Partnerships

Several authors (e.g., Dryfoos, 1994; Holtzman, 1995; Kowalski, 2006) advocate school partnerships as a way to strengthen and sustain communication. Partnerships are joint ventures involving schools and other agencies. These agencies range from businesses to other educational institutions (e.g., colleges) to other governmental agencies (e.g., a local recreation board). Holtzman (1995) concludes that the growth of partnerships reflected a realization that education is an investment in human capital. For example, employers need skilled workers, and successful schooling serves their interests. In addition, schools have been drawn to partnerships for at least two other reasons. Pragmatically, school officials realize that they have insufficient resources; philosophically, school officials realize that they have an obligation to work closely with the community (Kowalski, 2006).

The term *partnership* has many connotations. In truth, there are four levels of associations, all of which could be described as partnerships but each having a different level of commitment. These four levels, presented here, are applied to an example in which a school and local community college work together in the area of adult education (Kowalski, 2003; 2006):

1. *Networking.* In this level of association, the school district and community college officials merely agree to share information about what they are doing in adult education. No authority over adult education is relinquished by either institution.
2. *Coordination.* In this level of association, the school district and community college agree to do certain things in a coordinated manner. For example, they agree not to offer adult education classes on the same evening. However, neither institution relinquished authority.
3. *Cooperation.* In this level of association, the school district and community college agree to work together in certain areas of adult education. For example, they jointly teach courses. Some but not all authority is relinquished as one institution usually assumes a lead role.
4. *Collaboration.* In this level of association, the school district and community college agree to provide adult education jointly. That is, no decision is made without the approval of both parties. Obviously, considerable authority is relinquished.

Though each might be described as a partnership, the collaborative level is most likely to reduce duplication and increase quality of services. It also is the most reliant on effective, open communication, trust, and positive relationships.

Without sufficient planning and deliberation, partnerships are likely to fail. According to a study conducted by Miron and Wimpelberg (1989), of 450 school partnerships with local businesses, only 8 of them led to changes in instruction. Too often, school and business leaders jump at the opportunity to work together without asking and answering critical questions. Partnerships fail for a variety of reasons and poor communication is certainly one of them (Kowalski, 2006). Conversely, successful partnerships are usually characterized by long-term planning and high levels of involvement from all partners (Holtzman, 1995).

RELATIONSHIPS WITH THE SCHOOL BOARD

School boards represent the public and accordingly, communication with them and through them is critically important. As per normative practice in the education profession, the superintendent is most responsible for working directly with board members. He or she motivates, facilitates groups in collaborative decision making, and enables the participatory management of schools (Petersen & Short, 2002). As the superintendent's role transitions from the top of the organizational structure to the center of a complex network of interpersonal relationships, human skills of the district leader become fundamentally more critical (Henkin, 1993). Superintendents generally recognize the importance of interpersonal and communication skills, and boards of education continually confirm the association between strong interpersonal and communication skills and the effectiveness of school executives (Petersen & Short, 2002).

Research and administrative practice have routinely demonstrated that a poor relationship between the superintendent and the board of education deters school improvement, affects the quality of educational programs, weakens district stability and morale, impedes critical reform efforts such as district restructuring, reduces collaborative visioning and long-range planning, and eventually results in an increase in the "revolving door syndrome" of district leaders (Kowalski, 2006; Petersen & Short, 2002).

To avoid the development of negative relations between the superintendent and school board members, Petersen and Morrow-Williams (2005) recognize that interpersonal skills, such as being an effective communicator, are essential (p. 26). Townsend, Brown, and Buster (2005) echo this sentiment: "Communication and relationship building are the proactive behaviors of a skilled superintendent" (p. 85). The skilled superintendent knows that much of this communication and relationship building with school board members is apparent at school board meetings.

The superintendent, according to Townsend et al. (2005), must set the agenda to prevent the school board meetings from going in the wrong direction. It is the superintendent's responsibility to "take the lead to make sure the agenda furthers the board's role to govern, not manage" (p. 17). These authors suggested that board meetings and agendas revolve around five guiding principles:

1. Establishing a shared vision and devoting approximately four meetings a year to the topic.
2. Instituting appropriate structure to equip board members and the superintendent to enact policies.
3. Having a system of accountability.

4. Incorporating a sense of advocacy.
5. Serving to unite the parties involved. (pp. 21–22)

Communication with the school board, especially in smaller school systems, also involves principals and even teachers. Though board members have no individual authority and though they are supposed to communicate through the superintendent, they often visit schools or call school employees to exchange information. Consequently, superintendents should provide both employees and board members with guidelines regarding communication, especially communication that serves a general public need (Kowalski, 2006). This means having clearly delineated lines of communication that are also realistic.

RELATIONSHIPS WITH EMPLOYEES

Building and maintaining positive administrator-employee relations requires first and foremost a sense of community. Without a shared vision and common goals, school personnel may be left feeling rudderless and apathetic. An effective school leader clearly articulates a collective vision to students, staff, parents, and community.

Effects of Positive Employee Relations

Relationships are more likely to be positive in schools in which individual and group needs are being met (Greenberg, 1996) and positive behaviors are encouraged and rewarded (Hoy & Miskel, 2005). When administrators express interest in employee performance and respond favorably to employee accomplishments, teachers and other staff feel that they are valued and their efforts appreciated. Under these conditions, employees have higher levels of job satisfaction—a factor contributing to high productivity. In addition to recognizing achievement, the following three interventions are typically effective:

1. *Setting expectations.* Having expectations and clearly and frequently communicating them positively affects employee behavior (DuBrin, 1997).

2. *Involving employees.* Most school employees want to be involved in important matters that affect them and the overall welfare of students. This is yet another reason why concepts such as shared decision-making and democratic administration tend to improve school performance (Blase & Kirby, 2000).

3. *Using praise appropriately.* Though formal rewards are forms of praise, there are other ways that administrators can pay tribute to accomplishments. Thank-you notes, positive verbal comments at staff meetings, and recognition in school publications and Web pages are examples.

Communicating With Employees

Two-way communication between administrators and school employees is equally if not more important than it is between administrators and external publics. Faculty and staff typically want their voices heard, especially in relation to matters that affect them, students, and the community. In order to exchange information, administrators must know how to listen and interpret information. More specifically, listening has three elements: "what is heard, what is understood, and what is remembered" (Kowalski, 2006, p. 99). People often overestimate the quality of their listening skills, usually because they define listening narrowly as "hearing." Research has shown, however, that people who do not create accurate and complete mental pictures based on information heard do not comprehend or remember information fully (Bell, 1991; Paivio, 1969; 1979; 1986; Sadoski, 1983; Sadoski & Paivio, 2001).

Listening is an acquired skill, and even once it is mastered, administrators must exert discipline to apply it in their communication. Moreover, generalizations about what is effective listening have become more questionable in a society where many students, parents, and even employees have dissimilar cultural heritages. As an example, maintaining eye contact with a speaker has long been considered an effective listening technique; however, individuals in some cultures consider this behavior to be disrespectful, especially if the speaker is a person of authority. According to Brown and Kysilka (2002), there are also cultural differences with respect to information processing. For instance, some individuals are *field dependent*, whereas others are *field independent*. Field-dependent individuals respond "to information as a whole rather than as individual parts" (p. 75), a characteristic common among African Americans, Asian Americans, Latinos, and Native Americans. Field-independent individuals, in contrast, are able to "focus in on isolated facts and isolated tasks . . . [and] more easily sort significant information from less important details, working analytically and sequentially," a characteristic common among European Americans (p. 75).

Context orientation is another critical variable. Typically, field-dependent individuals tend to be members of *high-context* cultural groups in which "the context of a conversation is as important or more important than the actual words spoken" (Brown & Kysilka, 2002, p. 76). By comparison, field-independent individuals tend to be members of *low-context* cultural groups in which communicants expect that information will be conveyed directly, openly, and explicitly. The European American preference for low-context orientation correlates with a preference for direct verbal communication, one that "emphasizes values of openness, honesty, and forthrightness" (p. 82). High-context cultures, on the other hand, usually prefer an indirect mode of communication, one in which the message is hidden or disguised, often in an effort to save face, avoid embarrassment, or prevent confrontation.

In addition to cultural awareness, administrators should adhere to the three-step *PPE* approach when engaged in conversations. The method is described below using an example of a conversation in which a teacher is expressing concerns about textbooks to a principal.

1. *Paraphrasing.* Paraphrasing the speaker's comments enables the principal to provide immediate feedback to the teacher. For example, the principal makes the following comment, "So you received 22 books instead of the 25."

2. *Perception checking.* The principal clarifies her understanding of the teacher's message, usually by asking questions. For example, after listening to a series of statements, she asks, "Is the real problem then the fact that you had to delay starting the first instructional unit?"

3. *Empathizing with the speaker.* Being supportive is interpreted as effective listening. This is especially true when conversations center on concerns and problems. For example, toward the end of the conversation the principal tells the teacher, "I understand why not receiving a sufficient number of books caused you to be upset."

Most administrators know that their nonverbal behavior is important, but often overlooked is the fact that it is important to both speaking and listening. Spaulding and O'Hair (2004) summarize four functions of nonverbal communication;[1] the following three are highly relevant to listening:

1. *Expressing emotion.* Gestures, eye movement, and other forms of nonverbal communication indicate whether a person is committed to listening. For example, a principal who rifles through his desk drawers while a teacher is speaking indicates that the principal is probably emotionally detached from the conversation.
2. *Conveying interpersonal attitudes.* Nonverbal behavior can indicate a person's attitudes toward others. For example, a principal who repeatedly looks at his watch while a teacher is speaking to her may convey the negative message that she does not like the teacher and has no interest in his comments.
3. *Presenting one's personality.* Individuals interpret the nonverbal behavior to form impressions of others. For example, teachers may decide if a principal is caring, sincere, and ethical based on her behavior during conversations.

There are literally dozens of possible barriers to good listening. They range from being impatient to daydreaming to indifference toward others. Unfortunately, people usually do not learn to be good listeners naturally. Effective listening is an acquired skill that is as important to communication as is effective speaking (Spaulding & O'Hair, 2004).

CONCLUDING COMMENTS

Relationships are at the heart of effective school administration. Research demonstrates that dissatisfaction with superintendents and principals often centers on their perceived lack of human relations skills (Kowalski, 2003). This chapter examined four important categories of administrator relationships; those with the media, those with the public, those with school board members, and those with school employees. Though the quality and quantity of information exchanges may vary across these categories, the one constant is the expectation that administrators will engage consistently in open, ongoing, relational communication.

In order for current and future practitioners to meet this normative standard, two long-standing barriers must be confronted. First, administrators must reconsider traditional perspectives of organizational behavior, especially those nested in classical theory. The underlying assumptions of bureaucratic behavior lead superintendents and principals to view communication largely in relation to technical efficiency and managerial control. In reality, schools operate in democratic and highly political environments; consequently, behavior that limits open information exchanges is almost always viewed negatively. Second, administrators must accept a personal responsibility for building good communication skills. This means that they must understand communication as a science and have the ability to infuse and adapt this knowledge to their profession (Kowalski, 2005).

NOTE

1. The fourth function involves augmenting verbal messages and thus is not directly related to listening.

REFERENCES

Bell, N. (1991). Gestalt imagery: A critical factor in language comprehension. *Annals of Dyslexia, 41,* 246–260.

Berliner, D. C., & Biddle, B. J. (1998). *The lamentable alliance between the media and school critics.* Retrieved June 2, 2006, from www.aasa.org/publications/saarticledetail.cfm?ItemNumber=4488.

Blase, J., & Kirby, P. C. (2000). *Bringing out the best in teachers: What effective principals do.* Thousand Oaks, CA: Corwin.

Brown, S. C., & Kysilka, M. L. (2002). *Applying multicultural and global concepts in the classroom and beyond.* Boston: Allyn & Bacon.

Cambron-McCabe, N., Cunningham, L. L., Harvey, J., & Koff, R. H. (2005). *The superintendent's fieldbook.* Thousand Oaks, CA: Corwin.

Dryfoos, J. G. (1994). *Full-service schools: A revolution in health and social services for children, youth, and families.* San Francisco: Jossey-Bass.

DuBrin, A. J. (1997). *Human relations: Interpersonal job-oriented skills.* Upper Saddle River, NJ: Prentice Hall.

Ferrari, J. (2005). *5 tips for professional marketing materials.* Retrieved June 2, 2006, from www.entrepreneur.com/.

Gonring, M. P. (1997). Global and local media relations. In C. L. Caywood (Ed.), *The handbook of strategic public relations and integrated communication* (pp. 63–79). New York: McGraw-Hill.

Greenberg, J. (1996). *Managing behavior in organizations*. Upper Saddle River, NJ: Prentice Hall.

Henkin, A. B. (1993). Social skills of superintendents: A leadership requisite in restructured schools. *Educational Research Quarterly, 16*(4), 15–30.

Holtzman, H. (1995). Local partnerships as the source of innovative policy. In L. C. Rigsby, M. C. Reynolds, & M. C. Wang (Eds.), *School-community connections: Exploring issues for research and practice* (pp. 59–67). San Francisco: Jossey-Bass.

Hoy, W., & Miskel, C. (2005). *Educational administration: Theory, research and practice* (7th ed.). New York: McGraw-Hill.

Hyde, J. (2004) The internet & beyond-Mean business: 12 tips on writing better brochures. *Santa Cruz, CA: Persuasions Copywriting. Creative Search Media.* Retrieved September 4, 2006, from www.juliahyde.com/mw/issue-004.

Kowalski, T. J. (2003). *Contemporary school administration: An introduction* (2nd ed.). Boston: Allyn & Bacon.

Kowalski, T. J. (2004). Working with the media. In T. J. Kowalski (Ed.), *Public relations in schools* (3rd ed., pp. 251–273). Upper Saddle River, NJ: Merrill/Prentice Hall.

Kowalski, T. J. (2005). Evolution of the school superintendent as communicator. *Communication Education, 54*(2), 101–117.

Kowalski, T. J. (2006). *The school superintendent: Theory, practice and cases* (2nd ed). Thousand Oaks, CA: Sage.

Leinemann, R., & Baikaltseva, E. (2004). *Media relations measurement: Determining the value of PR to your company's success.* Burlington, VT: Gower.

Marconi, J. (2004). *Public relations: The complete guide.* Mason, OH: Thompson Learning.

Martin, M. W. (2000). *Does zero mean zero?* Retrieved June 2, 2006, from www.asbj.com/security/contents/0300martin.html.

Miron, L. F., & Wimpelberg, R. K. (1989). School-business partnerships and the reform of education. *Administrator's Notebook, 33*(9), 1–4.

Moy, P., & Pfau, M. (2000). *With malice toward all? The media and public confidence in democratic institutions.* Westport, CT: Praeger.

National School Public Relations Association. (2005a). *Don't wait for the media to call: Going active is the key to getting better news coverage.* Retrieved June 2, 2006, from www.nspra.org/CMV2N5Media.htm.

National School Public Relations Association. (2005b). *Villain, victim, or hero: Which role will you play when your next crisis strikes?* Retrieved June 2, 2006, from www.nspra.org/CMV2N5Villains.htm.

Paivio, A. (1969). Mental imagery in associative learning and memory. *Psychological Review, 76*, 241–263.

Paivio, A. (1979). *Imagery and verbal processes.* New York: Holt, Rinehart & Winston.

Paivio, A. (1986). *Mental representation: A dual coding approach.* New York: Oxford University Press.

Petersen, G. J., & Morrow-Williams, B. (2005). The board president and superintendent: An examination of influence through the eyes of the decision makers. In G. J. Petersen & L. D. Fusarelli (Eds.), *The politics of leadership: Superintendents and school boards in changing times* (pp. 23–50). Greenwich, CT: Information Age.

Petersen, G. J., & Short, P. M. (2002). An examination of the school board president's perception of the district superintendent's interpersonal communication competence and board decision-making. *Journal of School Leadership, 12*(4), 411–436.

Pinsdorf, M. K. (1999). *Communicating when your company is under siege: Surviving public crisis* (3rd ed.). New York: Fordham University Press.

Ridgway, J. (1996). *Practical media relations* (2nd ed.). Brookfield, VT: Gower.

Sadoski, M. (1983). An exploratory study of the relationship between reported imagery and the comprehension and recall of a story. *Reading Research Quarterly, 19*(1), 110–123.

Sadoski, M., & Paivio, A. (2001). *Imagery and text: A dual coding theory of reading and writing.* Mahwah, NJ: Erlbaum.

Spaulding, A. M., & O'Hair, M. J. (2004). Public relations in a communication context: Listening, nonverbal, and conflict-resolution skills. In T. J. Kowalski (Ed.), *Public relations in schools* (3rd ed., pp. 96–122). Upper Saddle River, NJ: Merrill/Prentice Hall.

Townsend, R. S., Brown, J. R., & Buster, W. L. (2005). *A practical guide to effective school board meetings.* Thousand Oaks, CA: Corwin.

11

School-Based Management and Communication

Research on school reform and restructuring suggests that new organizational arrangements are necessary for comprehensive school improvement. According to Clark and Meloy (1989), empirical evidence on creativity, innovation, and productivity supports the creation of organizational structures that promote freedom, self-control, and personal development. Organizational studies indicate that such nonbureaucratic characteristics as activity, variability, self-efficacy, empowerment, and disaggregation are more likely to be found in effective organizations than in their bureaucratic counterparts. Site-based management (SBM) and its central feature of shared decision making are touted by scholars as a way to establish climates that are conducive to authentic reforms. By adopting SBM and implementing it in accordance with its precepts, school administrators can engage in internal restructuring that aligns schools with their democratic heritage.

One of the most important arenas of communication in districts and schools is group decision making. Since the 1980s, SBM has become the most prevalent governance concept. The process is defined largely by two characteristics: the decentralization of authority and shared decision making. In theory, both characteristics are intended to ensure that important reform decisions will be based on the real needs of students and that these student needs will be met by site-based improvements. Utilizing the principle of directed autonomy, local school administrators are given greater leeway and discretion in determining how needs will be met and in using resources, but at the same time they are held accountable for meeting broad federal and state performance goals (Weiler, 1990). Success with this strategy, however, requires changes in how educators think about leadership, about their jobs, and about inclusion and involvement in schools. The process also requires new paths of leadership and the development and utilization of communication processes that ensure full inclusion and maximum understanding among all stakeholders.

SITE-BASED MANAGEMENT AS A RESTRUCTURING STRATEGY

Of the many proposed reform strategies, none is more comprehensive in scope than the movement toward school restructuring (Hill & Bonan, 1991). In fact, total school restructuring has the potential to significantly change the governance and operating structure of schools. The quintessential example of this potentiality is SBM—a concept of decentralization in which power and authority is redistributed and decision making is shifted from the district to school so that principals, teachers, parents, students, and other stakeholders can be involved more directly in governance (Marburger, 1985). Several states, including Kentucky and Texas, have enacted legislation to advance this initiative (Wagstaff & Reyes, 1992).

Philosophical Foundation

Site-based management is based on the assumption that localized, site-specific decision making will produce more effective decisions since local, campus decision makers are most aware of the specific needs of students. Both directly and indirectly, SBM broadens accountability for student success, invests citizens with a sense of ownership, creates a stronger focus on results and improvement, and builds a sense of community among all stakeholders (Heath & Vik, 1996; Mathews, 2006). Earlier, in chapter 7, the increasing antidemocratic trend of institutions in our society, including public schools, was examined. Notwithstanding the community schools movement of the 1960s, antidemocratic trends in educational governance continued largely unabated through most of the last half of the 20th century. Now, SBM provides an opportunity to develop genuine democratic pluralism in schools (Reyes, 1994). If properly pursued,

SBM revitalizes democracy, and as a result, stakeholders come together and reach consensus in democratic forums characterized by open and un-dominated discourse (Habermas, 1990). Bauman (1996) observes that in an information-based society, stakeholders excluded from participating in decision making usually become alienated. Site-based management is a process that can overcome or prevent disaffection and exclusion and, at the same time, provide an opportunity to make schools inclusive, partici-patory, and democratic institutions.

Promises and Potential Pitfalls

Site-based management is an initiative that is practiced in various ways and degrees across the country. Several of the largest school districts in the United States and Canada have adopted SBM, including large systems such as Miami–Dade County, Los Angeles, Edmonton, Chicago, Boston, and Wake County, North Carolina; however, the concept has not been im-plemented uniformly (Lindauer, Petrie, & Richardson, 1997). Even so, districts that have institutionalized SBM have adopted more democratic processes that involve a greater range of stakeholders in important deci-sions (Bauman, 1996).

Some scholars have been pessimistic about the long-term effects of SBM (Malen & Ogawa, 1988; Scribner, 1990). Doubts center primarily on three issues:

1. The extent to which SBM will permanently change patterns of au-thority, control, and power in schools
2. The effects of SBM on alienated and disenfranchised individuals
3. The public's comprehension of SBM

With respect to the first issue, scholars who have studied the culture of public schools (e.g., Fullan, 2001; Sarason, 1996) conclude that changing basic assumptions about the way schools should be organized and oper-ated will be a monumental task. With respect to effects, Scribner (1990) concludes that past reforms directed toward making schools more demo-cratic have produced few positive effects, especially for poor students and students of color. Finally, the fact that SBM exists in various iterations has made it a difficult concept for some to grasp (Hill & Bonan, 1991; Malen,

Ogawa, & Kranz, 1990; Wagstaff & Reyes, 1992), and a lack of under-standing often affects public acceptance. Organizational politics occur more frequently in situations characterized by ambiguity, substantial or-ganizational change, and uncertainty (Scribner, Fusarelli, Cain, & Pustka, 1993). Under such conditions, political actors utilize authority and influ-ence as micropolitical strategies to further their own self-interests and, thereby, to control the SBM process (Marshall & Scribner, 1991; Scribner et al., 1993).

Misapplications of SBM also can deter teacher professionalization, a condition deemed by many scholars to be essential to school improve-ment. Researchers (e.g., Darling-Hammond, 1994; Kowalski, 1995; 2004) note that while decentralization raises expectations of professionalization, misconstruing the concept or purposefully misusing it may actually weaken efforts to achieve this objective.

The knowledge base on SBM is continuously growing, largely because implementation efforts have been studied rather frequently. In a RAND study of five urban and suburban school systems deploying SBM, for ex-ample, Hill and Bonan (1991) found that changes evolved over time but incrementally, and the schools developed "distinctive characters, goals, and operating styles" (p. vi). The authors concluded that the degree to which power and decision-making authority were actually repositioned was crucial to success.

In their review of 83 empirical SBM studies, Leithwood and Menzies (1998) identified 4 distinct forms of SBM practice:

1. *Administrative control.* Decision making was decentralized to the principal but did not extend further.
2. *Professional control.* Teachers and principals, but not other stake-holders, controlled most decisions.
3. *Community control.* Parents and other community stakeholders con-trolled most decisions.
4. *Equal control.* Control was dispersed among all participants.

Only the last iteration, equal control, exemplifies the philosophical pur-pose of SBM. In order for it to be applied, educators must be willing to share authority, and community members must be willing to participate and assume responsibility for decisions (White, 1989).

Malen, Ogawa, and Kranz (1990) found that many SBM councils were mere ancillary advisors or pro forma endorsers rather than authentic decision-making groups. Member involvement was often limited to listening, advising, or rubber-stamping previously made administrative decisions; moreover, teachers did not wield significant influence (Malen & Ogawa, 1988). Several intervening variables have been found to be responsible for SBM councils maintaining rather than altering traditional influence relationships in schools. These factors include (a) the composition of the councils, (b) the relative power and role orientations of principals and other professionals, and (c) a congenial culture.

Site-based management threatens many school leaders because it alters traditional lines of authority and control in schools. Lieberman, Saxl, and Miles (1988) and Clune and White (1988) observe that calls for teacher participation in decision making resulted in considerable tension between teachers and administrators, especially in relation to the two groups assessing their respective normative roles. Undeniably, role ambiguity and confusion are inevitable as districts move to SBM (Van Meter, 1991). In part, tensions emanate from efforts to prevent SBM from being fully implemented. Administrators who philosophically oppose the concept, for example, may limit the participation of council members, perhaps by claiming that they lack expertise and experience. In addition, they argue they and not councils remain accountable for school productivity (Bacharach & Lawler, 1980; Malen et al., 1990).

When SBM fails, a lack of stakeholder involvement and poor communication are typically found to be pervasive problems. Despite rhetoric to the contrary, research (e.g., Hallinger, Murphy, & Hausman, 1992; Hallinger & Yanofsky, 1990; Kowalski, 1994; Murphy, Evertson, & Radnofsky, 1991) reveals that not all principals or teachers favor active parental and community involvement on these councils. Principals who exclude parents from school councils offer a myriad of excuses. The more common ones include (a) that parents often do not represent the entire community, (b) that parents will spawn power struggles, and (c) that many parents seek to be council members only because they have "an axe to grind."

Even when parents are council members, they may be excluded from meaningful participation. Councils divided into political factions and embroiled in power struggles typically suffer from poor communication. That is, information exchanges are largely one-way, nonfacilitative, and noninteractive. This communication breakdown makes it more likely that community representatives, regardless of whether they are parents of students, will be excluded from participating in consequential decisions. Their exclusion occurs because educators engage in asymmetrical communication—a process intended to benefit the educators but not the other council members. Therefore, the manner in which council members communicate helps determine if SBM is applied appropriately, especially in relation to shared decision making.[1]

Influence and Authority Domains

The scope of teacher involvement in SBM has been a matter of debate. Marburger (1985), for example, notes that much of the SBM and shared decision-making literature calls for teacher council members to be involved not only with curriculum but also with budget and personnel decisions. Research by Collins and Hansen (1991) verifies that teachers seek more influence on operational decisions pertaining to direct student instruction; however, they also found that the same level of interest did not exist in relation to involvement in managerial decisions. Evidence produced by SBM studies indicates that in many districts, unfortunately, teachers have not been included as full partners in either instructional or managerial decisions (Kreisberg, 1992).

Conley (1991) argues that SBM plans should clearly differentiate between decisions on which teachers have final authority and decisions on which teachers' involvement is limited only to influence (i.e., an advisory capacity in which they offer suggestions or recommendations). Bacharach and Lawler (1980) distinguish between authority and influence. They define the former as the ability to say yes or no to a particular decision; authority has a legal (legitimate or structural) basis granting an individual the right to make such decisions. They define influence as the capacity to shape decisions through informal or nonauthoritative means. Participation can range from the mere presentation of an opinion, where the locus of final authority rests elsewhere, to membership in a group that exercises final authority over an issue (Alutto & Belasco, 1972). The level of individual participation in decision making typically depends on individual status and expertise differences as well as the level of trust and support provided from superiors (Ritchie, 1974). According to Bacharach and Lawler (1980), there are three primary sources of influence:

1. Personal characteristics (charisma)
2. Expertise (knowledge and skills)
3. Opportunity (occasions that permit one to be influential)

Negative attitudes toward truly involving community members in SBM and shared decision making almost always produce considerable conflict. This is because community representatives, and especially parents, desire to be fully involved (Wagstaff & Reyes, 1992). Though parents are sometimes uncertain about their authority and responsibility as council members, they believe that they need to be involved and that their contributions are meaningful. This is why school administrators must ensure that all council members have equal authority and equal opportunities to participate in the decision-making process. Reyes and McCarty (1990) note that behavior in a social system, such as a school, may be largely governed by participants' perceptions of power. Therefore, power, not just the opportunity to participate, must be equitably distributed in the system (Schumaker, 1991). If school reform is to become a truly democratic enterprise which affords equal opportunities for all parties, then efforts must be devoted toward minimizing significant differences in knowledge, power, and resources among such parties (Scheurich & Imber, 1991).

Significant change in an organization requires ownership—that is, the opportunity to participate in defining change and the ability to adapt it to individual circumstances (David, 1989; Hill & Bonan, 1991). Discursive participation in consensual goal formation, however, is not a normal condition in most organizations (Clegg & Higgins, 1987). To be invariably told, rarely asked, infrequently consulted, and not be expected to participate in the formation of collective goals is hardly a secure basis for obtaining commitment (Clegg, 1989). To overcome this common problem, district and school administrators need to empower school councils and the teachers, parents, students, and community members who serve on them. This conclusion is consistent with recent research conducted in the private sector which found that engaged employees feel a profound connection to their work, drive innovation, and advance the organization's goals whereas disengaged employees do not (Krueger & Killham, 2005).

Operational Outcomes

Though the research about the effectiveness of SBM is mixed, in schools where shared decision making has been effectively deployed, SBM has demonstrated that it can change relationships among principals, teachers, parents, and other members of the community in schools. Typically, SBM increases the number of people participating in decision making and the types of decisions that are made collaboratively, especially those decisions affecting curriculum and instruction. The most significant impact SBM has had in the operation of schools, however, is in the area of improved communication and collaboration; influential councils are characterized by their collaborative, team approach to problem solving (Parker & Leithwood, 2000).

Wohlstetter (1995) and colleagues interviewed more than 500 people in 44 schools in 13 districts in the United States, Canada, and Australia and found that in schools where SBM worked, well-developed systems had been created "for sharing school-related information with a broad range of constituents" (p. 24). Information flowed freely; "decision making groups collected and dispensed information within the school and informed parents and the community" (p. 24). Furthermore, administrators "were systematic and creative in their efforts to communicate with parents and the community" (p. 24).

Historically, teachers and administrators have been primarily isolated in their workplace. Collectively, research on SBM reveals that increased interaction, though likely to spawn conflict in the short term, leads to improved communication and collaboration. This conclusion is reinforced by recent pressures to leave no child behind. New federal and state mandates to engage in data-driven decision making, for example, are not only causing school systems to improve databases and information management systems, they also are requiring educators to consult with each other more frequently (Kowalski, Lasley, & Mahoney, in press).

EFFECTIVE LEADERSHIP AND COMMUNICATION

Though support from the superintendent and other district administrators is important in SBM, principals largely determine whether the concept achieves its intended outcomes. A considerable amount of research has established that principals play a pivotal role in determining whether power is distributed and whether decision making is a participatory process (Doggett, 1990; Herman, 1989; Wagstaff & Reyes, 1992). The fundamental issue is not whether decision authority is decentralized but rather whether the redistribution of authority extends to council members and other teachers in the school (Conley & Bacharach, 1990). Not infrequently, superintendents decentralize authority only to discover that principals continue to behave autocratically (Herman, 1989).

Principal Leadership

Clearly, principals often determine whether SBM and its primary attributes are implemented as intended (Rutherford, 1991). Appropriate implementation requires both district-level commitment (from both the school board and superintendent) and effective leadership and facilitation from principals; however, principals alone usually determine the degree to which decision making is addressed as a democratic process (Wagstaff & Reyes, 1992). Again, such findings are consistent with research conducted in other types of organizations; employees' relationships with their supervisors has been found to be the primary determinant of engagement in the workplace (Krueger & Killham, 2005).

Principals have varying leadership styles; some are more effective in relation to SBM. Studying principals' leadership styles in relation to school councils, Etheridge, Hall, and Brown (1990) identify three dominant styles:

1. Laissez-faire
2. Authoritarian
3. Democratic

Principals who exhibited laissez-faire and democratic leadership styles facilitated cooperation and open communication in school councils, while authoritarian principals controlled the flow of information to school councils, inhibited communication among members, and limited involvement in decision making.

Principals in schools that have successfully implemented SBM are skilled in communication and conflict management. This is not unexpected since a process that emphasizes inclusion and collaboration tends to increase rather than reduce conflict and disagreement, at least in the short term (Henkin, Cistone, & Dee, 1999). In their study of 103 principals in a large urban school district, Henkin et al. (1999) found that administrators in SBM schools were more likely to resolve differences through communication, collaboration, and integrated problem-solving strategies than were administrators in traditional schools. Moreover, effective communication, collaboration, and integrated problem solving were found to be associated with higher levels of principals' satisfaction with teachers, site councils, and staff. In their study of high-poverty, high-performing schools along the Rio Grande valley in Texas, Wagstaff and Fusarelli (1999) also identify communication and collaboration within SBM councils as essential elements of school success. The authors concluded that SBM "facilitated open communication and collaboration by promoting the sharing of ideas among committee members, department heads, administrators, and teachers" (p. 20). They added that these schools were suffused with high levels of "coordinated planning and communication" and that leaders of those schools paid considerable attention, in the words of one principal, to "developing a lot of communication tools" (p. 20).

Not surprisingly, research (e.g., Smylie, 1992) also has found that teachers' willingness to participate in school decision making is influenced primarily by their relationships with their principals. Teachers are substantially more willing to participate in all areas of school decision making if they perceive their relationships with their principals as being open, collaborative, facilitative, and supportive. They are less willing to participate when they characterize the relationships as being closed, exclusionary, and controlling. Peel and Walker (1994) reach similar conclusions in their study of 26 principals in North Carolina who were engaged in SBM. The researchers found that teachers most supported principals who were firmly committed to sharing decision making among all stakeholders, were collaborative and encouraged risk taking, and who communicated clearly and often—sharing information and maintaining open lines of communication.

Collaboration and Communication

For school councils to operate effectively, several measures need to be pursued. The following are among the most important:

- Decision-making authority must be distributed as evenly as possible among as many participants as possible within the community served by the school.
- Serious attempts must be made to minimize power differentials among participants.
- Elected representatives must reflect the racial and ethnic composition of the community.
- Those participants who serve as elected representatives must act responsibly and must faithfully represent the desires of their constituents.
- The school site councils must possess comprehensive decision-making authority and be inclusive of all groups in the community.
- The councils must continuously monitor themselves to ensure that they remain representative of the community.
- All participants must believe that power sharing is not power loss.
- School leaders must have a high level of interpersonal relations and communication skills (Heath & Vik, 1996).

Rethinking traditional power relations can be quite challenging for school leaders because shared leadership is difficult to implement (Meadows, 1992). Faculty, staff, and administrators must change their mental models, adopt different values, and shift their focus. In order for shared leadership to succeed, superintendents and principals must reorient themselves—focusing more on relationships; cooperation and communication must become more important than competition; sharing must become more important than controlling. They must employ effective communication strategies and build "social networks among and between individuals and groups associated with schools" so that the social capital that accumulates as a result can be employed to achieve consensus and reconcile differences (Ortiz & Ogawa, 2000, p. 498). Utilizing communicative networks to share information relevant to decision making facilitates the building of trust and consensus. Such supportive processes are essential to SBM (Blase & Blase, 1999).

Unfortunately, when under intense pressure to produce immediate results, which seems to be a persistent reality, school leaders tend to forget or ignore this somewhat messy, diffused style of leadership, governance, and decision making. SBM is not an easy governance process to implement, particularly for principals because it increases the complexity of their role in schools (Ortiz & Ogawa, 2000). Principals are forced to undergo role transitions and can experience stress and strain as they transition from being the sole decision maker to a participant in the decision-making process. Factors such as experience and tenure, trust among staff, a congruence of personal leadership style with role changes, school-level autonomy, and support from central office (particularly the superintendent and the school board) were found to be crucial variables in reducing role strain among principals (Bredeson, 1993).

To provide proper support, superintendents must be inclusive and facilitative in their vision, planning, and policy development (Kowalski, 2005; Petersen & Kowalski, 2005). Superintendents must also possess political acuity and well-developed communications skills (Petersen & Kowalski, 2005). As Parker and Leithwood (2000) show, school leaders who adopt facilitative leadership styles and who maintain open lines of communication with council members are instrumental in creating more empowered, influential school councils—which is an intended outcome of the SBM process (Blase & Blase, 1999). Successful SBM councils have principals who have learned "to give up power in order to become 'one among equals'" (Blase & Blase, 1999, p. 485). Research on successful schools (regardless of SBM) consistently identifies facilitative leadership as a critical success variable (Wagstaff & Fusarelli, 1999).

Student Involvement

Ideally, and to a greater extent than currently practiced, students should be involved in their own education. Several research studies (e.g. Goodlad, 1984; McNeil, 1986; Silberman, 1970), however, have found that they are rarely invited to be active participants. As Kohn (1993) notes, schooling is typically about doing things *to* children, not working *with* them. As a result, schools systematically exclude students from involvement in significant decision-making processes. Kreisberg (1992) emphasizes the need to empower students in school operations. Any model of teacher empowerment that does not include the goal of empowering students as a central theme is not truly an empowerment model. In a democracy, the voices of all members are valued and heard. Some of the research on school-based management has found that in truly inclusive schools, students are involved in decision making. One principal in Wagstaff and

Fusarelli's study (1999) states, "I treat students the same way I treat adults," while another council member commented, "We allow them to be a part of decision making" (p. 26).

CONCLUDING COMMENTS

Research cited in this chapter demonstrates that SBM has not always opened or improved lines of communication among stakeholders in schools nor has it always led to the creation of high-functioning school councils. In some cases, this organizational concept has broadened the participatory character of decision making in schools, while in others it has not. Site-based management has decentralized decision making, but it has not democratized schools. SBM has given local school professionals (principals and teachers) a greater voice in decision making, but it has all too often excluded nonprofessionals (parents, community members, and students) from expanded participation in the decision-making process.

The failure of SBM to achieve all of its promises is not altogether surprising since, as Scribner and colleagues (1993) note, any intervention into the ongoing activities and processes of a school leads to change, disruption, a significant amount of uncertainty, and, inevitably, hostility and conflict. Therefore, effective communication is essential if SBM in general and school councils specifically are to operate as intended. According to Mathews (2006), taking time to involve the community in decision making (what he refers to as public-building) "may seem like going the long way around when schools face pressing problems," but these initiatives "can help shift some of the burden of accountability from educators alone to communities" (p. 39). Actively involving various "publics" in decision making is crucial in an age of divisiveness and constant criticism of public education (Petersen & Kowalski, 2005; St. John & Clements, 2004).

In the final analysis, decentralization and democratic leadership are worth the effort because broader participation can unleash the hidden power of schools, allowing them to function as truly democratic institutions. This "hidden power" often produces high-performing learning communities with collaborative, inclusive school cultures and open communication among all stakeholders (Wagstaff & Fusarelli, 1999). If schools are to become sites for building participatory democracy (which is the basic premise of SBM), administrators, teachers, staff, parents, community members, and students must be afforded the very sort of autonomy that is lacking in most public school systems. To achieve this, schools need to be organized so that they provide the opportunity for self-governing capacities (Beyer, 1992); the involvement of all relevant constituents is imperative. Parting with power is not easy, if only because doing so increases uncertainty and risk—factors that make decision making more precarious.

The issue of the preferred or optimal type of school governance may be more a matter of conflicting values and philosophy than of technical feasibility (Kirst, 1989). Conflict, however, is the essence of politics and a pervasive reality of school administration. Kirst advocates creating and sustaining an *influential political constituency*; SBM arguably offers the best possibility for creating this constituency. If schools are restructured in a manner suggested by this concept, they will be more inclusive and become learning communities reflective of our democratic heritage. The process is time-consuming and requires much effort and energy (Blase & Blase, 1999). However, although somewhat messy, perhaps organizationally inefficient, and difficult to implement, the inability of many school systems to significantly improve education for all students and reduce the achievement gap "argues for harder and more insistent work toward it [SBM], not for abandonment of the effort" (Hill & Bonan, 1991, p. 73).

NOTE

1. Some principals also use asymmetrical communication to exclude teachers from active participation in the decision-making process.

REFERENCES

Alutto, J. A., & Belasco, J. A. (1972). A typology for participation in organizational decision making. *Administrative Science Quarterly, 17,* 117–125.
Bacharach, S., & Lawler, E. (1980). *Power and politics in organizations: The social psychology of conflict, coalitions, and bargaining.* San Francisco: Jossey-Bass.
Bauman, P. C. (1996). *Governing education: Public sector reform or privatization.* Boston: Allyn & Bacon.

Beyer, L. E. (1992). Can schools further democratic practices? *Theory into Practice, 27*(4), 262–269.

Blase, J., & Blase, J. (1999). Implementation of shared governance for instructional improvement: Principals' perspectives. *Journal of Educational Administration, 37*(5), 476–500.

Bredeson, P. V. (1993). Letting go of outlived professional identities: A study of role transition and role strain for principals in restructured schools. *Educational Administration Quarterly, 29*(1), 34–68.

Clark, D. L., & Meloy, J. M. (1989). Renouncing bureaucracy: A democratic structure for leadership in schools. In T. J. Sergiovanni & J. H. Moore (Eds.), *Schooling for tomorrow: Directing reforms to issues that count*. Boston: Allyn & Bacon.

Clegg, S. R. (1989). *Frameworks of power.* London: Sage.

Clegg, S. R., & Higgins, W. (1987). Against the current: Sociology, socialism and organizations. *Organizational Studies, 8*(3), 201–221.

Clune, W. H., & White, P. (1988). *School-based management: Institutional variation, implementation, and issues for further research*. New Brunswick, NJ: Center for Policy Research in Education.

Collins, R., & Hansen, M. (1991). *School-based management/shared decision-making project 1987–88 through 1989–90*. Summative report.

Conley, S. C. (1991). Review of research on teacher participation in school decision making. *Review of Research in Education, 17*, 225–266.

Conley, S. C., & Bacharach, S. (1990). From school site management to participatory school site management. *Phi Delta Kappan, 71*(7), 539–544.

Darling-Hammond, L. (1994). Will 21st century schools really be different? *Education Digest, 60*(9), 4-8.

David, J. L. (1989, May). Synthesis of research on school-based management. *Educational Leadership*, 45–53.

Doggett, M. (1990). Leadership and competence: Keys to school-based management. *National Association of Secondary School Principals, 74*(526), 59–61.

Etheridge, C. P., Hall, M. L., & Brown, N. (1990). *Leadership, control, communication, and comprehension: Key factors in successful implementation of SBDM*. Paper presented at the Annual Meeting of the Mid-South Educational Research Association, New Orleans, LA.

Fullan, M. (2001). *Leading in a culture of change*. San Francisco: Jossey-Bass.

Goodlad, J. I. (1984). *A place called school: Prospects for the future*. New York: McGraw-Hill.

Habermas, J. (1990). *Moral consciousness and communicative action*. (T. McCarthy, Trans.). Cambridge, MA: MIT Press.

Hallinger, P., Murphy, J., & Hausman, C. (1992). Restructuring schools: Principals' perceptions of fundamental educational reform. *Educational Administration Quarterly, 28*(3), 330–349.

Hallinger, P., & Yanofsky, S. (1990, April). *Gearing up to change slowly: Restructuring roles and relationships at the district level.* Paper presented at the Annual Meeting of the American Educational Research Association, Boston.

Heath, J. A., & Vik, P. (1996). School site councils: Building communities of leaders. *Principal, 76*(2), 25, 28.

Henkin, A. B., Cistone, P. J., & Dee, J. R. (1999). Conflict management strategies of principals in site-based managed schools. *Journal of Educational Administration, 38*(2), 142–158.

Herman, J. J. (1989). A vision for the future: Site-based strategic planning. *National Association of Secondary School Principals, 73*(518), 23–27.

Hill, P. T., & Bonan, J. (1991). *Decentralization and accountability in public education.* Santa Monica, CA: Rand.

Kirst, M. W. (1989). Who should control the schools? Reassessing current policies. In T. J. Sergiovanni & J. H. Moore (Eds.), *Schooling for tomorrow: Directing reforms to issues that count.* Boston: Allyn & Bacon.

Kohn, A. (1993). Choices for children: Why and how to let students decide. *Phi Delta Kappan, 75*(1), 9–20.

Kowalski, T. J. (1994). Site-based management, teacher empowerment, and unionism: Beliefs of suburban school principals. *Contemporary Education, 60*(4), 200–206.

Kowalski, T. J. (1995). Preparing teachers to be leaders: Barriers in the workplace. In M. J. O'Hair & S. J. O'Dell (Eds.), *Educating teachers for leadership and change: Teacher education yearbook III* (pp. 243–256). Thousand Oaks, CA: Corwin.

Kowalski, T. J. (2004). The ongoing war for the soul of school administration. In T. J. Lasley (Ed.), *Better leaders for America's schools: Perspectives on the Manifesto* (pp. 92–114). Columbia, MO: University Council for Educational Administration.

Kowalski, T. J. (2005). Evolution of the school superintendent as communicator. *Communication Education, 54*(2), 101–117.

Kowalski, T. J., Lasley, T. J., & Mahoney, J. (in press). *Data-driven decisions and school leadership: Best practices for school improvement.* Boston: Allyn & Bacon.

Kreisberg, S. (1992). *Transforming power: Domination, empowerment, and education.* Albany: State University of New York Press.

Krueger, J., & Killham, E. (2005, December 8). At work, feeling good matters. *Gallup Management Journal.* Retrieved July 20, 2006, from www.gmj.gallup.com.

Leithwood, K., & Menzies, T. (1998). Forms and effects of school-based management: A review. *Educational Policy, 12*(3), 325–346.

Lieberman, A., Saxl, E., & Miles, M. (1988). Teacher ideology and practice. In A. Lieberman (Ed.), *Building a professional culture in schools*. New York: Teachers College Press.

Lindauer, P., Petrie, G., & Richardson, M. (1997). Teacher perception of Kentucky elementary principal leadership effectiveness and school-based council meeting effectiveness. *Research in the Schools, 4*(2), 39–47.

Malen, B., & Ogawa, R. (1988). Professional-patron influence on site-based governance councils: A confounding case study. *Educational Evaluation and Policy Analysis, 10*(4), 251–270.

Malen, B., Ogawa, R., & Kranz, J. (1990). What do we know about school-based management?: A case study of the literature. In W. H. Clune & J. F. White (Eds.), *Choice and control in American education: The practice of choice, decentralization and school restructuring* (pp. 112–132). New York: Falmer.

Marburger, C. L. (1985). *One school at a time: School-based management: A process for change*. Columbia, MD: National Committee for Citizens in Education.

Marshall, C., & Scribner, J. D. (1991). "It's all political": Inquiry into the micropolitics of education. *Education and Urban Society, 23*(4), 347–355.

Mathews, D. (2006). Putting the public back in public education. *Education Week, 25*(31), 39, 48.

McNeil, L. (1986). *Contradictions of control: School structure and school knowledge*. New York: Routledge & Kegan Paul.

Meadows, B. J. (1992). Nurturing cooperation and responsibility in a school community. *Phi Delta Kappan, 73*(6), 480–481.

Murphy, J., Evertson, C., & Radnofsky, M. (1991). Restructuring schools: Fourteen elementary and secondary teachers' perspectives on reform. *Elementary School Journal, 92*(2), 135–148.

Ortiz, F. I., & Ogawa, R. T. (2000). Site-based decision-making leadership in American public schools. *Journal of Educational Administration, 38*(5), 486–499.

Parker, K., & Leithwood, K. (2000). School councils' influence on school and classroom practice. *Peabody Journal of Education, 75*(4), 37–65.

Peel, H. A., & Walker, B. L. (1994). Empowering principal. *NASSP Bulletin, 78*(556), 41–42.

Petersen, G. J., & Kowalski, T. J. (2005). *School reform strategies and normative expectations for democratic leadership in the superintendency*. Paper presented at the Annual Meeting of the University Council for Educational Administration, Nashville, TN.

Reyes, P. (1994). *Cultural citizenship and social responsibility: A call for change in educational administration*. UCEA presidential address. Presented at the Annual Conference of the University Council for Educational Administration (UCEA), Houston, TX.

Reyes, P., & McCarty, D. J. (1990). Factors related to the power of lower participants in educational organizations: Multiple perspectives. *Sociological Focus, 23*(1), 17–30.

Ritchie, J. (1974). Supervision. In G. Strauss et al. (Eds.), *Organizational behavior: Research and issues*. Madison, WI: Industrial Relations Research Association.

Rutherford, B. (1991). *School-based management and school improvement: How it happened in three school districts*. Paper presented at the American Educational Research Association Annual Meeting, Chicago.

Sarason, S. B. (1996). *Revisiting the culture of the school and the problem of change*. New York: Teachers College Press.

Scheurich, J. J., & Imber, M. (1991). Educational reforms can reproduce societal inequities: A case study. *Educational Administration Quarterly, 27*(3), 297–320.

Schumaker, P. (1991). *Critical pluralism, democratic performance, and community power*. Lawrence: University Press of Kansas.

Scribner, J. D. (1990). *Liberating educational administration from hedgehog thinking: A planning proposal for the new millennium*. UCEA presidential address, 1990. Presented at the Annual Conference of the University Council for Educational Administration, Pittsburgh, PA.

Scribner, J. D., Fusarelli, L. D., Cain, A., & Pustka, B. (1993). *The micropolitical dynamics of restructured schools*. Paper presented at the American Association of School Administrators. Orlando, FL.

Silberman, C. E. (1970). *Crisis in the classroom: The remaking of American education*. New York: Random House.

Smylie, M. (1992). Teacher participation in school decision making: Assessing willingness to participate. *Educational Evaluation and Policy Analysis, 14*(1), 53–67.

St. John, E., & Clements, M. M. (2004). Public opinions and political contexts. In T. J. Kowalski (Ed.), *Public relations in schools* (3rd ed., pp. 47–67). Upper Saddle River, NJ: Merrill, Prentice Hall.

Van Meter, E. J. (1991, February). The Kentucky mandate: School-based decision making. *NASSP Bulletin*, 52–62.

Wagstaff, L. H., & Fusarelli, L. D. (1999). Establishing collaborative governance and leadership. In P. Reyes, J. D. Scribner, & A. P. Scribner (Eds.), *Lessons from high-performing Hispanic schools* (pp. 19–35). New York: Teachers College Press.

Wagstaff, L. H., & Reyes, P. (1992). *Report on school site-based management*. Paper presented to the State of Texas Educational Economic Policy Center, University of Texas at Austin.

Weiler, H. N. (1990). Comparative perspectives on educational decentralization: An exercise in contradiction? *Educational Evaluation and Policy Analysis, 12*(4), 433–448.

White, P. A. (1989, September). An overview of school-based management: What does the research say? *NASSP Bulletin*, 1–8.

Wohlstetter, P. (1995, September). Getting school-based management right: What works, what doesn't. *Phi Delta Kappan*, 22–26.

Author Index

Achilles, C., 86
Agee, W., 23
Algozzine, R., 11
Alutto, J., 214
Amundson, K., 70
Anderson, G., 12, 60, 70
Anderson, J., 157
Argyle, M., 43
Armistead, L., 27
Aronowitz, S., 130
Arriaza, G., 26
Ashford, S., 109, 110, 119, 121
Ault, P., 23
Axley, S., 12, 76

Bacharach, S., 153, 213, 214
Backlund, P., 93
Baikaltseva, E., 189
Baker, B., 26, 27, 63, 132
Barber, B., 129
Barbour, A., 93
Bauman, P., 8, 20, 28, 76, 158, 211
Beach, R., 27, 64, 66
Belasco, J., 214
Bell, N., 202

Benne, K., 74
Bennett, L., 126
Bennett, S., 126
Berger, P., 126
Berliner, D., 66, 187
Berrien, F., 67
Beverage, L., 88
Beyer, L., 130, 222
Biddle, B., 66, 187
Björk, L., 28, 64, 66, 67, 91, 95, 142
Blanchard, K., 180
Blase, J., 219, 220, 222
Blase, Joseph, 12, 60, 202, 219, 220, 222
Blumberg, A., 88
Blumer, I., 13, 77
Bolman, L., 40, 178
Bonan, J., 210, 211, 212, 215, 222
Bonoma, T., 169
Boulding, K., 176
Bourdieu, P., 67
Brashers, D., 12, 76
Bredeson, P., 41, 83, 220
Brockmeier, J., 64
Broom, G., 32

Subject Index

About the Authors

Theodore J. Kowalski is the Kuntz Family Chair in educational administration at the University of Dayton, Ohio. A former teacher, principal, superintendent, and college dean, he is the author of 29 books and over 180 book chapters, journal articles, and research studies.

George J. Petersen is professor and chair of educational leadership at California Polytechnic State University, San Luis Obispo. He was previously on the faculty at the University of Missouri and served as associate executive director of the University Council for Educational Administration.

Lance D. Fusarelli is associate professor of educational leadership at North Carolina State University, Raleigh. He was formerly on the faculty at Fordham University, New York.